Pope's imagination

For my students

DAVID FAIRER

Pope's imagination

MANCHESTER
UNIVERSITY PRESS

© David Fairer 1984

Published by Manchester University Press
Oxford Road, Manchester M13 9PL
and 51 Washington Street, Dover
New Hampshire 03820, USA

British Library cataloguing in publication data
Fairer, David
  Pope's imagination.
  1. Pope, Alexander—Criticism and
  interpretation
  I. Title
  821'.5   PR3634

Library of Congress cataloging in publication data
Fairer, David.
  Pope's imagination.
  Includes bibliographical references.
  1. Pope, Alexander, 1688–1744—Criticism and interpre-
tation. 2. Imagination in literature. I. Title.
PR3637.I4F34 1984   821'.5   84–832

ISBN 0–7190–1080–2

Phototypeset in Bembo by
Wilmaset, Birkenhead, Merseyside

Printed in Great Britain by
Butler & Tanner Ltd, Frome and London

Contents

Acknowledgements

Chapters 2 and 3 of this book are developments of two articles, 'Milton's Lady and Pope's Eloisa', *Southern Review* (Adelaide) xii (1979), 209–26, and 'Imagination in *The Rape of the Lock*', *Essays in Criticism* xxix (1979), 53–74. I am very grateful to the editors of these journals for permission to re-use a considerable amount of material from these essays.

Every book on Pope is to some degree a communal effort, and it is a pleasure to record my indebtedness to *all* the scholars and critics mentioned in the notes; small matters of disagreement often conceal the greatest debts, and in my critical discussion I have occasionally taken issue on particular points with scholars from whom I have learned the most.

Friends and colleagues in the School of English at Leeds University have been a constant source of help and encouragement, and parts of this work have benefited from the knowledge of Dr Ruth Morse, Dr Elizabeth Cook, Dr Shirley Chew and Dr Paul Hammond. Research has been a very enjoyable task, thanks partly to those congenial treasure-houses, The Brotherton Collection of Leeds University and the Bodleian Library, Oxford. I wish to thank the staff of both institutions for much assistance. I am also very grateful for helpful suggestions at various stages from Professor Robert Halsband and Mr Stephen Wall. Professor Michael V. DePorte's work on eighteenth-century abnormal psychology was the greatest stimulus to my researches. Mr Philip Wheatley of Balliol College, Oxford, gave me valued practical help. My biggest debt of all is to Dr Sandy Viner for his unsparing patience and care in preparing the typescript.

University of Leeds   *David Fairer*

Abbreviations

Introduction

I

Pope lived in an age which was fascinated by the power of imagination. Unlike the present age, which uses the term in relatively restricted senses, the early decades of the eighteenth century were a time when imagination was considered to have an influence, for good or ill, upon almost every aspect of life. Today we see little connection between space fantasy, a relish for grilled mutton kidneys, gambling, a rainbow, advertising, poetry, pride, pentecostalism, make-up, lunacy, disco light-effects, jewellery, charisma, video, gossip, children's toys, colour charts, wit, drugs, love, shell-collecting, a hall of mirrors, crowd hysteria, pornography, Christmas bunting, dreams, pigeon-breeding, studded leather jackets and garden gnomes. It is still possible nowadays to link some of these – jewellery and pride, disco and drugs, lunacy and garden gnomes – but this is largely a matter of personal association and is not sanctioned by physiological theory. Pope, however, would understand the list immediately as a twentieth-century anatomy of the imagination, a collection of objects and notions illustrating the faculty at work – its possibilities for delight and for deceit, its stimulation, danger and absurdity.

This book is written out of the conviction that modern criticism has not done justice to the richness and complexity of thinking about the imagination in the age of Pope. It is a lingering fallacy (though fortunately less prevalent nowadays) that the 'Augustan age' was uniquely distrustful of the imagination, and that the literary world in which Pope grew up was (to quote one of his most stimulating and sympathetic critics) 'relatively poor in imaginative opportunities'.[1] The early eighteenth century was indeed 'distrustful' of many areas of imaginative activity, but so were Spenser, Shakespeare, Jonson and Milton some generations earlier, and Pope is distrustful in very similar ways about similar things (and sometimes in very similar language). The point is that for Pope and his contemporaries 'imaginative activity' included virtually everything in which the mind of man took part. In its literary aspect it covered the private sublimities of reading Homer or Milton, or the *frissons* of semi-pornographic romances; it was (as we shall see) active in the public play of wit in the drawing-room, the gossip of the 'toy'-shop, the thrill of stage machinery in the theatre, the delight in burlesque puppet-shows at public fairs, or in the revelry of street pageants and firework displays; it was at the heart of the sexual instinct and the games of flirtation or *amour*, and was the medium through which the passions made their assault (whether pride, ambition, hope or love);[2] it was present at the highest level of literary creation and within the sordid walls of Bedlam; it was the province of the nun and the coquette, the virgin and the whore.

Over the past two centuries writers and critics have hived off something called the 'poetic' or 'creative' imagination into a private shrine, whose priestesses bear the names 'organic unity', 'esemplastic power' and 'visionary truth'. 'Fancy' has been relegated to an ornamented and mirrored boudoir, and 'fantasy' to a blacked-out room with projector and screen. To understand the age of Pope we have to break down these partitions and recover a sense of the imagination as a part of the human mind operating in many aspects of life and on many different levels. For Pope, the one faculty was present in the widest possible range of human experience, from divine ecstasy to society gossip, from female beauty to coprophiliac madness. Some of his finest poems work on the assumption that the imagination is at the heart of man's paradoxical nature, and is capable of many degrees of use and misuse. In the world of love (to take one example) it could, when properly focused, be an endless source of fresh delight and even of spiritual fulfilment; whereas employed in the wrong way it could enclose a person within moody selfishness and encourage unhealthy fantasising; it might breed superficiality, delusion, madness and self-destruction, and lead an individual to have wrong priorities and to fail in establishing deep relationships. To examine Pope's imagination, therefore, is not only to consider how he directs his own imagination within his poetry, but also to see how he explores the human mind at work in many areas of life. For him, the imagination of the poet is not somehow sealed off from the chaos of human experience by a distinctive title of its own.

Pope does not distinguish between the terms 'fancy' and

'imagination'. It is possible to count and categorise his use of the two words, but the result merely confirms his commitment to the paradoxical nature of the imaginative faculty and his avoidance of any distinction in terminology between what we might (over-simply) call its 'creative' and 'delusive' (or 'trivial') aspects. Scholarly investigations of the use of the terms 'fancy' and 'imagination' between 1660 and 1750 have yielded no clear results. Hobbes does not distinguish the terms.[3] Dryden was aware that a possible distinction was there to be made, but John M. Aden's analysis of the terminology of his earlier criticism (to 1672) demonstrates how interchangeable the two terms were for him, and how frequently he used them synonymously.[4] Robert D. Hume shows that in Dryden's later career both words tend to be replaced by 'invention', 'as the first term in the creative process'.[5] John Bullitt and W. J. Bate are not able to clarify the position in the period before 1750, but they do demonstrate how after that date certain writers (J. G. Cooper, William Duff, Dugald Stewart) discriminate between the terms in a gradual movement towards Coleridge's crucial distinction.[6]

It was the developing interest in 'the Sublime' which seems to have encouraged writers during the second half of the eighteenth century to recognise a difference in the use of the words 'fancy' and 'imagination'. By 1794 a shift in emphasis could be perceived between the 'boundless IMAGINATION' of *Paradise Lost* and the 'exquisite FANCY' of *The Rape of the Lock*.[7] As late as 1783, however, James Beattie found it appropriate to use the terms interchangeably:

According to the common use of words, Imagination and Fancy are not perfectly synonymous. They are, indeed, names for the same faculty, but the former seems to be applied to the more solemn, and the latter to the more trivial, exertions of it. A witty author is a man of lively Fancy; but a sublime poet is said to possess a vast Imagination. However, as these words are often, and by the best writers, used indiscriminately, I shall not further distinguish them.[8]

Pope in this regard seems to have followed Addison, who at the beginning of his 'Pleasures of Imagination' essays in *The Spectator* (1712) speaks of 'the Imagination or Fancy (which I shall use promiscuously)'.[9] In Pope's poetry the word 'fancy' was metrically more useful, but in both verse and prose the two terms could be used synonymously to avoid repetition.[10]

A representative critical document here is his Preface to *The Iliad* (1715), an essay which Maynard Mack has rightly called 'a paean to the supremacy of imagination'.[11] Pope recognises in Homer the supreme imaginative artist and tries to convey something of his power. In doing so he uses the terms 'Invention', 'Imagination' and 'Fancy' within the same paragraph (additional italics are mine):

It is to the Strength of this amazing *Invention* we are to attribute that unequal'd Fire and Rapture, which is so forcible in *Homer*, that no Man of true Poetical Spirit is Master of himself while he reads him . . . the Reader is hurry'd out of himself by the Force of the Poet's *Imagination*. . . . 'Tis however remarkable that his *Fancy*, which is every where vigorous, is not discover'd immediately at the beginning of his Poem in its fullest Splendor: It grows in the Progress both upon himself and others, and becomes on Fire like a Chariot-Wheel, by its own Rapidity. Exact Disposition, just Thought, correct Elocution, polish'd Numbers, may have been found in a thousand; but this Poetical *Fire*, this *Vivida vis animi*, in a very few.[12]

Unlike Dryden, whose Preface to *Annus Mirabilis* (1667) attempts in a well-known passage to disentangle the terms 'invention', 'imagination' and 'fancy',[13] Pope in this paragraph is clearly refusing to differentiate between the three words. It is more important for his purposes to distinguish the power of the imaginative faculty (which these three terms express) from the controllable, conscious, discriminating faculty ('Exact Disposition, just Thought, correct Elocution, polish'd Numbers').

Likewise in the section describing the copiousness of Homer's similes Pope again employs all three terms without attempting to distinguish them (the italics are mine): 'It is owing to the same vast *Invention* that his Similes have been thought too exuberant and full of Circumstances'; 'his *Fancy* suggested to him at once so many various and correspondent Images'; 'the Extent and Fecundity of his *Imagination*; to which all things, in their various Views, presented themselves in an Instant'.[14]

Occasionally Pope can disconcert us by placing the highest level of the creative imagination up against the most delusive and destructive aspects of (what we nowadays term) fantasy. An instance of this is the way the malign figure of Dulness in *The Dunciad* is made to recall Homer himself. The mark of true genius, for Pope, is exemplified by the ability of Homer's imagination to pull everything into its own sphere: 'This strong and ruling Faculty was like a powerful Star, which, in the Violence of its Course, drew all things within its

Vortex.'[15] The image is memorably recalled in *The Dunciad*, where the goddess Dulness draws to herself 'a vast involuntary throng, / Who gently drawn . . . / Roll in her Vortex' (iv, 82–4),[16] and it is she who has the power to make 'no Man . . . Master of himself'. Pope's return in such a context to an image which he had earlier used of Homer's greatness may seem a grotesque parody, until we realise that both Homer *and* Dulness are figures of universal power who draw everything into themselves – the supreme poet of imagination, and the tyrannous queen of fantasy and illusion. Nowadays we build bulwarks of theory to keep them apart; Pope, over the gap of years, exploits the paradox.

This is not to suggest that Pope was woolly-minded on the subject, or that he did not perceive different aspects or levels of imaginative activity. Quite the contrary. It is precisely because he found the paradoxical nature of man so fascinating and artistically fruitful that he was able, indeed anxious, to preserve such contradictions within the human mind. The imagination is the source of Belinda's coquettry *and* her prudery, of the agony *and* ecstasy of Eloisa, of the many kinds of contrariety observed in *Epistle to a Lady*, and of the powerful burlesque creativity of Dulness. Paradox is the key, and so it is inevitable that Pope will wish to preserve a single faculty as one source of man's self-contradiction. If only mankind could (he seems to imply) separate imagination from fancy and fantasy – if only we could distinguish truth from error, the sublime from the ridiculous:

> He hangs between; in doubt to act, or rest,
> In doubt to deem himself a God, or Beast;
> In doubt his Mind or Body to prefer,
> Born but to die, and reas'ning but to err;
> Alike in ignorance, his reason such,
> Whether he thinks too little, or too much:
> Chaos of Thought and Passion, all confus'd;
> Still by himself abus'd, or disabus'd;
> Created half to rise, and half to fall;
> Great lord of all things, yet a prey to all;
> Sole judge of Truth, in endless Error hurl'd:
> The glory, jest, and riddle of the world!
>
> (*Essay on Man*, ii, 7–18)

Nowadays a theory of the imagination (like a theory of any kind) is regarded as a certificate of validation for a creative artist, and it is fashionable to nod with approval when we see older writers groping their way towards a Coleridgean synthesis. Symptomatic is James Engell's recent study, *The Creative Imagination. Enlightenment to Romanticism* (Cambridge, Mass. and London, 1981), which takes the 'essential idea' of imagination to be a romantic one, and charts the growth of the embryo towards its 'integrated whole' in Coleridge. Inevitably perhaps, a synthesising approach like this leads Professor Engell to oversimplify (and occasionally misrepresent)[17] ideas which blur the picture. His statement that 'the Enlightenment created the idea of the imagination' may hold for the particular line of development he follows; but it might be said to ignore the power which an *un*synthesised view (such as Pope's) could have for a creative artist.

How far is a poet's concept of imagination an expression of, and how far a determinant of, his view of the relationship between himself and the world? Whatever the case, Pope, no less than Coleridge, had an understanding of the imagination which expressed this relationship. It is presumptuous to assume that one poet's concept is the 'truer' or more artistically fruitful. If a poet wishes to explore the tragi-comedy of man's pride and self-deception, then he will be less well served by a synthesising imagination, whereas he will mine inexhaustible irony from a faculty which is able to be alternately penetrative and superficial, revelatory and deceptive, creative and chaotic, inspired and mad. In writing about Pope's imagination it is impossible to avoid such use of antithesis (just as Pope's own thoughts fall so naturally into couplets). Pope himself was even antithetical in his attitude towards antithesis: it could stir within him disgust at its ambivalence (Sporus the 'vile antithesis'), joyous humour at its grotesque folly (Timon's 'huge heaps of littleness'), sorrow at its self-destructiveness (Narcissa in *Epistle to a Lady*), or delight at its inexhaustible fascination ('Woman's at best a Contradiction still' (*Epistle to a Lady*, 270)).

It would therefore be a fatuous enterprise to present Pope as having a self-consistent theory of the imagination. The truth is that for him, and for the tradition within which I want to place him, the notion of the imagination was a very large, loose, and baggy one. These are not terms of reproach. It was 'large' because it involved *every* aspect of human awareness; 'loose' because it shaded off into many other theoretical areas such as dream-theory, theories of lunacy, the physiology of melancholy, theological issues, etc; and 'baggy' because it was capacious enough to contain within itself so many apparently contradictory views of man. If Pope seems to be veering from empiricism to puritanism, to platonism, to neo-stoicism, then that is neither a weakness of this book nor an indictment of Pope as a thinker.

He is at his greatest when he is capable of being in doubts and uncertainties. The 'chameleon' poet is an idea Pope certainly understood (it is a traditional one), and his own poetry, as we shall see, is obsessed with shifting colours, merging identities and the play of imaginative sympathy. (In this area the one poet to whom, apart from Milton, he is most akin is the figure of John Keats.) But Pope is also a poet for whom the making of distinctions is an urgent concern, and it is the tension within his work between imaginative sympathy and moral judgment – between a freer and a more stable element – which gives it much of its power. *Eloisa to Abelard* places and judges its heroine in terms of Milton's lady and the imagination's noblest devotions, and yet it ends with Pope exploring the issue of the 'sympathetic' poet who will share her griefs; *The Rape of the Lock* is a poem of love as well as a satire, and is an exercise both in compliment and exposure; *Epistle to a Lady* manipulates artistically both the sympathy and distaste of the reader; and *The Dunciad* (arguably Pope's most 'creative' poem) is about *un*creation, about the meeting-point of delight and horror, and our own imaginative kinship with the dunces is a necessary part of our wider understanding of the whole.

It is this theme which has determined my choice of works for discussion. The four poems on which the book focuses make the working of the imagination an integral part of their subject, and considered together I believe they give a special insight into that aspect of Pope's art. Other fine poems, where imagination is powerfully at work but not part of the subject-matter (e.g. *Windsor Forest*, the epistles to Burlington and Bathurst, the Imitations of Horace, the Homer translation), are peripheral to this inquiry.

II

This book is, therefore, primarily a study of four of Pope's most visually exciting poems spanning the earlier and later stages of his career: *Eloisa to Abelard* (1717), *The Rape of the Lock* (1714), *Epistle to a*

Lady (1735), and *The Dunciad Variorum* (1729). They are each works
of considerable imaginative power, and this comes partly from
Pope's ability to externalise in description the mental world his
characters inhabit – the solitary gloom of Eloisa's convent sur-
rounded by a landscape of grottos and caverns, the contrast between
the glittering world of Belinda's beauty and the chilly, misty palace
of her spleen, the colourful sketchbook of women's characters, and
Dulness's domain of chaos, pantomime and urban nightmare.

However, these four poems have been chosen not simply because
they are imaginative creations themselves, but because they are in
various ways *about* the workings of the imagination as Pope and his
contemporaries understood it – how it can affect an individual's
moral or spiritual status and have far-reaching implications for a
society and its literature. I wish to show that in each poem the
functioning and abuse of the imagination is a major theme helping to
determine its argument, shape and imagery. I shall also argue that in
each case Pope is writing within a discernible tradition of thought
about a particular aspect of imaginative activity, and that he was
deeply concerned, as a poet and as a man, with the proper use of a
faculty which set its mark on the experience of every individual.

Chapter Two, for example, considers Pope's heroic epistle *Eloisa
to Abelard* within the terms of Renaissance theories about the paradoxical nature of the imagination and the duality of Body and Soul
which they assumed. Chapter Three turns to faculty psychology and
its influence on the empiricism of Hobbes and Locke, a tradition that
encouraged the dichotomies of beauty-truth and imagination-
reality; *The Rape of the Lock* is seen as inheriting with this tradition a
whole range of imagery (to do with colour, scent, sound and
superficial light-effects) which supports the psychological drama of
the poem. Chapter Four places *Epistle to a Lady* within the
seventeenth-century debate about the nature of woman, which by
Pope's day had become associated with an ungoverned imagination.
The final chapter takes further the imagination's tendency towards
anarchy and chaos, its capacity for metamorphosis, confusion, and
undisciplined activity – aspects which were coming to be interpreted
in terms of mental 'process', an idea represented in *The Dunciad
Variorum* by the virtuosity of Dulness and her infantile worshippers.
These four chapters will attempt in turn to sketch the nature of the
tradition, and then to proceed, towards the second half of each
chapter, to a reading of the individual poem.

In trying to avoid encasing Pope within a tidy 'thesis' I run the risk of appearing to make the notion of imagination a nebulous one. But since Pope regularly uses the *cloud*[18] as an image for the workings of imagination (whether lit by rainbow-colours or sinking into an all-embracing mist) this is inevitable and necessary. In his poetry the beams of imagination frequently play upon shifting clouds (it is part of their teasing uncertainty), and unless something of the same 'nebulous' quality of the faculty is picked up by the reader, then Pope will have been falsified. If it seems that each chapter locates the imagination differently, then again that is deliberate. To use modern terminology, the 'fantasising' of Eloisa *is* importantly different from the 'fancifulness' of Belinda – but unless we recognise how 'imagination', 'fancy' and 'fantasy' can shade into each other, we shall miss many powerful ironies in Pope's poetry. I wish to tease out the ambiguities within the faculty of imagination – not to make it an artificially stable concept.

A related aim is therefore to explore Pope's ideas in terms of the varied theory and practice of Renaissance and seventeenth-century poetry, and thereby, I hope, to illuminate Pope's literary relations with his English past. Source-hunting can be a pleasant exercise of the scholar's own imagination, but the many analogues quoted in the course of my discussion are not offered as direct sources for Pope's ideas (although a few of them may be), but rather as examples of the various conventions of thought and expression with which he is working. I offer them in the hope that they will enrich our understanding of Pope's mind and that their arguments, images and associations will act as useful glosses to the poems concerned. Through such parallels this book engages deliberately with the wider issue of Pope's literary relationship to his predecessors and contemporaries. It may at first seem disconcerting to find so many analogues drawn from the century preceeding 1660, but this is because for too long the 'Augustan age' has been somewhat set apart from earlier periods of English literature. Since the eighteenth century (and Dr Johnson was partly responsible for this) there has been a tendency to see Pope as belonging to an 'Augustan tradition' separable from the 'native tradition' of Spenser–Shakespeare – Milton. Viewing Pope from the vantage-point offered by these four poems, he appears firmly *within* his native tradition, and such compartmentalising begins to look false to the place that the early eighteenth century occupies in the development of English poetry.

By this assertion I do not mean to underplay Pope's enormously creative engagement with the poets of Greece and Rome, but I do believe that an emphasis on the classical tradition has occasionally distorted the picture (for example, attention has rightly been given to Eloisa's links with the heroines of Ovid and Corneille, but none to her ironic kinship with Milton's Lady). Young poets of the decade following Pope's death may have seen themselves as re-establishing the 'school of Milton' after the 'school of Pope',[19] but in the poems discussed here Pope himself is the pre-eminent representative of the 'school of Milton'. The extent of Milton's influence on Pope has been generally recognised by critics,[20] but sometimes without the realisation that Pope, like Milton, was touched by neoplatonism, Renaissance medical and philosophical theory, and even Puritanism. Pope deeply understood Milton and the traditions within which his great predecessor wrote, and he expected his readers to appreciate his own re-working of Miltonic themes. A recurrent issue, therefore, is the *rapport* between Pope and Milton in their understanding of the imagination and their shared concern with right and wrong ways of seeing.

The four poems are not discussed in chronological order, partly because the present arrangement seemed to work best, but also because my argument is 'chronological' only in the sense that I detect a shift in Pope's treatment of the imagination between 1717 and 1729. In *Epistle to Dr Arbuthnot* (1735) he reminisced about the course of his career: 'That not in Fancy's Maze he wander'd long, / But stoop'd to Truth, and moraliz'd his song . . .' (340–1). The two earlier poems, *Eloisa to Abelard* and *The Rape of the Lock*, can indeed be seen as taking a generous view of the imaginative faculty. Eloisa is finally granted a degree of victory within her imagination, and the 'truth' of Clarissa is partially overridden by the fanciful transformation of Belinda's beauty into an eternal star. In the two later poems, however, the theme of imagination is handled with greater moral rigour: *Epistle to a Lady* stresses how it must be tethered by 'Fixed Principles', and *The Dunciad Variorum* ends with a vision of universal darkness – the final result of not seeing clearly. In this sense Pope did strike out from the delightful maze, and though he never ceased to marvel at the imagination's vitality he came increasingly to understand its deceptions and dangers.

To sum up: as well as identifying particular themes in these individual poems, I also want to establish certain general points: (1)

that Pope was intensely interested in how imagination worked within himself and others; (2) that he understood its effects and manipulated them for artistic ends; (3) that in some of his finest poems he explored the nature of imaginative activity, through character and also through the responses of the reader; (4) that he absorbed a number of earlier traditions of thought about the imagination and examined their implications in his own poetry; (5) that the endless ambiguities between (and within) these various theories were preserved by him, and used as a means of engaging with man's contradictory nature – that he highlighted such ambiguities and drew poetic power from them; finally (6) that in this important aspect of his writing Pope is clearly working within the native tradition of English literature, 1550–1700.

By way of prelude to an examination of the poems, I wish in a brief first chapter to look at a few of Pope's letters, where he engages with some of the themes we shall be considering later. Through them it should be possible to convey how consciously 'aware' he was of imaginative activity, and to demonstrate his fascination both with the workings of his own imagination and with his power to manipulate other people's.

ONE

Pope's imagination

As a young man Pope seems to have had a hyperactive imagination, and from the beginning of his poetic career he felt its power very strongly. In his early correspondence he exploits it in many different ways. The tone may vary from the flirtatious to an amused self-examination, but always there is a note of self-consciousness, perhaps because he saw the imagination as something in which a person 'indulged'. Even in his youthful letters it functions within an appropriate context, and the most whimsical fancy is artistically controlled. But always the keynote is 'paradox'; Pope's fascination with the imagination springs from his awareness of the ironies of his own nature and those of his fellow men. He realises that it is a dangerous and renegade power, that it can transcend physical limitation (few poets felt this more than he) and that it may offer a satanic temptation of the most urgent kind. He knows its kinship with madness, but there is never the suspicion that he does not understand what his imagination is doing, or that he cannot, in his writing, direct it. To trace briefly some of his attitudes towards the imagination over the course of his poetic career is to recognise the depth of his interest in its workings and his obvious sensitivity to its literary effects.

On 5 December 1712 he wrote to his friend John Caryll:

Like a witch, whose Carcase lies motionless on the floor, while she keeps her airy Sabbaths, & enjoys a thousand Imaginary Entertainments abroad, in this world, & in others, I seem to sleep in the midst of the Hurry, even as you would swear a Top stands still, when tis in the Whirle of its giddy motion. 'Tis no figure, but a serious truth I tell you when I say that my Days & Nights are so much alike, so equally insensible of any Moving Power but Fancy, that I have sometimes spoke of things in our family as Truths & real accidents, which I only Dreamt of; & again when some things that actually happen'd came into my head, have thought (till I enquird) that I had only dream'd of them.[1]

We are not far here from the vortex image: his mind whirls round, and yet at the point of dizziest activity he seems insensible; in fact he is divided between body and spirit, between the carcase on the floor and the witches' sabbath of his mind. The grotesqueness of the witch simile fits the tone of fascination and slight uneasiness with which Pope contemplates the paradox. Dream and reality have merged together, but the artistic control is there in the way he gives the paradox a suitable image. For all the uneasiness there is also delight: he knows that this is not madness, and yet his contrasting of 'figure' with 'serious truth' assumes that truth and imagination are not normally in alliance. In this passage Pope is simultaneously indulging a fancy and controlling an image.

Pope's imagination could certainly entertain him with other worlds, and when he was in a poetical mood immediate reality easily disappeared; as he told his friend Jervas: 'Poetry . . . takes me up so intirely that I scarce see what passes under my nose, and hear nothing that is said about me' (16 Aug. 1714). It was of course a commonplace of the age that an unchecked imagination was little else than madness,[2] and this belief explains two remarks recorded by Joseph Spence among his anecdotes of Pope. Spence reported that the poet's sister had spoken plainly to him of her brother's 'maddish way', and that Edmund Smith had not been in the young poet's company long before concluding: 'Igad that young fellow will either be a madman or make a very great poet'.[3] Pope's many humorous glances at his own dreaminess enact the well-known words of Shakespeare's Theseus: 'The lunatic, the lover, and the poet, / Are of imagination all compact' (*MND*, V.i.7–8). They are in part a conscious twitching of his poetic mantle.

Pope's awareness of the tradition of the visionary poet perhaps lies behind his self-consciousness about the issue of imagination, and such a feeling could only be encouraged by the fact that he was from youth troublesomely short-sighted. It was left to the old Restoration wit William Wycherley to point out the flattering parallels to his young friend: 'you may better bear the weakness of your owtward sight, since it is recompenc'd by the strength of your immagination and inward penitration, as your Poetic Forefathers were down from Homer to Milton' (Wycherley–Pope, 19 Jan. 1708).

From relatively early in his career Pope felt the paradox of man's position between a physical and spiritual existence, and this riddle is partly seen in terms of the imagination, which removes him to worlds beyond, but only to remind him of the physically real. The result is a habitual awareness of incongruity and inconsistency. The opening words of his letter to Caryll, 14 August 1713, are interesting in this respect:

I have been lying in wait for my own imagination this week and more, and watching what thoughts of mine came up in the whirl of fancy . . . You can't wonder my thoughts are scarce consistent, when I tell you how they are distracted! Every hour of my life, my mind is strangely divided. This minute, perhaps, I am above the stars, with a thousand systems round about me, looking forward into the vast abyss of eternity, and losing my whole comprehension in the boundless spaces of the extended Creation, in dialogues with Whiston and the astronomers; the next moment I am below all trifles, even grovelling with Tidcombe in the very center of nonsense . . . Good God! What an Incongruous Animal is Man? how unsettled in his best part, his soul; and how changing and variable in his frame of body? The constancy of the one, shook by every notion, the temperament of the other, affected by every blast of wind. What an April weather in the mind! In a word, what is Man altogether, but one mighty Inconsistency.

Such a letter should not be taken too solemnly (on one level it is a witty description of his available reading matter) but Pope has made out of it a journey into spiritual contradiction: the 'whirl' of imagination can bring divine vision, but also find its way to the solid core of nonsense beneath all human experience. The power of the mind recalls the weakness of the body.

In some of his later letters Pope returns to the theme of his own divided nature – a crippled, imprisoning body, but a free and companionable soul; a life within reality transcended by a life in imagination: 'In sincere truth I often think myself (it is all I can do) with your lordship: and let me tell you my life in thought and imagination is as much superior to my life in action and reality as the best soul can be to the vilest body' (Pope–Bathurst, 18 Dec. [?1730]). Writing to the Earl of Orrery, he puts this opposition in specifically Pauline terms, and the word 'carcase' movingly reappears: 'Were not my own Carcase (very little suited to my Soul) my worst Enemy, were it not for the *Body of this Death*, (as St Paul calls it) I would not be seperated from you . . .' (10 May 1736). And six years later, to the same friend, he speaks of 'my frequent Dreams, & Escapes of Soul toward you: for I often imagine myself with you' (27 Aug. [1742].[4] This recollects the dilemma he had explored in *Eloisa to Abelard*, and the resemblance is not accidental, since it is that poem which is Pope's most creative expression of the conflict between a life in the body and a life in the soul, and the imagination's potential for transcending everyday reality.

A related paradox for Pope was that of human pride. So many of man's thoughts could be seen as the fantastic offspring of vanity and error; man's self-awarded greatness is thus largely a creation of his own imagination, and the cloudy worlds of politics, philosophy or poetry only encourage this self-deception:

half the things that employ our heads deserve not the name of thoughts, they are only stronger dreams or impressions upon the imagination; our schemes of government, our systems of philosophy, our golden words of poetry, are all but so many shadow images and airy prospects, which arise to us but so much the livelier and more frequent as we are more overcast with the darkness, wrapt in the night, and disturbed with the fumes of human vanity. (Pope–Caryll, 13 July 1714)

This idea found poetic form years later in *The Dunciad Variorum*, where Pope describes how Theobald (later Cibber) lies upon the lap of maternal Dulness and is conveyed 'on Fancy's easy wing' into the world of vision:

> Hence the Fool's paradise, the Statesman's scheme,
> The air-built Castle, and the golden Dream,
> The Maid's romantic wish, the Chymist's flame,
> And Poet's vision of eternal fame. (iii, 9–12)

Both passages convey the folly of ambition and pride which tempts the imagination of every individual. Pope knows how schemes, dreams and airy nothings flourish in the foggy landscape of man's ignorance – the landscape which *The Dunciad Variorum* will explore so powerfully.

As an artist Pope had flirted with a wild 'scheme' of his own. In later life he told Spence that he once 'had some thoughts of writing a Persian Fable in which I should have given a full loose to description and imagination. It would have been a very wild thing if I had executed it, but might not have been unentertaining.'[5] His attraction to the 'Persian tales' had apparently begun as early as 1711,[6] and even twelve years later he was recommending the subject to Judith Cowper:

I have long had an inclination to tell a Fairy tale; the more wild & exotic the better, therfore a *Vision*, which is confined to no rules of probability, will take in all the Variety & luxuriancy of Description you will. Provided there

be an apparent moral to it. I think one or 2 of the Persian Tales would give
one Hints for such an Invention . . . a Piece of this fanciful & Imaginary
nature I am sure is practicable. (26 Sept. 1723)

Pope is conscious that this would be an artistically renegade exercise,
that Miss Cowper could indulge herself and not be restrained by
thoughts of truth to nature or the probabilities of the real world; the
rules could be disregarded, and the moral need only be 'apparent'. In
another mood, and to another correspondent, Pope might have
attacked this as dangerous irresponsibility, where the 'fanciful &
Imaginary' has usurped the real and true; but here his combined tone
of confession and indulgence tells us that he sees this as a congenial
task well suited to a young lady with little experience of the world.
One aspect of Pope's sense of artistic decorum (for him always a
living principle) is his awareness that the poetic imagination is
entitled to break 'the rules' – when this is consciously done and the
context calls for it. The idea is clearly seen in a letter to Lady Mary
Wortley Montagu, where Pope is faced with describing something
which outrages order and common sense – in this case the jumble of
dwellings at Stanton Harcourt from where he writes:

You must expect nothing regular in my description of a House that seems to
be built before Rules were in fashion. The whole is so disjointed, & the parts
so detachd from each other, and yet so joining again one can't tell how; that
in a poetical Fitt you'd imagine it had been a Village in Amphions time,
where twenty Cottages had taken a dance together, were all Out, and stood
still in amazement ever since. (Sept. 1718)

The image is decorously outrageous, a deliberate fancy introduced
with a sense of enjoyment in breaking the rules for a 'regular'
description. He establishes his critical justification and then proceeds
to link the confusion of the buildings with a confusion in his own
poetic mind. In his *Epistle to a Lady* many years later he adopts a
similar tone of gusto and daring in employing an irregular
imaginative style for describing the characters of women – again
with a proper sense of its decorum for a series of people who seem to
conform to no rule.

It is no coincidence that the four poems discussed in this book all
have women for their leading characters. Eloisa, Belinda and the
goddess Dulness seem an incongruous trio, but they are linked for
Pope's purposes by their capacity to indulge and inspire the
imagination. At the surface they may appear to inhabit contrasting

worlds, but each contains at a more profound level the capacity for chaos – Belinda's Cave of Spleen is not different in kind from the Cave of Poverty and Poetry where *The Dunciad Variorum* opens, and Eloisa's melancholic mental prison is not too far distant either. The world of beauty and vision is rooted in something darker and more chaotic. Pope associated women with the imaginative faculty, partly because he accepted the widely-held view of his day that woman was by nature more 'fanciful' than man, but also because of a deeper fascination which frequently led him to direct his imagination towards them in intriguing ways.

On 12 November 1711 Pope wrote to his friend Henry Cromwell about the impossibility, as he saw it, of his art's ever being able to do justice to his imagination. Artistic frustration merges into a kind of sexual teasing as he describes the coquettish behaviour of the muses: 'Those Aeriall Ladies just discover to me enough of their Beauties to urge my Pursuit, and draw me on in a wandring Maze of Thought, still in hopes (& only in hopes) of attaining those favors from 'em, which they confer on their more happy admirers elsewhere.' The muses behave as the sylphs do in *The Rape of the Lock* when they lure Belinda's admirers into the labyrinths of fancy. In his very next sentence he explores the idea that there is something treacherous about the imagination, that when the poet consciously confronts the 'gilded Clouds' of his vision and tries to give it artistic form it collapses in front of him like an emotional girl:

We grasp some more beautifull Idea in our Brain, than our Endeavors to express it can set to the view of others; & still do but labour to fall short of our first Imagination. The gay Colouring which Fancy gave to our Design at the first transient glance we had of it, goes off in the Execution; like those various Figures in the gilded Clouds, which while we gaze long upon, to seperate the Parts of each imaginary Image, the whole faints before the Eye, & decays into Confusion.

The image is of a disastrous flirtation. He thinks he has fought off their other admirers, that he has at last attained their favour by a glance; but when he tries to make them his own they faint away in confusion. Women? Or his imagination? In *An Essay on Criticism* (published in the same year as this letter) Pope repeats the idea that colours can betray:

> When the ripe Colours *soften* and *unite*,
> And sweetly *melt* into just Shade and Light,

> When mellowing Years their full Perfection give,
> And each Bold Figure just begins to *Live*;
> The *treach'rous Colours* the fair Art betray,
> And all the bright Creation fades away! (488–93)

The painting, its softness and sweetness increasing as it mellows to maturity, takes on the qualities of a beautiful woman whose looks will finally fade with age. In *The Rape of the Lock* Pope similarly brings together shifting colours, a maze, flirtation, betrayal and confusion in the relationship between Belinda and her sylphs, where the power and precariousness of the imagination are specifically seen in feminine terms.

Pope is fascinated by the vulnerability of women, and by their distance from him. Their weakness lies in their fancies – they are in no *physical* danger from him, but in his imagination he can come intimately and embarrassingly close to them. *The Rape of the Lock* gains considerable power from this paradox. The Sun-like, divine Belinda awes her worshippers at a distance, but the sylph can recline on the 'nosegay in her breast' and explore the 'close Recesses' of her mind. Another aspect of Pope's imagination can, in the form of Umbriel, actually flit inside Belinda's spleen to watch her unconscious in its primal workings. In a letter to Broome, 31 Dec. 1719, he senses his power to exploit women's imaginations, and tells his friend how he will set about luring a lady to pay a visit: 'I will tell Mrs Betty Marriot such wonders of the enchanted bowers, silver streams, opening avenues, rising mounts, and painted grottos, that her very curiosity shall bring her to us . . .' He is jokingly aware of what a woman will do to satisfy her imagination and he hints that he will play the part of a drawing-room Othello wooing his Desdemona. The idea is itself fanciful and playful and to that extent innocent. But, as so often with Pope, there is a serpent lying in the grass. How 'innocently' should we take his phrases ('silver streams, opening avenues, rising mounts')? It could be that his imagination expresses itself unconsciously; but more likely he is relishing the juxtaposition of his own sexual awareness with the innocence of Betty Marriot, lover of romantic scenery. Pope seems to enjoy the way in which his imagination can transform an innocent scene into a sensual one, and he understands the satanic aspect of this idea. In the whole of literature there is no starker contrast than that between the innocent, unfallen Eve and her tempter Satan; and yet Satan was able, through Eve's imagination, to enter the very cells of her mind and create her troubling dream. Pope felt this particular contrast powerfully on one occasion when he found himself sharing a coach with a young lady. To break down her reticence he offered her some fruit:

In short, I tempted, and she Eat; nor was I more like the Devil, than she like Eve . . . I put on the Gallantry of the old Serpent, & in spite of my Evil Forme, accosted her with all the Gayety I was master of . . . I had the pleasantest Journey imaginable, so that now, as once of yore, by means of the *forbidden Fruit*, the *Devil* got into *Paradise* . . . (Pope–Cromwell, 11 July 1709)

Pope recognises the incongruity of this meeting between the stunted cripple and the beautiful woman. But through his imagination her innocence becomes vulnerable; she is accosted by his wit just as she has (probably unbeknown to herself) been tempted and enjoyed by his 'fancying' her.

In a letter to *The Guardian*, 24 March 1713, Pope gives a comical turn to the temptations of imagination. In the person of 'a Mad Doctor' specialising in the cure of frenzies, he writes to advertise his '*Grand Elixir*', a potion which is the medicinal equivalent of what Dr Johnson calls 'the whispers of fancy';[7] it is an 'intellectual Oyl; which applied at the Ear seizes all the Senses with a most agreeable Transport'. The Doctor takes it upon himself

to confer an agreeable Madness on my Fellow-Creatures, for their mutual Delight and Benefit. Since it is agreed by the Philosophers, that Happiness and Misery consist chiefly in the Imagination, nothing is more necessary to Mankind in general than this pleasing Delirium, which renders every one satisfied with himself, and persuades him that all others are equally so.[8]

We recall that, like Satan's flattery, the oil is 'applied at the Ear'. In this context the satanic temptation may have become light-hearted and cheering, but Pope hints at the more serious issue of man's need for illusion, when he adds that 'it restores and vivifies the most dejected Minds, corrects and extracts all that is painful in the Knowledge of a Man's Self'. In his later work Pope will confront the painfulness of self-knowledge and challenge the pleasing delusions of the imagination, but here the Miltonic reference is all part of the joke.

Pope was capable of writing flirtatious letters, and he was apparently amused by the thought that what was in reality mere paper could, through the medium of the lady's imagination, be transformed to something more dangerous. This paradox lies behind his witty insistence upon the innocence of the material itself when he writes to Betty Marriot:

Cast your eyes upon Paper, Madam, there you may look innocently: Men are seducing, books are dangerous, the amorous one's soften you, and the godly one's give you the spleen: If you look upon trees, they clasp in embraces; birds and beasts make love; the Sun is too warm for your blood, the Moon melts you into yielding and melancholy. Therefore I say once more, cast your eyes upon Paper . . . (?1714)

Pope relishes the idea that if all she sees is paper, then she will be safe. He felt strongly the satanic power of the imagination, and there is, even in his most playful exploitations of it, a sense that he knows he is flirting with something dangerous. Whenever he writes about the imagination (in his letters or his poetry) the themes of delusion, treachery, temptation and fall are never far away.

The most imaginative of Pope's letters are those he wrote to Lady Mary Wortley Montagu during her absence with her husband in the Near East. He noticed that his feelings for her grew warmer in proportion to her distance from him, and this was because his imagination ('a generous Piece of Popery') was left free to roam after her:

Methinks it is a noble Spirit of Contradiction to fate and fortune, not to give up those that are snatchd from us, but follow them with warmer Zeal, the farther they are removd from the sence of it . . . 'Tis a generous Piece of Popery that pursues even those who are to be Eternally absent into another world; let it be right or wrong, the very Extravagance is a sort of Piety . . . (10 Nov. 1716)

It is no contradiction really, since Pope knows well how the imagination can transcend time and space, and he seems to take pleasure in charming her from such a vast distance. He can even extend the gap into infinity:

Since your Body is so full of fire, and capable of such Solar motions as your Letter describes, your Soul can never be long going to the Fixed Stars (where I intend to settle) Or Else you may find me in the milky way, because Fontanelle assures us, the Stars are so crowded there that a man may stand upon one, and talk to his friend on another. (10 Nov. 1716)

In return, he delights in the way her descriptive letters can carry him across hundreds of miles to the scenes she is enjoying: 'The poetical manner in which you paint some of the Scenes about you, makes me despise my native country and sets me on fire to fall into the Dance about your Fountain in Belgrade-village' (autumn 1717). It is typical of Pope that in his very next sentence he should recognise a literary precedent for the illusion he is enjoying: 'I fancy myself, in my romantic thoughts & distant admiration of you, not unlike the man in the Alchymist that has a passion for the Queen of the Faeries. I lye dreaming of you in Moonshiny Nights exactly in the posture of Endymion gaping for Cynthia in a Picture.' He knows that Ben Jonson's Dapper, along with the other gulls, was deluded by his imagination into becoming a figure of utter ridicule as he knelt before the Queen of the Fairies in a vain belief in the transforming power of the Alchemist's art (which parallels in that way the power of the imagination). Pope exploits the fancy with a conscious awareness of its literary ancestry and a delight that Lady Mary will share the joke.

This sense of amusement at the imagination's folly, the willing suspension of his scepticism, combined with his understanding of how beauty and its agent are capable of making disagreeable truths evaporate – all this seemed to be awaiting the moment of disillusion-ment and the recognition that imagination can cheat and betray. One such moment came with his quarrel with Lady Mary. Whether the cause was her laughter at his declaration of love (as Lady Louisa Stuart recorded)[9] or something less dramatic, what had been a stimulus to his amorous imagination became a source of utter distaste. Pope saw how the imagination could be akin to ugliness as well as beauty, and hate as well as love, and in his satire he came increasingly to stress this other side. The tactics are those of someone who knows how to exploit the precariousness of the imagination and is able by a word or phrase to push delight over into distaste, so that a brilliant transformation is not entirely achieved and disagreeable ideas still cling. He knows how incongruity can slip into something threatening, how sensuous effects can cause uneasiness as well as pleasure, and how the awesome can easily become the shocking.

Lady Mary ('Sappho') makes her appearance in *Epistle to a Lady* as a distasteful rather than delightful paradox. Images of the captivating imagination (fragrance and glittering diamonds) are now merged with physical dirt and grease, as he uses her for an example of contradiction:

> . . . As Sappho's diamonds with her dirty smock,
> Or Sappho at her toilet's greasy task,

> With Sappho fragrant at an ev'ning Mask:
> So morning Insects that in muck begun,
> Shine, buzz, and fly-blow in the setting-sun. (24–8)

The surface charm is still there, but Pope's imagination has now turned to the *process* behind the finished product. Here she is a Swiftian 'goddess' labouring at the messy and painful task of her toilette, the word 'fragrant' becoming heavy with the wrong associations. She is still a creature of his imagination, but now belongs to the darker 'muck' where the imagination breeds, just as butterflies are hatched from dirty grubs. (This is the world of process explored in *The Dunciad Variorum*.) Pope's early poem 'Phryne' (the Greek for toad) looks in a very similar way behind the bride who shines 'In Di'monds, Pearls, and rich Brocades . . . / And flutters in her Pride':

> So have I known those Insects fair,
> (Which curious *Germans* hold so rare,)
>   Still vary Shapes and Dyes;
> Still gain new Titles with new Forms;
> First Grubs obscene, then wriggling Worms,
>   Then painted Butterflies. (19–24)

Perhaps the most famous butterfly in Pope is Lord Hervey ('Sporus'), the 'painted Child of Dirt' in *Epistle to Dr Arbuthnot* (1735). Pope's notorious portrait is an exercise in not allowing the imaginative transformation to be completed or the illusion to be preserved. Hervey retains traces of the elements (earth and water) from which he sprang, as the reptile must always return to the muddy water. Pope's tactic is to leave Hervey's metamorphosis incomplete, so that he becomes an 'amphibious Thing', the 'familiar Toad' of Satan squatting at Eve's ear and infecting her imagination (the image meant a great deal to him):

> His Wit all see-saw between *that* and *this*,
> Now high, now low, now Master up, now Miss,
> And he himself one vile Antithesis.
> Amphibious Thing! that acting either Part,
> The trifling Head, or the corrupted Heart!
> Fop at the Toilet, Flatt'rer at the Board,
> Now trips a Lady, and now struts a Lord.
> *Eve*'s Tempter thus the Rabbins have exprest,
> A Cherub's face, a Reptile all the rest . . . (323–31)

Some of Pope's most powerful satire comes when he explores in this way the imagination as process; the illusion is shattered and beauty is shown to be still embedded within the medium of its creation.

On other occasions the method is similar. In the Cave of Spleen (Canto iv of *The Rape of the Lock*) and in the setting for *The Dunciad Variorum*, Pope describes the murky, misty areas where images have not fully achieved themselves, whether in the 'nameless somethings' waiting for generation in chaos, or the comic 'living *Teapots*' inhabiting the foggy grotto of Belinda's unconscious. This represents, as it were, the underside of Pope's imagination – the earthy grotesqueness beneath the airy beauty, the dark internal world of the gnomes beneath the sylph-world with its surface play of light and colour. Each is a province of the imagination, and Pope, as we shall see, had many literary and philosophical precedents for this duality. We shall notice how other writers besides Pope were concerned that the imagination should emerge from the amorphous internal world (the base earth) towards the lucid level of aspiration or transcendence, and that Pope was not the first poet to explore how the imagination could regress to its origins within the chaotic unconscious. Shakespeare had shown in *Othello*, for example, how close a fantasist is to primitive chaos, and how the loss of faith in an illusion might bring disintegration as it sinks from an extreme of faith/love to one of despair/distaste ('when I love thee not, / Chaos is come again', III,iii,92–3).[10] Something of a reverse movement is discernible in Cleopatra (another Shakespearean figure who interested Pope).[11] Throughout her play she exemplifies the imagination's metamorphosing power (upon her own identity and other people's); she is an example of that 'serpent of old Nile' which is bred in the mud by the action of the sun;[12] and while to her enemie she remains embedded in the Egyptian clay, the dramatist allows her to achieve a final metamorphosis and fly free of her lower elements ('I am fire, and air; my other elements / I give to baser life', V,ii,288–9) so that she ends with the fantasy intact. These two Shakespearean fantasists are linked by this image of the Egyptian serpent (the worm of fantasy generated within the muddy unconscious): Cleopatra's 'pretty worm of Nilus' finally releases her from mortal reality,[13] but Othello's Egyptian handkerchief (bred by 'hallow'd' worms and exerting a hypnotic hold over lovers' fancies)[14] becomes the destructive serpent of jealousy. Pope's fascination with the 'equivocal generation' of reptiles is just one aspect of his interest in the relationship between imagination and the creative principle, and his concern as an artist with the equivocal nature of imaginative activity.

Of the poems discussed in the coming chapters, the two earlier ones (*Eloisa to Abelard* and *The Rape of the Lock*) bring into question the illusions in which the heroines live; they confront the possibility of chaos and disintegration, only to end with gestures of sympathy by which the poet allows the fancy to stand – indeed places himself within it. *Epistle to a Lady*, however, catalogues the self-destructiveness of fanciful *de*lusions, ending with a conscious restraining of the imaginative impulse, and *The Dunciad Variorum* explores the imagination's capacity for chaos by showing how created things, if illusion rules, are in danger of imploding into original matter. If Pope's imagination *was* in some ways a woman, then she was at times a fallen woman, at times a redeemed woman: she was sometimes Eve, victim of a satanic dream; sometimes the Lady in the *Maske* awaiting the release of her soul into a higher sphere. At all times she was elusive, troubled, brilliant. She delighted him, but frustrated him. Pope followed her, served her, and finally grew disillusioned with her.

TWO

The paradox of the imagination:
Eloisa to Abelard

I

From its first publication in his *Works* of 1717, Pope's Ovidian epistle *Eloisa to Abelard* became one of his most admired and influential poems. Even towards the end of the eighteenth century when critics were questioning whether Pope had any right to be called a poet at all, *Eloisa to Abelard* remained a favourite with readers and critics alike. Joseph Warton (whose *Essay on Pope* of 1756 helped to establish the decline of Pope's reputation) singled out this poem for its pathos;[1] pre-romantic poets of the 1740s and 1750s, in rebellion against Pope's moralising satiric verse, stole phrases and images from it, and Eloisa mourning against a tombstone was a popular melancholic icon.[2]

Modern criticism has learned how to value Pope the satirist (the master of tone and classical allusion) and along with this revaluation has grown a dislike for the histrionics of *Eloisa to Abelard*, for its unironic wholeheartedness, its imaginative commitment to the woman's predicament, and what is seen as Pope's unhealthy interest in his heroine's self-arousal (one critic has described the poem as a 'rhapsodic fantasy of masturbation and release').[3] It has become an established view that Pope does not manage to distance himself from his heroine, that he somehow sanctions her 'fantasising' and fails to maintain the kind of detachment from her which would allow him to stand free and 'place' Eloisa by controlling the situation and tone.[4] In order to find this control other critics have stressed the poem's artful rhetoric and the way in which Pope the 'accomplished rhetorician' imposes form on 'almost chaotic subject matter'.[5] Each of these approaches, however, betrays a degree of embarrassment at the extent to which Pope writes from inside Eloisa's imagination. The poem is in danger of being forced towards the extremes of fantasy or rhetorical exercise.

A way out of this impasse is perhaps to confront the 'fantasy' issue head-on and investigate the terms upon which Pope explores the movements within Eloisa's mind. Artistic control may then be seen not merely in terms of rhetorical structure, but in the extent to which Pope charts and evaluates her visions and 'places' them in relation to a long tradition of thought about contemplative activity. In order to understand the true quality of Pope's art in *Eloisa to Abelard*, and to appreciate the nature of the poem's irony, it is important to examine its relationship to Renaissance theories of the imagination, and in particular to the early poems of Milton.

Jean Hagstrum has remarked that Pope was 'intellectually and spiritually a son of the Renaissance and its seventeenth-century afterglow'.[6] This is said specifically of the poet's pictorial skills, but the words apply equally well to Pope's *inward* sight. The 'afterglow' particularly evident in *Eloisa to Abelard* is that cast by Milton, the greatest seventeenth-century explorer and challenger of Renaissance ideas (and for Pope and his contemporaries England's great imaginative poet). In *Eloisa to Abelard* Milton is not merely an 'influence', but a necessary frame of reference within which Pope intends his poem to be read. It exhibits a deeply Miltonic concern with the right and wrong ways of seeing, and with this concern in mind it is possible to isolate an important theme which determines the character of the poem and gives a moral urgency to the heroine's fantasies. This is Eloisa's struggle in the course of the epistle to redirect her imagination away from its enslavement to physical passion and frustrated melancholia towards a divine contemplation.[7] My approach will be by way of the physiological and psychological background to this topic as discussed by Renaissance and early seventeenth-century theorists of the imagination. This will lead to an exploration of how Milton handles the theme in 'L'Allegro', 'Il Penseroso' and the *Maske*. With this context established it will be possible to show how Pope consciously associates his own poem with these Miltonic fictions, and to offer a reading of *Eloisa to Abelard* in this light.

II

For a Renaissance writer the faculty of 'fancy' or 'imagination' (Greek *phantasia*, Latin *imaginatio*) occupied one of the three cells which made up the human brain.[8] The commonest arrangement described *imaginatio* as dwelling in the front chamber, with *ratio* in the middle and *memoria* behind,[9] and this is allegorised by Spenser in his description of the Castle of Alma in Book II of *The Faerie Queene*, where he pictures the melancholy figure of Phantastes sitting in a room rather tastelessly decorated 'With sondry colours, in the which were writ / Infinite shapes of thinges dispersed thin' (II, ix, 50). This is the front chamber of the turret, and its walls are painted with such things 'as in the world were never yit' as well as representations of 'idle fantasies': 'Infernall Hags, Centaurs, feendes, Hippodames, / Apes, Lyons, Aegles, Owles, fooles, lovers, children, Dames'. Flies buzz around, symbolising 'idle thoughtes and fantasies, / Devices, dreames, opinions unsound, / Shewes, visions, sooth-sayes, and prophesies . . .' (II, ix, 51), and in the midst of it all sits the swarthy Phantastes, brows contracted, eyes staring, a man immediately recognisable as being born under Saturn, 'full of melancholy . . . That mad or foolish seemd' (II, ix, 52). Spenser places the emphasis on the folly and nightmare of the imagination. 'Lyons, Aegles, Owles' may suggest its capacity for power, aspiration and wisdom, but the list immediately slips to 'fooles, lovers, children, Dames'. In this passage Spenser also hints at the paradoxical nature of the faculty, its ability to draw together contradictory ideas (the Centaur), its links with idleness, sleep and madness, and its tendency towards either superficial 'shewes' or more penetrative 'visions', superstitious 'sooth-sayes' or more divine 'prophesies'. The visualising aspect of mental activity, which imagination represents, was of course reliant on the healthy functioning of the mind as a whole. It was not good or evil in itself, but its capacity for either depended on the activity in which it was involved and the sanctions placed upon it.

Under the terms of Renaissance faculty psychology[10] the imagination carried on its function as the brain's image-making sensorium within the 'sensitive soul' of man. It was thus able to act independently of the higher 'rational soul' (seat of the conscious faculties of the mind, the reason and will), though in a healthy mind the conscious rational faculties would combine to assert their lordship over the imaginative faculty. When a man's body was functioning normally (that is, when he was awake, sober, sane, dispassionate, and settled in his humours) the imagination carried out the useful function of organising the input of sense-experience into images, submitting its findings to the rational faculty which would analyse, evaluate, accept or reject. This relationship would often work well, but there was danger in that the 'rational soul' (because conscious) was intermittent in its operation. It ceased to function, for example, in sleep, when will and reason were suspended. But the imagination never rested, with the result that in sleep it could have things all its own way, as described by Robert Burton:

> In time of sleep this faculty [Phantasy or Imagination] is free, and many times conceives strange, stupend, absurd shapes, as in sick men we commonly observe . . . In melancholy men this faculty is most powerful and strong, and often hurts, producing many monstrous and prodigious things . . . In poets and painters imagination forcibly works, as appears by their several fictions, antics, images . . . In men it is subject and governed by reason, or at least should be . . . when the common sense resteth, the outward senses rest also. The phantasy alone is free . . . as appears by those imaginary dreams, which are of divers kinds, natural, divine, demoniacal, etc., which vary according to humours . . . (I, i, 2, vii)[11]

Burton sees no *generic* difference between illness, madness, melancholia, nightmares, the imaginations of the poet, and 'divine' dreams. Anything which suspended the power of the reason and will (whether drink, amorous passion, an excess of melancholy vapours, or divine *afflatus*) excited and released the anarchic *phantasia*. The activity of the imagination always had this potential for chaos. The world of dreams was only the most prevalent example. A body in the grip of a particular passion (pride, jealousy, ambition or whatever) could likewise overthrow the will and leave the way open for wild fantasies, and an excess of alcohol would bring similar illusions. The imagination was a good servant but a bad master.

Shakespeare seems to have been exploring such ideas in *The Tempest*.[12] Prospero, whose private cell may conceivably have links with the *cellula phantastica* within the poet's brain, has the ability to conjure up spirits 'to enact [his] present fancies' and then to allow the vision to dissolve in air again. But the man with power over the miraculous Ariel (who recalls the swiftness, insubstantiality and hypnotic power of the imagination) must also acknowledge as his the figure of Caliban, the rebellious servant–monster and 'thing of darkness'. Caliban delights in the physical world of the island and in a parody of the divine imagination discovers the 'celestial liquor' alcohol and takes a drunken butler for his god. In his last words Caliban recognises his folly and determines henceforth to 'seek for grace'.

The neoplatonic duality of body and soul, and the consequent placing of man between the angel and the beast, naturally encouraged the conviction that the imagination reflected man's paradoxical nature. It could raise him higher or pull him down according to the extent to which it followed the spirit or the flesh. Gianfrancesco Pico della Mirandola (nephew of the more famous Giovanni and friend of Ficino) expounded this idea in his treatise *De Imaginatione* (1501):

> For if phantasy shall deliberately resist the pleasures which allure the senses, and drag them to things infernal, and shall strive to draw them to things celestial, it will lead thither the rebellious sense, unwilling and reluctant though this be. But if, yielding to the senses, phantasy shall decline to apply itself to the business of virtue, so great is its power that it afflicts the body and beclouds the mind.[13]

Eloisa to Abelard, a poem which shows (Pope tells us in The Argument) 'the struggles of grace and nature, virtue and passion', gains much power from such a conflict within Eloisa's imagination.

In addition, therefore, to its basic task of providing raw material for the judgmental faculty (*ratio*), imagination could obey a nobler call and assist the higher 'intuitive' reason (*mens*) by aiding the mind in contemplation. St Augustine had denied that the essence of divine love could be seen by the physical eyes, nor could it be 'thought of in the spirit by means of an image like a body [i.e. through the imagination]; but only in the mind, that is, in the intellect, can it be known and perceived'.[14] However, many Renaissance writers conceded that when properly disciplined and directed the imagination was a valuable aid to the intellect.[15] Gianfrancesco Pico showed a hearty distrust of the imaginative powers of the mind, but even he asserted their vital role in contemplation:

> Imagination enters into alliance with all the superior powers, inasmuch as they would fail in that function which nature has bestowed upon each of them unless imagination support and assist them. Nor could the soul, fettered as it is to the body, opine, know, or comprehend at all, if phantasy were not constantly to supply it with the images themselves. (p. 33)

For Pico, the imagination was given to man in order to allow communication between body and soul, 'through which the soul, even when united to the body, should perform its own functions' (p. 41), 'nevertheless it is irrational and devoid of correct judg-

ment, unless aided by the guidance of a superior power. Hearkening
to this, imagination beatifies man; disobedient to it, imagination
dooms him' (p. 43).

Imagination, therefore, could be at the service of the soul or of the
body, and depending on its master it could bring images of air and
spirit, or images of earth and flesh. At the beatific close of the
Paradiso Dante gazes upon the Eternal light through the power of
'l'alta fantasia' (xxxiii, 142); in such a way the divine aspect of
imagination could accompany intellect on the platonic ascent. An
archetype of this contemplative flight is the platonist Philo's
description of the ascent of mind to God:

when on soaring wing it has contemplated the atmosphere and all its phases,
it is borne yet higher to the ether and the circuit of heaven, and is whirled
round with the dances of planets and fixed stars . . . And so, carrying its
gaze beyond the confines of all substance discernible by sense, it comes to a
point at which it reaches out after the intelligible world, and on descrying in
that world sights of surpassing loveliness . . . it is seized by a sober
intoxication, like those filled with Corybantic frenzy . . . it seems to be on
its way to the Great King Himself; but, amid its longing to see Him, pure
and untempered rays of concentrated light stream forth like a torrent, so that
by its gleams the eye of the understanding is dazzled.[16]

Here intoxication, frenzy and a dazzled understanding are in the
service of a lofty vision, and the imagination takes on the quality of
air, the highest element; the sinful earth of man's physical nature has
been transcended. At the other extreme of imaginative activity is
John Aubrey's description of James Harrington's 'phancy'; here the
associations are quite different: the rarefied ether is replaced by
human sweat, the element of earth, from whose heat insects are bred:

he grew to have a phancy that his perspiration turned to flies, and sometimes
to bees . . . a fly or two, or more, might be drawn-out of the lurking holes
by the warmeth; and then he would crye out, 'Doe not you see it apparently
that these come from me?' 'Twas the strangest sort of madnes that ever I
found in any one: talke of any thing els, his discourse would be very
ingeniose and pleasant.[17]

Both *The Rape of the Lock* (in its contrast between airy sylphs and
earthy gnomes) and *the Dunciad Variorum* (with its description of
grotesque creativity) exploit such elemental contrasts within the
imagination, and Eloisa is keenly aware of the two poles as her mind
swings between images of the ethereal and the physical.

The contrast could also be seen in less extreme terms, so that the alternative was not madness and physicality, but a delight in superficial show and false beauty. In his 'Hymne of Heavenly Beautie' (1596) Spenser, for example, makes an explicit contrast between the heavenly delight of true vision (via the 'inward ey') and those 'idle fancies' which merely distract and deceive:

> So full their eyes are of that glorious sight,
> And senses fraught with such satietie,
> That in nought else on earth they can delight,
> But in th'aspect of that felicitie,
> Which they have written in their inward ey . . .
> Ah then my hungry soule, which long hast fed
> On idle fancies of thy foolish thought,
> And with false beauties flattring bait misled,
> Hast after vaine deceiptfull shadowes sought,
> Which all are fled, and now have left thee nought . . . (281–92)

This directing of the imagination away from superficial pleasures and 'false beauties' on to those higher objects of 'infinite delight' (258) and divine 'extasy' (261) was part of the training for the contemplative life (a theme touched on in Milton's 'Il Penseroso'), and indeed Gianfrancesco Pico, in discussing the 'diseases and imperfections of phantasy which hinge upon temperament' (p. 59), remarks that the matter is particularly perilous for 'those devoted to the contemplative life, who give free rein to the imagination' (p. 61). Pope's Eloisa will show these dangers very clearly.

The important distinction I wish to make, therefore, is between what will be termed the 'divine' imagination and the 'base' imagination,[18] and it is important to stress that this is a distinction not of kind, but of function. The 'divine' imagination is the highway of the gods, its operation a glimpse of heavenly truth from the soul's tower, piercing mysteries beyond the reach of earthly men. The term 'base' imagination, however, is intended to subsume the nightmarish 'damned' imagination, but also other lower levels of functioning of the faculty: the imagination when it simply offers harmless pleasure (L'Allegro's 'unreproved pleasures'), when it delights in rustic superstitions, when it is triggered off by the outer physical senses, when it is stirred by wine or a disturbance of the humours, when it is the slave of the passions, or aroused by the 'decaying sense,'[19] as Hobbes called it, of memory (and not the 'divine' memory which the soul has of its home) – when it is content not to rise above the things of this world. This is a comprehensive bundle of ideas, but such aspects all belong to the imagination *when it is not functioning at its highest level*. From the viewpoint of a thoroughgoing neoplatonist, all these aspects of the imagination (whatever harmless beauty they might evoke) helped to yoke the soul to the things of this world, the world of Nature and not of Grace. In this view man's immortal soul was trapped in the prison of the flesh, and any degree of attachment to the world of Nature (that is, to the things of this sublunary world) helped to imbrute the soul and hinder its final ascent towards God. The 'base' image could either help to dress the world in gorgeous colours or pander to the flesh's desires; both effects led man away from the divine. When the imagination acted at its highest level, however, it could help to set before the soul the image of the suffering Christ, the eternal bliss of Heaven, the beauty of the angels, and it could in such ways be the handmaid of man's intellect by helping to bring the *gnosis*, or knowledge of the divine forms, which for the neoplatonist were the true reality. 'Therefore we can without difficulty affirm that not only all the good, universally, but also all the bad, can be derived from the imagination' (Pico, p. 43).

As we have seen, the favourite candidate for imaginative excess was the melancholy man ('In melancholy men this faculty is most powerful and strong').[20] During the late sixteenth and early seventeenth century, when the cult of melancholy was at its height, there was a related interest in the links between melancholy and imagination, and within the former there was seen a similar contrast between its divine and damned aspects. It has been recognised by scholars that Renaissance melancholy had two guises, the 'Galenic' and the 'Aristotelian'.[21] The first was base, self-destructive, nightmarish and mad; the other noble, lofty, heroic and godlike. One tradition, taking its cue from the ancient medical lore of Galen, stressed the unfortunate characteristics of melancholy, with its mad delusions and depression of spirits which could only be aroused into cheerfulness by wine. The counterpart of this was so-called 'Aristotelian' melancholy, godlike in its aspirations, fitting a man for heavenly contemplation. Thomas Walkington, in *The Optick Glasse of Humors* (1607), points a neat contrast between these two melancholies: 'The melancholick man is said of the wise to be *aut Deus aut Daemon*, either angel of heaven or a fiend of hell: for in whomsoever this humour hath dominion, the soule is either wrapt up into an *Elysium* and paradise of blesse by a heavenly contemplation, or into a direfull hellish purgatory by a cynicall meditation . . . (f. 64b)

It comes as no surprise to find that this contrast between 'divine' and 'damned' melancholy is paralleled by a similar contrast between the 'divine' and 'damned' aspects of the imaginative faculty, the imagination of heavenly contemplation and the imagination of passion and delusion. For Walkington the former melancholy was 'the nurse of contemplation, the pretious balme of witte and pollicy: the enthousiasticall breath of poetry, the foison of *our best phantasies*' (f. 68a, my italics), while the sufferers from the latter 'are not only out of temper for their organs of body, but their minds also are so out of frame and distract, that they are in bondage to many ridiculous passions, imagining that they see and feele such things, as no man els can either perceive or touch' (ff. 69a–69b). Or, as Levinus Lemnius (1576) puts it, black melancholy 'disquieteth the mynde, wyth sundry straung apparitions, and phantasticall imaginations.'[22] According to the traditional proverb, *sub Saturno nati aut optimi aut pessimi.*[23]

The theme of these Renaissance theories of the imagination, therefore, is overwhelmingly one of paradox: the faculty inspired by divine melancholy could also be imprisoned by nightmare and drunken delusion;[24] it could transcend the senses or be tied to the base promptings of the flesh. Pope's humanist fascination with the paradoxical nature of man[25] felt very much at home among such contradictions, and his interest in the workings of the imagination allowed him to appreciate the opportunities this paradox gave for internal psychic drama (Renaissance *psychomachia*), where a battle might be fought within an individual torn by the conflicting claims of spirit and flesh. *Eloisa to Abelard* is Pope's response to such potentialities. But many of these ideas came to him filtered through the work of Milton, whose Ludlow *Maske* explores just such a struggle. Therefore, a brief consideration of Milton's treatment of this theme in his early poetry is a necessary transition to Pope's development of these ideas in *Eloisa to Abelard*.

III

It has been pointed out by Lawrence Babb that Milton's diptych 'L'Allegro' and 'Il Penseroso' enacts a distinction between 'damned' and 'divine' melancholy.[26] The first is exorcised at the opening of 'L'Allegro':

> Hence loathed Melancholy
>   Of *Cerberus*, and blackest midnight born,
> In *Stygian* Cave forlorn
>   'Mongst horrid shapes, and shreiks, and sights unholy,
> Find out som uncouth cell,
>   Where brooding darknes spreads his jealous wings . . . (ll. 1–6)[27]

This is of course quite different from the 'divine' melancholy celebrated by Il Penseroso, who at night 'unspheres' the spirit of Plato in his lonely tower and aspires at the end of the poem 'to somthing like Prophetic strain.' The tendency throughout 'Il Penseroso' is towards divine vision; the poet invokes the figure of heavenly contemplation:

> Com pensive Nun, devout and pure,
> Sober, stedfast, and demure,
> All in a robe of darkest grain . . .
> And looks commercing with the skies,
> Thy rapt soul sitting in thine eyes. (31–40)

'Damned' and 'divine' melancholy are therefore clearly differentiated in terms of the effect each has upon the imagination: one is a nightmare, the other a holy vision.

If 'L'Allegro' exorcises the 'horrid shapes' and 'sights unholy' of 'damned' melancholy, the opening lines of 'Il Penseroso' also banish the 'base' imagination – not the hellish visions associated with 'damned' melancholy, but the frivolous fancies bred in an idle, pleasure-loving mind:

> . . . fancies fond with gaudy shapes . . .
>   As thick and numberless
>   As the gay motes that people the Sun Beams,
>   Or likest hovering dreams . . . (6–9)

(This is very apt for the fancies which L'Allegro delights in.) Both poems, then, exorcise a wrong kind of imagination. Milton is distinguishing the highest possible level of vision (that which can attain contemplation of the divine – the 'Prophetic strain' alluded to at the end of 'Il Penseroso') from, firstly, its opposite (where sanity and salvation are at stake), and secondly from the pleasurable fancy which may, on L'Allegro's terms, be condoned if only for the delight that it gives.

In Milton's *Maske* (1634) Comus combines within himself each of these aspects of the 'base' imagination; indeed, it is inevitable from his lineage that he should. He is, after all, the half-brother of Euphrosyne (Mirth) celebrated in 'L'Allegro' (both are children of Bacchus) and so he shares the rhythms and delights of that poem:

> Jest and youthful Jollity,
> Quips and Cranks, and wanton Wiles . . .
> Com, and trip it as ye go
> On the light fantastick toe . . . (26–33)

Like Mirth, he welcomes 'Jollity', liberty and pleasure. But whereas Mirth's mother is Venus, his is Circe, not an instrument of the harmless, delightful imagination, but a force with the transforming power of evil, possessing arts to pervert the soul and lure it away from God towards the snares of the flesh, with their threat of bestiality and damnation. Comus therefore inherits both aspects of the 'base' imagination. He presents a façade of light-hearted mirth, delighting (like L'Allegro) in the enchanted world of Nature ('on the Tawny Sands and Shelves, / Trip the pert Fairies and the dapper Elves', 117–18); but he brings with this an alliance with the forces of darkness, invoking Cotytto 'That ne're [is] call'd, but when the Dragon woom / Of Stygian darknes spets her thickest gloom' (131–2). By uniting both these aspects of the 'base' imagination he provides the most formidable of all adversaries for the being who enshrines in the masque the power of highest 'divine' imagination.

Imprisoned in Comus' chair, physically at his mercy, her senses assailed by Comus' heady vision of the earth's fruitfulness, with the magician's bestial victims before her, the Lady remains committed to her inner vision. She is one of those who

always reserve in themselves a privat roome, where to the tempests of Fortune cannot reach. There it is, where the soule retires, to maintaine her selfe in an eternall serenity . . . Here finally it is, where wee conserving the image of things delightfull, shall have meanes to have nought but goodly thoughts; . . . wee may . . . give contentment to our minde, while our senses are on the rack, and entertaine our Idea on beauty, at such time as foulnes shalbe the object of our eyes.

(Jacques du Bosc, *The Compleat Woman*, trans. N. N. (London, 1639), pp. 40–1)

It is through her imagination that the Lady is able to conserve 'the image of things delightfull'. The 'divine' imagination places the 'Idea' before her, thereby counteracting the lure of the immediate senses which Comus has set for her, so that she tells him: 'Thou canst

not touch the freedom of my minde / With all thy charms, although
this corporal rinde / Thou hast immanacl'd' (662–4). (Like any
aspiring, chaste soul, she has contempt for the decaying flesh which
traps her, and for the bodily senses which tie her to it.) Plato saw the
glories and the dangers of the kind of divine vision that overruled the
five senses. As he expressed it in the *Ion*: '. . . the poet is a light and
winged and holy thing, and there is no invention in him until he has
been inspired and is out of his senses, and reason is no longer in
him.'[28] The Lady in Milton's *Maske* is in this way *out of her senses*,
whereas Comus is trapped in his. In George Herbert's words (in
'The Pulley') he 'rest[s] in Nature, not the God of Nature'. By being
enslaved to the created world through his senses (the world of
Nature, not of Grace), Comus is spiritually crippled, and the very
baseness of his imagination conveys this. He is a being who can
achieve vision only through drunkenness and passion, a heady
swimming vision of the world's fertility, or grotesque magical
fancies. Part of his function as antimasque is this parodying of the
lofty imagination, as when he declares to his animal-headed
followers: 'We that are of purer fire / Imitate the Starry Quire' (111–
12). Thomas Walkington (writing in 1607) has words which can be
applied very well to Comus' false inspiration:

the melancholick man therefore is saide to be borne under leaden *Saturne* the
most disastrous and malignant planet of all . . . this humor if it be not oft
holped with mirth or wine: or some other accidentall cause which is
repugnant to his effect, it will cause nature to droupe . . . Even so the soule
being pressed downe with the ponderous waight of melancholy, and as it
were a thral unto this dumpish humor, is rouzed up with wine and meriment
especially, and infraunchist againe into a more ample and heavenly freedom
of contemplation . . . (ff. 65a–66a)

In the debate scene Comus tempts the Lady with 'all the pleasures /
That fancy can beget on youthfull thoughts, / When the fresh blood
grows lively' (668–70) (the mechanical, 'base' imagination aroused
by the awakening senses). But the Lady rejects such a cordial,
declaring that her mind is far removed from the delights such a being
has to offer. Comus' argument breaks down at the point where the
Lady simply asserts her vision, revealed to the inner sense but hidden
from the outer senses of her enemy:

> Thou hast nor Eare, nor Soul to apprehend
> The sublime notion, and high mystery

> That must be utter'd to unfold the sage
> And serious doctrine of Virginity . . . (784–7)

Even her word 'apprehend' belongs with the lofty intellect, not the senses. Comus' reaction to this is predictable. As he offers her the cup once again, he translates her lofty inner 'apprehension' into the cruder, physical terms of his own 'base' imagination, remarking cynically that "tis but the lees / And setlings of a melancholy blood' (809–10).[29] In other words, he thinks of her divine vision in terms of the 'base' imagination, as resulting from a disturbance of her body's humours: for him her visions are the products of black melancholy for which wine offers easy relief. If Comus 'rests in Nature', then the Lady (using Sir Philip Sidney's words this time) 'doth grow in effect into another nature',[30] that is, from the level of Nature to the level of Grace. Her spiritual well-being is signalled by her powers of 'divine' imagination. The darkness of the wood, the purity of her mind, her abdication from what du Bosc's treatise (p. 41) calls 'the clamorous commerce of the senses', all release her imagination for the higher vision of spiritual truth.

This tension between the 'base' imagination and the 'divine' imagination is dramatically enacted at the Lady's first entrance, when Comus casts his vicious fancies into the air before her in the form of his magic dust:

> Thus I hurl
> My dazling Spells into the spungy ayr,
> Of power to cheat the eye with blear illusion,
> And give it false presentments . . . (153–6)

As the Lady enters, her eye is assailed so that she is temporarily in the grip of the enchanter's 'base' imagination, and for a moment she takes on Comus' own language:

> What might this be? A thousand fantasies
> Begin to throng into my memory
> Of calling shapes, and beckning shadows dire,
> And airy tongues, that syllable mens names
> On Sands, and Shoars, and desert Wildernesses. (205–9)

This is a perversion of the imagination because it is a degradation of the memory. The Lady's mind is now troubled by *Hobbesian* memory ('decaying sense') rather than uplifted by *neoplatonic* memory (the immortal human soul's dim recollection of God). It is by virtue of this latter memory that the mind of man yearns towards

things lofty and infinite.[31] The former memory, by filling the mind
with confused impressions ransacked from the untidy store-room
of the senses, is the food of the 'base' imagination. But the Lady's
possession by Comus' imagery is only momentary. At this crucial
instant her pure mind is granted a higher vision:

> O welcom pure-ey'd Faith, white-handed Hope,
> Thou hovering Angel girt with golden wings,
> And thou unblemish't form of Chastity,
> I see ye visibly . . .
>   (213–16)

In this way the higher imagination drives out the lower, as the
Lady's soul powerfully asserts its own memory. In neoplatonic
terms: the Lady's intellect is awakened by the memory of her divine
origin and is granted a vision of the truth through the lens of her
'divine' imagination.

It is significant that Comus' first challenge to this chaste,
wandering soul is a visual one, and that her first triumph is a vision
of her spiritual protectors – that Faith is 'pure-ey'd', that Hope is a
golden-winged angel, and that the very *Form* of Chastity is placed
before her. 'I see ye visibly' she exclaims (216) as if to counteract
any suggestion that this is a triumph of intellect alone. No, her
'divine' imagination places them powerfully before her. The Lady's
chastity is, of course, not a merely physical technicality, but
involves the status of her soul; it involves the dedication of her life
to her soul's aspirations. And the Attendant Spirit's promise to her
at the close of the másque, as she emerges triumphant from Comus'
challenge, is a hint at the soul's final marriage to its long-sought
love, typically conveyed as the uniting of Cupid with Psyche
('After her wandring labours long', 1007).[32] The imprisoned soul
has, during the course of the masque, been released through grace-
given 'higher' vision. At the moment of her 'taking' by the
magician her mind remains free; the eye of her soul is uncoloured
by her captor's sensuality.

The motionlessness of the Lady in Comus' chair is an evil
enactment of the raptness and stillness of the soul before divine
beauty. The Lady's imprisonment is a parody of the true 'raptness'
or 'rapture' (which Comus feels when he hears the Lady sing), and
similarly we are meant to discern a fine distinction between the
song of his evil mother Circe (which would 'take the prison'd soul',

256) and the other truly sublime 'taking' by the Lady's harmonies (whereby 'even Silence / Was took e're she was ware', 557–8). In this sense the action of Comus in seizing and imprisoning the Lady is the anti-masque parody of 'rapture'. The Lady 'enraptures' Comus, and his response is to seize (*rapio*) the Lady. Comus must affix the Lady by glue to the chair, rather than Orpheus-like, by true poetry, charm her into a genuine motionlessness of the outward senses. Comus, by his attempt to 'ravish' the Lady, *physicalises* the concept just as in his poetry his argument of Nature physicalises, and his imagination is bred by base physical instincts. The Lady's 'ravishment' is of a higher order, as Comus himself recognises when the sounds of her Echo-song float through the air towards him:

> Can any mortal mixture of Earths mould
> Breath such Divine inchanting ravishment?
> Sure somthing holy lodges in that brest,
> And with these raptures moves the vocal air . . . (244–7)

This is a 'taking' which is at the same time a 'freeing' of the soul. Laurentius (p. 86) speaks of 'a kinde of divine ravishment, commonly called *Enthousiasma*, which stirreth men up to plaie the Philosophers, Poets, and also to prophesie: in such maner, as that it may seeme to containe in it some divine parts'. By her own divine vision the Lady transforms the dark and hideous wood into a place alive with her spiritual protectors. The transformatory quality of the masque form is brilliantly used by Milton to show the right and wrong transforming visions – the Lady's grace-given vision granted to the contemplative chaste soul, and Comus' visionary palace full of drunken revellers physicalised into beasts.

Milton's use of such ideas in 'Il Penseroso' and the *Maske* provides the necessary context for a full understanding of Pope's intentions in *Eloisa to Abelard*. Pope's poem too is about the soul, and about the flesh, full of alternating ideas of imprisonment and release; it is about vision physicalised and distorted by passion. Above all, it is a letter written under the pressure of hateful black Melancholy, in which a woman dedicated to a life of chaste contemplation finds herself living in the flesh, her imagination distracted from its true object. Understood in this way, it becomes a moving drama in which Eloisa's imagination is the battleground.

IV

Like Milton's Lady, Eloisa is a physical prisoner; but unlike her
Miltonic counterpart she is imprisoned by her imagination too. The
divine vision of the Lady's soul allowed her mind to break free from
Comus' power; but Eloisa's vision within her cell makes her feel her
imprisonment all the more strongly. Eloisa's visions do not deny the
flesh and assert the soul; instead they endanger the soul and assert the
power of the flesh with terrible force. Eloisa's prison is, ironically,
the Convent of the *Paraclete* (the Holy Ghost) whose image is the
bird-like, immortal human soul, which disdains earthly ties and
yearns to fly back to its creator. But Eloisa's senses still long for her
lover Abelard. Her soul cannot achieve the flight, and throughout
the poem it is continually sinking back to earth as Abelard reasserts
himself within her imagination. Her plight, in Pope's version of
Comus' hideous wood, is a true nightmare because she is incapable
of the right, divine, transforming vision. The whole poem is a
struggle between her contemplative soul and her 'base' imagination,
bred by her solitude and her inner love-melancholy, nourished by
the Miltonic landscape, activated by physical passion. Eloisa
expresses her dilemma in the opening four lines of her letter:

> In these deep solitudes and awful cells,
> Where heav'nly-pensive, contemplation dwells,
> And ever-musing melancholy reigns;
> What means this tumult in a Vestal's veins? (1–4)

This prison should by right be a place of contemplative release,
'heavn'ly-pensive', the setting for the kind of imaginative transcendence evoked in 'Il Penseroso' and the *Maske*, where the chaste soul
leaves the flesh behind. But Eloisa is immediately startled by her
awakening physical awareness (the 'tumult' in her veins) which is to
have such a powerful effect on her imagination as the poem
proceeds.

In Milton's *Maske* the Elder Brother had assured the younger that
their sister would be protected *by means of her divine vision*:

> Vertue could see to do what vertue would
> By her own radiant light, though Sun and Moon
> Were in the flat Sea sunk. And Wisdoms self
> Oft seeks to sweet retired Solitude,
> Where with her best nurse Contemplation
> She plumes her feathers, and lets grow her wings . . . (373–8)

Such 'sacred rayes of Chastity' (424) will guide her bird-like soul through the most threatening surroundings:

> Yea there, where very desolation dwels
> By grots, and caverns shag'd with horrid shades,
> She may pass on with unblench't majesty . . . (428–30)

This is of course the same landscape (physical and spiritual) as that surrounding Eloisa, and Pope clinches the parallel by quoting line 429: 'Ye grots and caverns shagg'd with horrid thorn!' (20) she cries to the imprisoning walls of her Convent, making the plight of Milton's Lady her own. What should have been a divine, 'heav'nly-pensive' contemplation ('looks commercing with the skies, / Thy rapt soul sitting in thine eyes', as Milton puts it in 'Il Penseroso', 39–40) has become the wrong kind of 'raptness' – an imprisoning of her soul within the flesh. The 'tumult' in her veins is a disastrous intrusion of the physical, turning what should have been the 'divine' melancholy of 'Il Penseroso' into the hateful melancholia of the splenetic woman. An extension of this passage from 'Il Penseroso' sustains the parallel (Milton, it should be remembered, is addressing 'divinest Melancholy'):

> looks commercing with the skies,
> Thy rapt soul sitting in thine eyes:
> There held in holy passion still,
> Forget thy self to Marble . . . (39–42)

This idea is beautifully used by Pope when Eloisa addresses the stone statues which gaze down at her from the shrines: 'Tho' cold like you, unmov'd, and silent grown, / I have not yet forgot my self to stone' (23–4). Once again the Miltonic allusion establishes the full significance of Eloisa's plight. Unlike the Lady she cannot achieve such a negation of the body. Comus had threatened his captive: '. . . if I but wave this wand, / Your nervs are all chain'd up in Alabaster, / And you a statue . . .' (659–61). But Milton and Pope understand the emptiness of this threat for a soul which simply asserts its total independence of the body. Eloisa, however, can gain no such release, and the calm statues in the shrines look down on her, building up the irony of her inability to become statuesque.[33]

How did Eloisa fall? She fell, at the very beginning, in her imagination, just as Milton's Eve fell for the first time when Satan breathed his fancies in at her ear while she slept ('Assaying by his Devilish art to reach / the Organs of her Fancie, and with them forge

/ Illusions as he list', *Paradise Lost*, iv, 801–3). Eloisa's active girlish imagination led her astray when she fell in love with her teacher Abelard:

> My fancy form'd thee of Angelick kind,
> Some emanation of th' all-beauteous Mind.
> Those smiling eyes, attemp'ring ev'ry ray,
> Shone sweetly lambent with celestial day:
> Guiltless I gaz'd . . . (61–5)

Her love originated in the imagination as some spiritual emanation of the deity. It began as a kind of divine mysticism, but rather than raising her mind towards God, this started a descent (or really, as Eloisa sees it, a retrogression) towards physical passion: 'Back thro' the paths of pleasing sense I ran, / Nor wish'd an Angel whom I lov'd a Man' (69–70). In other words, what began as a vision of her *inner* sense[34] (the imagination) soon ran through the outward, physical senses, so that she ceased to strive for what was unseen, delighting rather in what was physically present.[35] In a kind of reversal of the platonic ascent, her love led her away from the divine: 'Dim and remote the joys of saints I see, / Nor envy them, that heav'n I lose for thee' (71–2). Now in her lover's absence her powerful 'base' imagination brings Abelard physically before her. It co-operates with her passion and reawakens the 'stubborn pulse' (27) of her physical nature, the rhythmic insistence of her body as against the quiet harmony of her soul. Richard Sibbes had warned against allowing imagination to arouse the affections:

Now the reason why *imagination* workes so upon the soule, is, because it stirres up the *affections* . . . and our affections stirre the humors of the body, so that oftentimes both our soules and bodies are *troubled* hereby . . . / . . . wee must take heed wee suffer not things to passe suddenly from *imagination* to *affection*. (*The Soules Conflict with Itselfe*, 1635, pp. 233, 257)

There now begins a powerful progression of ideas in the poem turning on images of freedom and imprisonment. Eloisa is trapped by her senses, but her love apes the liberty of the imagination: 'Love, free as air, at sight of human ties, / Spreads his light wings, and in a moment flies' (75–6). Such images of free movement were regularly associated with the workings of the imagination (like the soul, it could be a 'light and winged and holy thing') but the freedom that Eloisa is gaining in this part of the poem turns into the kind of denial of responsibility and earthly ties which is associated with the apotheosis of that great lover Cleopatra:

> Should at my feet the world's great master fall,
> Himself, his throne, his world, I'd scorn 'em all:
> Not *Caesar*'s empress wou'd I deign to prove;
> No, make me mistress to the man I love . . . (85–8)

The world may be well lost, but the Miltonic ancestry of Pope's poem shows the irony of this imagined freedom, 'When love is liberty, and nature, law' (92); for what does she see? 'Alas how chang'd! what sudden horrors rise! / A naked Lover bound and bleeding lies!' (99–100). She sees an Abelard emasculated and imprisoned. The imagery of enslavement (the ironical result of her ranging imagination) now associates itself with her own predicament, and her awakened memory recalls to her mind the picture of the day they both knelt at the foot of the altar when she took her vows. She sees them both as victims (line 108). This juxtaposition of ideas of freedom and imprisonment movingly captures the irony of Eloisa's situation; her imagination is free to roam, but only brings to her images of physical enslavement and passion. It does not release her from the body, but only confirms her bondage to it. At such moments her imagination, her memory and her passion work in league with each other. By being the slave of her physical passion, her imagination is clearly abdicating its possible 'divine' role.

There are moments in the poem when Eloisa shows herself capable of 'divine' vision, but it is the tragedy of her predicament that such spiritual images merge with those of her lover. The divine is regularly fused with the fleshly. Sir John Davies, in his poem *Nosce Teipsum*, describes how the imagination is able to merge sense-impressions together:

> . . . *Phantasie*, neare handmaid to the mind,
> Sits, and beholds, and doth discerne them all;
> Compounds in one, things diverse in their kind . . . (1085–7)

Davies held that 'imagination or fantasy' possessed also an elementary judging power. More usually, however, this discrimination was regarded as a separate faculty called 'estimation' or 'sensible reason',[36] and the imagination was considered not to possess this power of separating and distinguishing. Thomas Hobbes was stating a widely-accepted theory when he claimed in *Leviathan* (1651) that the activity of the imagination was a conjoining one. It

linked images together, whereas the 'judgment' discriminated and
separated. Hence imagination and judgment worked in opposite
directions, the one merging (or synthesising), the other separating
(or analysing). Speaking of thoughts Hobbes says: 'Those that
observe their similitudes . . . are sayd to have a *Good Wit*; by which,
in this occasion, is meant a *Good Fancy*. But they that observe their
differences, and dissimilitudes; which is called *Distinguishing*, and
Discerning, and *Judging* between thing and thing . . . are said to have
a *good Judgement* . . . (I, viii). In the later *De Homine* Hobbes
expresses the distinction more epigrammatically: 'judgment subtly
distinguisheth among similar objects while fancy pleasingly con-
founds dissimilar objects'.[37] The imagination's ability to 'confound'
unlike ideas is a recurrent theme in Pope's work, as we shall see in
later chapters. At various moments in *Eloisa to Abelard* the heroine's
imagination exemplifies such a merging, as she declares when she
kisses the name 'Abelard':

> Dear fatal name! rest ever unreveal'd,
> Nor pass these lips in holy silence seal'd.
> Hide it, my heart, within that close disguise,
> Where, mix'd with God's, his lov'd Idea lies. (9–12)

('Idea' is virtually synonymous with 'image', in that images
automatically raised ideas in the mind.)[38] Abelard's image merges
with that of God within her;[39] it was after all originally the
imagination which formed him 'of Angelick kind.' Such a
confounding occurs regularly throughout the poem: the vision of
the naked lover, bound and bleeding, comes merged into the figure
of the suffering Jesus; Abelard mounts like the risen Christ; and
when Eloisa describes the walls of the convent as 'vocal with the
Maker's praise' (140) we recall that she has just described how
Abelard himself 'rais'd these hallow'd walls' (133), an act which she
goes on to link imaginatively with the God of Isaiah xxxv who
causes the desert to bloom ('the desert smil'd, / And Paradise was
open'd in the Wild', 133–4). It is wrong to see such ideas as
oppositions; they are rather fusings within Eloisa's imagination.

  In fact, her great struggle as the poem proceeds is to attempt to
force these disparate images into opposition. In other words, her
inner struggle with her imagination is to push these divine and
sensual images towards opposite poles. Only after they have become
separated can Eloisa choose the higher.[40] This interpretation would

seem to make sense of the almost wilful way in which Eloisa sees things in terms of opposition. Lines 177–206, for example, show not merely the recourse of a Racine or Corneille heroine,[41] but a deliberate prising apart of those images of God and Abelard which she had declared were merged within her. Such terrible opposition is part of her recovery. This justifies the wilful nature of her struggle, almost as though it hardly mattered which of the two images fully possessed her. At line 126 she cries:

> With other beauties charm my partial eyes,
> Full in my view set all the bright abode,
> And make my soul quit *Abelard* for God.

She longs for the divine vision wholly to obliterate the sensual vision. But at line 281 she is pleading for the image of Abelard to superimpose itself on the divine image and thereby blot it out:

> Come, if thou dar'st, all charming as thou art!
> Oppose thy self to heav'n; dispute my heart;
> Come, with one glance of those deluding eyes,
> Blot out each bright Idea of the skies.
> Take back that grace, those sorrows, and those tears,
> Take back my fruitless penitence and pray'rs,
> Snatch me, just mounting, from the blest abode,
> Assist the Fiends and tear me from my God!

Such histrionics serve a spiritual purpose, in that opposition is a preparation for choice.

It is made clear in the poem that Eloisa's psychic situation is one of black melancholy. Her imagination is no longer set upon meditation, but is responding to the gloomy natural surroundings which merge with her own sorrowful feelings. Such a fusion gives power to one of the most influential passages in the poem:

> . . . o'er the twilight groves, and dusky caves,
> Long-sounding isles, and intermingled graves,
> Black Melancholy sits, and round her throws
> A death-like silence, and a dread repose:
> Her gloomy presence saddens all the scene,
> Shades ev'ry flow'r, and darkens ev'ry green . . . (163–8)

Thomas Walkington explains how black melancholy tends to isolate an individual and impels him to seek this kind of landscape: 'it causeth men to bee aliened from the nature of man, and wholly to

discarde themselves from all societie, but rather like heremits and
olde anchors [=anchorites] to live in grots, caves, and other hidden
celles of the earth . . .' (f. 68a). The effect upon the imagination of
black melancholy is described (aptly for this poem) by Andreas'
Laurentius:

> The melancholike man . . . is alwaies disquieted both in bodie and spirit, he
> is subject to watchfulnes, which doth consume him on the one side, . . . for
> if he think to make truce with his passions by taking some rest, behold so
> soone as hee would shut his eyelids, hee is assayled with a thousand vaine
> visions, and hideous buggards, with fantasticall inventions, and dreadfull
> dreames . . . (*A Discourse of the Preservation of the Sight*, trans. Richard
> Surphlet (London, 1599, p. 82)

This is particularly apposite to Eloisa's melancholy situation, where
her resting-place is a place of restlessness, and where her hateful
dreams are far from being the golden ones of the pure soul. Eloisa
points the contrast between her own visions and those granted to the
truly chaste (in body and mind):

> Grace shines around her with serenest beams,
> And whisp'ring Angels prompt her golden dreams.
> For her th'unfading rose of *Eden* blooms,
> And wings of Seraphs shed divine perfumes;
> For her the Spouse prepares the bridal ring,
> For her white virgins *Hymenaeals* sing;
> To sounds of heav'nly harps, she dies away,
> And melts in visions of eternal day.
>   Far other dreams my erring soul employ,
> Far other raptures, of unholy joy:
> When at the close of each sad, sorrowing day,
> Fancy restores what vengeance snatch'd away,
> Then conscience sleeps, and leaving nature free,
> All my loose soul unbounded springs to thee. (215–28)

The figure of the 'blameless Vestal' is lit by the 'eternal sun-shine' of
Grace, and her divine dreams (described above) bring the joys of
Heaven vividly before her in a mystical vision of the soul's marriage
to Christ. But Eloisa's dreams are the response of her erring nature,
and she explicitly contrasts her baser imagination with the Vestal's
vision. Hers is the anarchic assertion of imagination during sleep –
significantly, when her conscience is laid to rest. This resembles
Eve's dream as interpreted by Adam in *Paradise Lost* (v, 100–12:
see below, p. 56), the type of the troublesome, erring illusion

which deceives the mind and leaves nothing but unease and despair on waking. Eloisa is at this point closer akin to Eve than to the Lady in the *Maske*. She is not a chaste soul, but is gripped by the passions, the surest arousers of the 'base' imagination. All she is capable of is a vision which is a parody of the release of the soul, a mere 'soft illusion' bred by a disturbed mind:

> To dream once more I close my willing eyes;
> Ye soft illusions, dear deceits, arise! . . .
> I shriek, start up, the same sad prospect find,
> And wake to all the griefs I left behind. (239–48)

Sir Thomas Browne, in his essay 'On Dreams', distinguished between demonic and divine dreams:

A good part of our sleepes is peeced out with visions, and phantasticall objects wherin wee are confessedly deceaved. The day supplyeth us with truths, the night with fictions and falshoods . . . wherin the soberest heads have acted all the monstrosities of melancholy . . . [whereas] Virtuous thoughts of the day laye up good treasors for the night, whereby the impressions of imaginarie formes arise . . . preparatory unto divine impressions . . .[42]

Eloisa's dreams are akin to 'the monstrosities of melancholy', a projection into the night of her daytime frustrations. A closer parallel to Pope's poem is a passage from John Dennis's *The Passion of Byblis* (London, 1692). This translation from Ovid's *Metamorphoses* ix (it had also been translated by John Oldham in 1681) tells the story of Byblis' doomed incestuous love for her brother Caunus, and therefore her situation has some links with the hopeless passion of Pope's Eloisa. The passage in question presents Byblis' doubts about the status of her dreams:

> But what import, or what are then my Dreams,
> The fond Results of Hypochondriack Steams?
> Or do they as divinely' inspir'd presage?
> The Gods forbid! The Gods repel this Rage!
> The Gods this Fever of my Soul assuage! (p. 6)

But Byblis, 'her lab'ring Fancy to Distraction wrought' (p. 21), is unable to control her passion and imagines an erotic climax similar to that in Pope's poem: '*Caunus* will kiss me as I panting lye, / To his sweet Lips, as to its Heav'n, my parting Soul will fly' (p. 7). Again, the physicalised vision of the lover parodies the ascent of the soul.

Eloisa's restlessness contrasts starkly with the holy calm of the 'blameless Vestal' (207) whose tears and sighs are very different from her own. The balance of Pope's lines reflects the 'equal periods' of the virgin's existence:

> Eternal sun-shine of the spotless mind!
> Each pray'r accepted, and each wish resign'd;
> Labour and rest, that equal periods keep;
> 'Obedient slumbers that can wake and weep';
> Desires compos'd, affections ever ev'n,
> Tears that delight, and sighs that waft to heav'n. (209–14)

Here (line 212) Pope takes over verbatim a line from Crashaw's 'Description of a Religious House and Condition of Life', and in doing so he perhaps wants us to appreciate how ironic that poem becomes when applied to Eloisa's condition. Crashaw describes how the calm and quietness of the religious life is conducive to the ascent of the soul:

> . . . reverent discipline, & religious fear,
> And soft obedience, find sweet biding here;
> Silence, and sacred rest; peace, & pure joyes;
> Kind loves keep house, ly close, and make no noise . . .
> The self-remembring SOUL sweetly recovers
> Her kindred with the starrs; not basely hovers
> Below: But meditates her immortall way
> Home to the originall sourse of LIGHT & intellectual Day. (30–9)

Once again Pope, by a sensitive allusion, is able to increase the irony of Eloisa's predicament. While she lacks 'sacred rest' and 'pure joyes', her lover Abelard experiences the calm which is denied to her, but only because he has been castrated:

> For thee the fates, severely kind, ordain
> A cool suspense from pleasure and from pain;
> Thy life a long, dead calm of fix'd repose;
> No pulse that riots, and no blood that glows. (249–52)

In her imagination Abelard appears cold and statuesque; he possesses for her an unearthly peace which seems to contradict nature: 'Still as the sea, ere winds were taught to blow, / Or moving spirit bade the waters flow . . .' (253–4). Perhaps we are here expected to remember that the moment of creation was the imposition of order and distinction upon the original chaos. Certainly Eloisa's imagination now surges up again at its most chaotic as she recalls the religious service. Still restlessly at work, it runs amok and dismembers the whole scene. It is a thrilling, orgasmic climax in which her soul is again trapped in physicality – here in a heavily sexual ambiguity:

> What scenes appear where-e'er I turn my view!
> The dear Ideas, where I fly, pursue,
> Rise in the grove, before the altar rise,
> Stain all my soul, and wanton in my eyes!
> I waste the Matin lamp in sighs for thee,
> Thy image steals between my God and me,
> Thy voice I seem in ev'ry hymn to hear,
> With ev'ry bead I drop too soft a tear.
> When from the Censer clouds of fragrance roll,
> And swelling organs lift the rising soul;
> One thought of thee puts all the pomp to flight,
> Priests, Tapers, Temples, swim before my sight:
> In seas of flame my plunging soul is drown'd,
> While Altars blaze, and Angels tremble round. (263–76)

In line 272 their 'souls' meet in a final ecstatic merging and the parody of 'release' is complete. The chaos in this description has puzzled some critics. Brendan O Hehir has argued that Pope can be acquitted of 'stating the absurd' once it is realised that the tears and the clouds of incense combine to affect her vision, so that she is here 'reporting accurately and naturalistically what in fact she saw' (the point has been accepted by more recent critics).[43] Such a naturalistic explanation may have some point, but Eloisa's skill as an accurate reporter is not the issue here. Pope is more interested at this moment in what the passage tells us of her mind and emotions, and however much her eyes may sting we should not ignore the disorders within her imagination.

After this climactic union the 'base' imagination lessens its grip. Eloisa dismisses Abelard from her ('Ah come not, write not, think not once of me', 291) and she bids adieu to the 'Long lov'd, ador'd ideas' (296) which are still in her mind's eye. In lines 297–302 she even has a degree of allegorical vision, of Hope and Faith (noticeably lacking 'Chastity' to make up the Trinity which protected Milton's Lady):

> Fresh blooming hope, gay daughter of the sky!
> And faith, our early immortality!
> Enter each mild, each amicable guest;
> Receive, and wrap me in eternal rest! (299–302)

'Mild' and 'amicable'–they are less animated figures than those her 'base' imagination has created, but they do bring her a little nearer her Miltonic counterpart. At this point in the poem Eloisa leaves memory behind, surrendering the stored images of her lover ('Thy oaths I quit, thy memory resign' 293) so that her 'base' imagination is now without the food that nourished it. In line 303 she moves towards a vision of the future, as she finally turns towards a meditation on death and imagines the words of one of those 'pitying saints' described at the beginning of the poem. This voice of human sympathy speaks to her from the shrine above her head and summons her on her journey. Eloisa's imagination responds joyfully to the hope which beckons:

> I come, I come! prepare your roseate bow'rs,
> Celestial palms, and ever-blooming flow'rs.
> Thither, where sinners may have rest, I go,
> Where flames refin'd in breasts seraphic glow. (317–20)

It is a more refined and 'divine' vision than Eloisa has yet achieved, closer to the 'golden dream' granted to the Vestal.[44] As this meditation proceeds, the moment of death becomes imaginatively present to her, and Abelard reappears to give (as she pictures it) a final ecstatic kiss:

> Thou, *Abelard*! the last sad office pay,
> And smooth my passage to the realms of day:
> See my lips tremble, and my eye-balls roll,
> Suck my last breath, and catch my flying soul! (321–4)

It is at this crucial moment that Eloisa dismisses such a fancy with a triumphant exclamation:

> Ah no–in sacred vestments may'st thou stand,
> The hallow'd taper trembling in thy hand,
> Present the Cross before my lifted eye,
> Teach me at once, and learn of me to die. (325–8)

In place of the echo of Othello's perdition[45] she receives within her imagination Abelard the priest, holding Christ's cross before her face for her eyes to focus on at the moment of death. No longer can she say, as she did earlier, 'Not on the Cross my eyes were fix'd, but you' (116). Her imagination is no longer febrile, but calm and determined, achieving at last something like the true Christian *simplicity* as understood by Savonarola: '[A man will achieve

Christian simplicity] if all things which his intellect knows or contemplates are God, or related to God . . . [and] If his imagination (*phanthasia*) holds always before his eyes Christ Crucified . . .'[46] Gianfrancesco Pico stressed the importance at moments of imaginative tumult of concentrating the mind upon a single image: 'If the imagination is too mobile and loose, we must seek a single image, or a few on which to dwell, in order to be at ease from that tumult and varying concourse of impressions' (p. 61). Eloisa's 'Ah no' is a moving illustration of this idea.

Seeing the poem in terms of the imagination (as this chapter has tried to do) establishes a context for a sympathetic evaluation of Eloisa's spiritual state at the poem's close.[47] This reading suggests that she does achieve some resolution of her mental struggle, in that she at last reaches the right level of vision. After all, the spiritual state of Milton's Lady (with whom I have tried to draw some fruitful parallels) had been seen in such terms, and she is the presiding figure behind Pope's poem. We suspect, of course, that beyond the confines of the poem her imagination will sink back into being once more an instrument of her frustrated passions. But the poet draws back from the scene at this instant, just as Eloisa herself reaches an aloof, almost dispassionate, awareness: 'O death all-eloquent! you only prove / What dust we doat on, when 'tis man we love' (335-6). As she distances herself from her clamorous senses, flesh becomes mere dust, and she can now contemplate the joys of heaven which await Abelard, and see love transposed from the pulsating human frame on to a higher level:

> In trance extatic may thy pangs be drown'd,
> Bright clouds descend, and Angels watch thee round,
> From opening skies may streaming glories shine,
> And Saints embrace thee with a love like mine. (339-42)

Eloisa's *faith* and *hope* have finally raised her beyond the demands of Nature towards the realm of Grace, in a manner described by Gianfrancesco Pico: 'The light of Faith . . . is of the greatest service to either type of imagination. It supports and conducts each by the hand, sweeping each up, so to speak, and elevating it above its own nature' (p. 89).

I believe that by being so clearly allied to Milton's *Maske*, Pope's *Eloisa to Abelard* tackles a similar question of the right and wrong ways of seeing – the temptation for the imagination to cherish passion and the senses, rather than transcend them. It is this struggle which lies behind Pope's poem. It is a *psychomachia* engaged upon Miltonic terms, and one of the concepts which generates its force is a dualistic view of the imagination, for which there is clear Renaissance precedent. The poem is a battleground for the 'divine' and 'base' functions of the imagination, and, if the poem ends with a feeling that the struggle has been temporarily resolved, then it is within Eloisa's imagination that this has been achieved.

THREE

Truth and the imagination:
The Rape of the Lock

I

If *Eloisa to Abelard* is a struggle within the imagination of its heroine, *The Rape of the Lock* challenges the imagination with the claims of the real world. The landscape (mental and physical) of Eloisa is totally composed and coloured by her melancholy, but outside Belinda's imaginative world we glimpse the realities of smallpox, old age, and the bustling life of business and judgment where 'Wretches hang that Jury-men may Dine' (iii, 22). This sensed presence of an uncomfortable truth, of a world beyond Belinda's imaginative influence threatening to judge it, is integral to the meaning of the poem. *The Rape of the Lock* makes important use of this opposition between imagination and truth. The plot itself juxtaposes Belinda, her ally Ariel, and their instrument the lock, against Clarissa, her ally the Baron, and their instrument the scissors. The scissors cut through the lock, the Baron drives away Ariel, and Clarissa challenges Belinda with the uncomfortable truth.

The conviction that the imagination tends to present things as they *appear*, and not always as they *are*, and its consequent stress on the role of the directing and discriminating judgment, is central to the empiricist philosophy of Hobbes and Locke. In this chapter I aim to trace this particular tradition of thinking about the imagination from its sources in Renaissance faculty psychology, and also to take a brief look at some of the literary analogues which share these habits of thought and exploit a similar range of imagery. *The Rape of the Lock* will then be considered as a work which, like *Eloisa to Abelard*, confronts a human dilemma. The engagement of fantasy with reality is the heart of the poem's meaning: as 'incongruity' it is the source of its delightful mock-heroic wit; as 'conflict' it generates the psychological drama.

II

The previous chapter explored the paradox of the imagination, which at its highest could act as the handmaid of the contemplative intellect, bringing the *gnosis* or divine vision of the true 'reality', but which could also be the vehicle of melancholic delusions and spiritual error. The tendency of the imagination towards either extreme depended on whether it served the aspirations of the soul or the promptings of the body. Such a view naturally assumed a notion of the duality of flesh and spirit and of the spirit's claims to apprehend the truth, and was therefore suited to neoplatonic theories of the nature of man. In the empiricist philosophy of Hobbes, however, such a duality is absent: reason does not possess 'higher' intuitive powers, but is a quasi-mathematical 'reckoning'[1] in the quest for the empirically known. Truth is not transcendental, but observable, with close links to judgment and our modern term 'good sense'. Divorced from the higher powers of the soul, which Hobbes denies, imagination is an indispensable but untrustworthy vehicle of experience. Hobbes's imagination (he uses the terms 'imagination' and 'fancy' interchangeably though he notes a subtle distinction in their etymologies)[2] is 'decaying sense', the vast store of images already perceived by the senses, and therefore absolutely vital for the formation of our attitudes, experiences and expectations in life. It has, for Hobbes, 'produced very marvellous effects to the benefit of mankinde', but only when 'guided by the Precepts of true Philosophy'.[3] Without such a guide and direction, imagination deceives and confuses ('without Steddinesse, and Direction to some End, a great Fancy is one kind of Madnesse', *Leviathan*, I, viii). Imagination is not a sufficient means of discovering the truth: that procedure is the concern of judgment:

In a good History, the Judgement must be eminent; because the goodnesse consisteth, in the Method, in the Truth, and in the Choyse of the actions that are most profitable to be known. Fancy has no place, but onely in adorning the stile . . . In Orations of Prayse, and in Invectives, the Fancy is praedominant; because the designe is not truth, but to Honour or Dishonour . . . In Hortatives, and Pleadings, as Truth, or Disguise serveth best to the Designe in hand; so is the Judgement, or the Fancy most required . . . In Demonstration, in Councell, and all rigorous search of Truth, Judgement does all . . . (I, viii)

Imagination as a merging power and judgment as a discriminating power are, as we saw in the previous chapter,[4] understood by Hobbes as opposites; but judgment is *in itself* commendable, whereas imagination needs the help of judgment to be virtuous in its effect.[5] Truth is here clearly the province of judgment alone: imagination is left with the superficialities of disguise, ornament and metaphor (metaphors are 'utterly excluded' from truth, since 'they openly professe deceipt', I, viii).

In denying to the imagination the power of judgment, Hobbes's thinking is in line with the traditional views of Renaissance faculty psychology. He does not conceive the issue in terms of the various powers of the human soul,[6] but his attitude towards the imagination's potential for deception is similar. As the previous chapter mentioned, faculty psychology understood imagination to be an aspect of man's 'sensitive soul' and therefore active independently of the 'rational soul'. Its role was as an image-making faculty, not a faculty for evaluating reality. Because like the passions it functioned within the 'sensitive soul', it lacked the moral sense whereby things could be judged true or false, right or wrong. In the seventeenth century Richard Sibbes, the puritan divine, linked this irrationality to amorality when he wrote that 'the principall use' of the imagination was '*properly* to judge what is comfortable or uncomfortable, what is pleasing or displeasing to the outward man, (not what is *morally* or *spiritually* good or ill)' (*The Soules Conflict with Itselfe*, 1635, p. 250). Important questions of morality and value (the truth about the *inner* man) were to be decided by a person's conscious rationality, not by his imagination.

The faculty psychology of a hundred years before still made sense to Augustan writers (as the latest mechanistic theories did not),[7] and in Milton they had a poet who offered them a rigorous and moving exploration of the imagination's power for good and ill, and the role of the 'higher' faculties in overruling it. For Pope (here as in other ways the heir of the Miltonic–humanist tradition) the truth could not be affirmed until the imaginative faculty had submitted its findings to the rational faculty, which acted upon the received images by applying to them the judgment of the reason.[8] Such a compartment-alising of the mind made the imagination responsible to the judgment *whenever truth was required*. If truth did not press its demands, or if the rational faculty was in any way suspended, then the imagination (which never rested) was left remarkably free.

These ideas are expounded by Milton's Adam in a speech of some significance for *The Rape of the Lock* as well as for the scheme of *Paradise Lost*. Satan has infected the organs of Eve's fancy while she sleeps, causing her to have a dream of temptation and fall. When Adam hears her story he instructs her in this basic Renaissance lore:

> . . . But know that in the Soule
> Are many lesser Faculties that serve
> Reason as chief; among these Fansie next
> Her office holds; of all external things,
> Which the five watchful Senses represent,
> She forms Imaginations, Aerie shapes,
> Which Reason joyning or disjoyning, frames
> All what we affirm or what deny, and call
> Our knowledge or opinion; then retires
> Into her private Cell when Nature rests.
> Oft in her absence mimic Fansie wakes
> To imitate her; but misjoyning shapes,
> Wilde work produces oft, and most in dreams . . . (v, 100–12)

Imagination creates 'Aerie shapes' which are undefined and lack meaning until reason (here not higher intuitive reason, but closer to Hobbes's discriminating judgment) sorts them out and structures ('frames') them into something knowable, so that we can judge their truth and affirm or deny them. When the reason is absent imagination will work alone, mis-joining shapes and producing grotesque absurdities.

Throughout *Paradise Lost* Milton presents Satan as the enemy of truth, and as such it is fitting that he should be an exploiter of the imagination. Simply by his many changes of shape (as cormorant, serpent, toad, mist etc.) he apes the imaginative power, and is able to enter Eve's fancy and play havoc there. Demons were traditionally believed to have the ability to manipulate the imagination, especially in dreams, and Satan exemplifies this.[9] He is appropriately compared with the will o' the wisp or *ignis fatuus*, that 'delusive Light' which 'misleads th' amaz'd Night-wanderer from his way' (ix, 640).[10] Likewise his rhetoric makes telling use of imagery in order to sweeten his flattering lies – his love-song to Eve in her dream is an exercise in fanciful unreason.[11] As a serpent his shining eyes, golden neck and bright crest weave and circle in front of her 'to lure her Eye' (ix, 518). Once again, he knows Eve's weakness and is quick to exploit it. His 'glozing' words flatter her pride and create in her mind a quite false picture of the colourful 'alluring fruit' (ix, 588), 'of fairest colours mixt, / Ruddie and Gold' (ix, 577–8). Dennis Burden has rightly pointed out that the ordinary fruit of the Tree of Knowledge is only made provocative by Satan's description[12] – an excellent example of how the imagination is Satan's ally at important stages in Eve's fall. Being the embodiment of truth, however, Milton's God inevitably shuns imagery. Unlike Satan he has no need to deceive, and so the truth comes from him plain and unornamented. The Renaissance critic Tomitano pointed out that 'Metaphors are . . . little esteemed in doctrine, which is content with its severe and pure simplicity',[13] and Hobbes, we recall, said: 'as Truth, or Disguise serveth best to the Designe in hand; so is the Judgement, or the Fancy most required' (*Leviathan*, I, viii). In the characters of Satan and God, therefore, Milton has dramatised logically and powerfully the opposition between imagination (deceit) and reason (truth).

The imagination was considered especially dangerous because it set up false values within the mind. What the imagination declared to be 'good' was usually only an appearance of good, and very often demonstrably evil (as Milton's Eve found to her cost). Richard Sibbes sums up the matter thus:

the *imagination* setteth a great price upon sensible good things [i.e. what is pleasing to the senses]; and the *judgement* it self since *the fall*, untill it hath an higher light and strength, yeeldeth to our *imagination*; hence it comes to passe that . . . the very worst things, if they bee attended with respect in the world and *sensible* contentments, are *imagined* to bee the greatest good . . . (p. 228)

(The fall of Belinda, like the fall of Eve, will show the significance of these words.) An author who frequently explores the way imagination can cherish false values is Ben Jonson. The gulls in *Volpone* and *The Alchemist*, for example, all follow an *ignis fatuus* (Sir Epicure Mammon, Dapper, Corbaccio etc.) which distorts their sense of value and turns them into ridiculous fantasists. In his poem 'Fair Friend . . .' (*The Under-wood*, lxxx) Jonson puts the matter succinctly when he remarks:

> It is like Love to Truth reduc'd,
>   All the false values gone,
> Which were created, and induc'd
>   By fond imagination. (17–20)

It is clear that Jonson recognises the importance of distinguishing mere 'opinion' from the truth, and this can only be done by allowing reason to challenge imagination: '*Opinion* is a light, vaine, crude, and imperfect thing, settled in the Imagination; but never arriving at the understanding, there, to obtaine the tincture of Reason.'[14]

Imagination plays with light and empty images, preferring the pleasures of self-delusion to the unsettling truth. In this way the mind becomes fascinated and involved with the imagination, so that an individual easily persuades himself that reality conforms with his desires. Matthew Prior discusses the delusions of wit in these very terms:

> Atoms You cut; and Forms You measure,
> To gratifie your private Pleasure;
> 'Till airy Seeds of casual Wit
> Do some fantastic Birth beget . . .
> The happy Whimsey You pursue;
> 'Till You at length believe it true.
> Caught by your own delusive Art,
> You fancy first, and then assert. (*Alma*, iii, 29–38)

In 'The Turtle and the Sparrow' Prior points out how different the imagination can be from the thing itself (and significantly for *The Rape of the Lock* he is talking here about the 'meer Coquet'): 'nor avails it much / If true or false, our troubles spring / More from the fancy than the thing' (296–8). So far as the imagination is concerned, 'true or false' is irrelevant. Because imagination is engaged with the outward appearances of things, and our sensuous appreciation of them, the fancy-reality contradiction can be seen even more starkly, in terms of beauty and truth. Prior again puts this concisely: 'So shall I court thy dearest Truth, / When Beauty ceases to engage . . .' ('An Ode' ('While blooming Youth'), 49–50).

The relationship between the ideas we have of things and the real qualities of the things themselves is perhaps the central issue in the philosophy of John Locke. In *An Essay Concerning Human Understanding* (1690) Locke theorises about the qualities of the objects we perceive and how our perceptions of them are formed. His argument is lengthy and covers many different aspects of mental activity; however, one particular distinction which he makes is especially relevant to this discussion of the imagination and to an understanding of Pope's imagery in *The Rape of the Lock*. Locke is careful to distinguish between those qualities which 'are utterly inseparable from the body, in what estate soever it be . . . viz.

solidity, extension, figure, motion or rest, and number' (II, viii, 9) and 'such qualities which in truth are nothing in the objects themselves but powers to produce various sensations in us . . . as colours, sounds, tastes, etc.' (II, viii, 10). These Locke names, respectively, 'primary' and 'secondary' qualities. A division there-fore is inevitable between qualities which are clearly 'real', in that they are actually possessed by the object, and those qualities which exist in our own minds as we perceive the object. Locke does not of course develop out of this a theory of 'subjective truth' or 'truth of the imagination' (it was the romantic age which produced those); instead, he tends to see 'primary qualities' as being closer to objective reality: 'the ideas of primary qualities of bodies are resemblances of them, and their patterns do really exist in the bodies themselves, but the ideas produced in us by these secondary qualities have no resemblance of them at all. There is nothing like our ideas existing in the bodies themselves' (II, viii, 15). It is easy to see how this distinction comes to exemplify that between objective truth and subjective imagination. The former is something stable and knowable, the latter is evanescent and uncertain.

Locke's distinction was not new. It had been clearly formulated by Galileo, who held that only the measurable properties of matter could be said to be 'real': other so-called properties (colour, sounds, smells etc.) were 'unreal' subjective illusions.[15] Hobbes also focuses on the properties of sound and colour to make a similar point which specifically associates such conceptions with the imagination: 'when any thing is *Seen* by us, we reckon not the thing it selfe; but the *sight*, the *Colour*, the *Idea* of it in the fancy: and when any thing is *heard*, wee reckon it not; but the *hearing*, or *sound* onely, which is our fancy or conception of it by the Eare: and such are names of fancies' (I, iv).

In this context it is no surprise to find that imagination and colour were becoming closely associated. In *Spectator* 413 (24 June 1712) Addison described 'that great Modern Discovery, which is at present universally acknowledged . . . Namely, that Light and Colours, as apprehended by the Imagination, are only Ideas in the Mind, and not Qualities that have any Existence in Matter.' So easily could imagination seem to create colours within the mind. Abraham Cowley specifically sees the figure of Fancy in terms of shifting colours and Miltonic 'Aerie shapes':

> Here in a robe which does all colours show,
> (The envy of birds, and the clouds gawdy *bow*)
> *Phansie*, wild *Dame*, with much lascivious pride
> By twin-*Chamelions* drawn, does gaily ride.
> Her coach there follows, and throngs round about
> Of Shapes and airy *Forms* an endless rout.
>   (*Davideis*, ii, 439–44)

This characterisation of 'Phansie' as being led by chameleons (an image which conveys the right picture of shifting colours) obviously appealed to Nicholas Rowe, who re-worked the description in his *Callipaedia* (1712):

> An *airy Nymph* appear'd, whose splendid Show
> Out-shone the Colours of Heaven's *gaudy Bow*;
> *Phantasia* hight, who, with lascivious Pride,
> By twin *Camelions* drawn, does gaily ride. (iii, 105–8)

Rowe expands Cowley's reference to that other image for the imagination, the gaudy rainbow, which adds to shifting colour the idea of insubstantiality, a disembodied beauty that can come and go without being physically caught or touched. Colour is imagination's realm because it is shifting, uncertain and accidental, a 'secondary' quality (in Locke's terms) which 'exists' as an idea in the mind, and hence it is a fitting image for a theory of the imagination which juxtaposes the airy, insubstantial pleasures of beauty with the realities of plain and solid truth.

Another earlier characterisation of 'Fancy' which influenced the way poets visualised the quality is the allegorical figure who leads the procession of the Masque of Cupid in Spenser's *Faerie Queene*:

> His garment neither was of silke nor say,
>   But painted plumes, in goodly order dight,
>   Like as the sunburnt *Indians* do aray
>   Their tawney bodies, in their proudest plight:
> As those same plumes, so seemd he vaine and light,
>   That by his gate might easily appeare;
>   For still he far'd as dauncing in delight,
>   And in his hand a windy fan did beare,
> That in the idle aire he mov'd still here and there. (III, xii, 8)

Spenser's 'Fancy', like Jonson's 'Opinion', is light and vain; his coloured peacock-plumes dance in the wind and the airy fan is his emblem. Early seventeenth-century masque-costume, with its waving colours, plumes and tinsel, was regarded in the strictest sense as 'fancy dress'. It was suitable clothing for an art form which by its magical transformations, its imagery of soul and body, its aerobatics, cloud-work and generally glittering illusion, exploited more than any other the medium of imagination.[16]

Lying behind *The Rape of the Lock*, therefore, is a long tradition of thought about the imagination, from Renaissance faculty psychology through to the empirical philosophy of Hobbes and Locke, whereby imagination and judgment serve different ends, one in the realm of beauty and 'secondary qualities', the other in the real knowable world of 'truth'. According to this tradition, imagination is wayward, pleasure-loving, amoral, superficial and sets up false values; whereas judgment presents a truth which is stable and objectively known. Parallel with this philosophic tradition is the literary tradition. In the work of a handful of poets, Spenser, Jonson, Milton, Cowley, Rowe and Prior, we have seen how the distinction between imagination and judgment could be seen as a clash between beauty and truth, and how a cluster of imagery grew up around the figure of 'Fancy', consisting of shifting colours, airiness, shape-changing and vanity: the chameleon and the rainbow.

In his final version of *The Rape of the Lock* (1717) Pope appears to sum up this tradition in a poem which shows how imagination is inevitably falsifying (either delightfully or distressingly so), a colouring which can distort the truth by blurring its outline and dimensions, and substituting the beautiful, though secondary, qualities from within our own minds. In *The Rape of the Lock* the truth presses its demands upon the imagination. The tension between these two elements lies behind the clash of personalities within the poem, making it at several levels a drama of the mind. Although the poem is not an allegory exactly, it is more allegorical in character than has usually been allowed. It is concerned with the imagination as a beautiful, amoral, irresponsible and alluring thing, a cluster of adjectives as apt for Belinda as for the sylphs, and it is by way of this parallel between heroine and mythology that I want to begin exploring the work's allegorical elements, and to offer an approach which can reconcile our appreciation of its imaginative world with an evaluation of its human concerns.

III

The most important feature of Pope's transformation of his poem
from the two-canto version of 1712 to the extended five cantos of
1714 is the introduction of the machinery of the sylphs.[17] It is
generally agreed that as a result of their presence 'Belinda's world is
shot through with . . . exquisitely shimmering beauty',[18] that they
are brilliant, dazzling, and a triumphant exercise of the poet's artistic
imagination. Nevertheless, John Dennis's accusation that the
machinery does not affect the 'action' of the poem[19] raised the
recurring question as to whether the sylphs are integrated into its
structure. One way round this problem has been to detect in them
certain symbolic qualities so that they relate to the social world over
which they preside. Reuben Brower's list of what the sylphs 'stand
for' ('feminine honour, flirtation, courtship, the necessary rivalry of
man and woman')[20] risks overkill. Geoffrey Tillotson takes a more
external, literary approach when he considers that the sylphs
exemplify Le Bossu's prescription for the machinery of epic: 'the
sylphs are "theological" (they represent "good" and "bad"),
"physical" (they roll planets and attend to the weather), and
"allegorical" or "moral" (the machines include Spleen)'.[21] But the
sylphs, being removed from the world of moral judgments,
represent neither 'good' nor 'bad'. They delight in beauty without
judging it, being as concerned to protect earrings and fan as they are
to preserve chastity. To them a 'dire Disaster' is an aesthetic one,
outraging decorum rather than morality:

> Whether the Nymph shall break *Diana*'s Law,
> Or some frail *China* Jar receive a Flaw,
> Or stain her Honour, or her new Brocade,
> Forget her Pray'rs, or miss a Masquerade . . . (ii, 105–8)

As with Keats's poetic imagination, which 'has as much delight in
conceiving an Iago as an Imogen' (Keats to Woodhouse, 27 Oct.
1818), so with the amoral sylphs. Neither are the sylphs physical
beings: they are all light and colour, and Pope goes out of his way to
stress their disembodied character as 'Transparent Forms, too fine
for mortal Sight' (ii, 61).

To understand the sylphs fully it is necessary to examine them in
terms of the imagery we have seen as conventionally associated with

the imagination. Pope himself is clearly aware of this tradition, since he repeatedly uses colour as the medium in which the imagination operates:[22] 'There sober Thought pursu'd th'amusing theme / Till Fancy colour'd it, and form'd a Dream (Donne, *Satire IV*, 188–9). (The thought is Pope's, not Donne's.) He can talk of love as 'drest in Fancy's airy beam' (Horace, *Odes* iv, i, 41), and describe how the imagination, in allegiance with the passions, can colour and misrepresent what a person sees:

> All Manners take a tincture from our own,
> Or come discolour'd thro' our Passions shown.
> Or Fancy's beam enlarges, multiplies,
> Contracts, inverts, and gives ten thousand dyes.
> (*Epistle to Cobham*, 25–8)

Pope regularly stresses the shifting, insubstantial quality of the imagination, 'Where Beams of warm *Imagination* play, / The *Memory*'s soft Figures melt away' (*Essay on Criticism*, 58–9). And as light is extinguished at the close of the four-book *Dunciad*, the fragile colours of fancy are the first victims of endless night: 'Before her, *Fancy*'s gilded clouds decay, / And all its varying Rain-bows die away' (1743 *Dunciad*, iv, 631–2). In this context it is necessary to quote again from a passage discussed in Chapter One,[23] where Pope describes how tantalising a poet's imagination can be:

We . . . do but labour to fall short of our first Imagination. The gay Colouring which Fancy gave to our Design at the first transient glance we had of it, goes off in the Execution; like those various Figures in the gilded Clouds, which while we gaze long upon, to seperate the Parts of each imaginary Image, the whole faints before the Eye, & decays into Confusion. (Pope–Cromwell, 12 Nov. 1711)

What are the sylphs, then, but Pope's most powerful and sustained image for the imagination?

> Some to the Sun their Insect-Wings unfold,
> Waft on the Breeze, or sink in Clouds of Gold.
> Transparent Forms, too fine for mortal Sight,
> Their fluid Bodies half dissolv'd in Light.
> Loose to the Wind their airy Garments flew,
> Thin glitt'ring Textures of the filmy Dew;
> Dipt in the richest Tincture of the Skies,
> Where Light disports in ever-mingling Dies,

> While ev'ry Beam new transient Colours flings,
> Colours that change whene'er they wave their Wings. (ii, 59–68)

The imagery of rainbows, 'airy Garments', glitter, tinted clouds, and every kind of 'transient' colour, merges here into a brilliant insubstantial pageant. The vision will not hold still. The restless, dazzling charm of the imagination associates itself with Belinda, whose eyes as well as mind are 'sprightly' and 'unfix'd' (ii, 9–10), and it is this uncertain beam which sets itself up within the poem as the rival of the sun. To gaze in Belinda's face annihilates moral judgments.

Geoffrey Tillotson is in fact closer to the centre of the poem when he acknowledges the uncanny way in which it tends to demoralise the critic: 'The criticism the poem provides is sometimes more a picture than a criticism. It is so elaborate, shifting, constellated, that the intellect is baffled and demoralised by the aesthetic sense and emotions' (p. 120). One of the main effects of Pope's introduction of the sylphs into his poem is indeed to give it this moral complication. Any censure of coquettish 'levity' of heart is deflected onto the sylphs who 'contrive it all' (i, 104), and (working against Belinda this time) we withdraw our approval of female purity once we are told "Tis but their *Sylph*, the wise Celestials know, / Tho' *Honour* is the Word with Men below' (i, 77–8). This kind of ethical alternative is obviously too clear-cut for such a work as *The Rape of the Lock*. Its moral subtlety goes deeper because it exploits the inherent ambiguity of the imagination itself, which enters the poem with the sylphs. They suspend our approval and our disapproval: 'levity' and 'honour' are concepts implying the operation of the judgment by 'Men below' (in this context merely 'erring Mortals' ironically 'blind to Truth', however much they may agree on their evaluations). Such concepts are annihilated by the sylphs, who are 'Spirits, freed from mortal Laws' (i, 69), the masters of 'Fancy's maze' whose skilfully manipulated distractions help to preserve the women they patronise: 'Oft when the World imagine Women stray, / The *Sylphs* thro' mystick Mazes guide their Way . . .' (i, 91–2). Note the irresponsibility whereby the judgment of the world becomes a fancy, and the judging word 'stray' is transformed to a delightful stroll.

An interesting comparison here, which illustrates how Pope handles the amorality of the sylphs, is provided by some lines from Henry Vaughan's poem 'The Daughter of Herodias' which condemn Salome for perverting the seriousness of music:

> Vain, sinful art! who first did fit
> Thy lewd loathed *motions* unto *sounds*,
> And made grave *music* like wild *wit*
> Err in loose airs beyond her bounds?

The echo of this stanza in *The Rape of the Lock* reinforces the idea that Pope's sylphs, though they flirt beautifully with the sinful, are at the same time detached from it. The sylphs' fusion of music and movement, their 'loose airs' are errant merely in terms of motion; they expose morality's favourite words (err, loose, wild, beyond bounds) as the metaphors of movement which they are. The ambiguous *vanity* and *art* of Belinda are rendered harmless through her association with the sylphs, who are *empty* and *decorative* as well as *proud* and *scheming*. Vaughan's adjective 'sinful', however, glues the concepts together with a moral label ('Vain, sinful art!'), highlighting the way the sylphs, in contrast, loosen such words from their moral context.

In such ways the sylphs literally 'demoralise', enacting the amoral role of the imagination by dissolving the tidy human boundaries between virtue and vice. In a threatening world, says Pope, girls are not guided by neat moral imperatives, but by their imaginations, and luckily for them, such a lack of human commitment is the very thing that preserves them. The imagination of the coquette offers so many distractions that she avoids falling victim to her admirers: the sylphs bombard women's hearts with images, leaving them delighted, distracted and uncommitted. 'Fancy's maze' protects them, in that one image drives away another before things get too serious:

> With varying Vanities, from ev'ry Part,
> They shift the moving Toyshop of their Heart;
> Where Wigs with Wigs, with Sword-knots Sword-knots strive,
> Beaus banish Beaus, and Coaches Coaches drive. (i, 99–102)

The eighteenth-century 'toy shop' was 'a fancy shop' (*OED*) and 'toy' an 'odd fancy' (Johnson). One toy shop at 'The Three Rabbits, near Durham-Yard in the Strand' sold, among other trinkets: necklaces, ivory eggs, purses, garters, cane-strings, snuff-boxes, counters for cards, combs, tassels for men's neckcloths, silver buckles, buttons, powder-boxes and puffs, and 'all Sorts of Scissars'[24] – in fact, most of the small objects which crowd into *The Rape of the Lock*.

Pope's machinery of imagination, naturally expressing itself in
terms of shifting lights, finds a striking parallel in the decoration he
lavished on his Twickenham grotto. One early visitor delighted
in Pope's magical invention in such terms as might have been used
of the sylphs:

> Mr *Pope*'s poetick Genius has introduced a kind of Machinery, which
> performs the same Part in the Grotto that supernal Powers and
> incorporeal Beings act in the heroick Species of Poetry. This is effected by
> disposing Plates of Looking glass in the obscure Parts of the Roof and
> Sides of the Cave, where a sufficient Force of Light is wanting to discover
> the Deception, while the other Parts, the Rills, Fountains, Flints, Pebbles,
> &c. being duly illuminated, are so reflected by the various posited
> Mirrors, as, without exposing the Cause, every Object is multiplied, and
> its Position represented in a surprising Diversity.
>
> (*The Newcastle General Magazine*, Jan. 1748. the 'Epistolary Descrip-
> tion' is reproduced by Maynard Mack, *The Garden and the City* (1969),
> pp. 237–43)

This appears to enact Pope's description of 'Fancy's beam',
which 'enlarges, multiplies, / Contracts, inverts, and gives ten
thousand dyes'. Pope's 'poetick Genius' resides in the perfect
union of his art and his imagination: the disposition and workmanship within the grotto are skilful, but the poet has created for
the beholder a place of deceit where objects are perceived by the
senses not as they really are, but as through the distorting,
enhancing glass of the imagination. The 'Machinery' of 'incor-
poreal Beings' (described above) fulfils a role parallel to that of the
sylphs in *The Rape of the Lock*, throwing varied and surprising
angles of light on the objects within: the cause of the aura is
hidden, but the effect is to represent the objects now transformed
as if by the imagination of the beholder. Just as the sylphs enact
the imagination in Pope's poem, surrounding Belinda with playful
light-effects (so that the object herself is won over from the world
of Nature), so the beautiful deception of Pope's concealed art
within the grotto substitutes fancy's beam for truth.[25] William
Mason made this very point in his poem *Musaeus* (1747), in which
Milton compliments Pope on his grotto, only to be told by the
poet in reply that the place merely recalls 'the toys of thoughtless
youth [,] / When flow'ry fiction held the place of truth; / When
fancy rul'd . . .'[26] (p. 17).

The scene of Belinda at her dressing-table is a ritual of the

enhancement of Nature, in which the imagination co-operates once
more with art. She presides at a sacrament of transformation:

> This Casket *India*'s glowing Gems unlocks,
> And all *Arabia* breathes from yonder Box.
> The Tortoise here and Elephant unite,
> Transform'd to *Combs*, the speckled and the white. (i, 133–6)

The rites are those of narcissistic pride, and the heroine is clearly
arming herself for battle, but the presence of the imagination in this
passage should warn the reader against reciting the moral too
solemnly. Modern critics are agreed that the values of Belinda's
society are confused, and the line 'Puffs, Powders, Patches, Bibles,
Billet-doux' (i, 138) is frequently quoted as symbolising this
disarray. Geoffrey Tillotson and Maynard Mack agree that the line
betrays a 'moral disorder' in the heroine's social world, and this is
certainly true.[27] But at this moment of the poem the emphasis is
perhaps less on 'society' than on the particular *inner* world of the
coquette. This world may outrage our moral preconceptions and
strain decorum to breaking-point, but the disorder is fundamentally
an imaginative profusion, and during this scene Belinda is becoming
a creature of the imagination. For the moment ethical judgments are
suspended, and the disarray is not 'sad' (a critic's word), but
delightful.[28]

The necessary gloss to this passage is provided by Pope himself, in
an anonymous letter contributed to *The Guardian*, No. 106 (13 July
1713),[29] a few months before he completed the extended version of
The Rape of the Lock. Its parallels with the poem are remarkable. In
his dream Pope peers through the window in his mistress's breast
and tries to sketch the confusion within her heart as one image
rapidly chases out another: 'The first Images I discovered in it were
Fans, Silks, Ribbonds, Laces, and many other Gewgaws, which lay
so thick together, that the whole Heart was nothing else but a Toy-
shop' (Ault, p. 131). Such disorder betrays the lack of hierarchy
within the imagination. Pope is desperate to discover where he as a
human being stands amongst all this female frippery, but he has to
contend with some unexpected rivals for her attention. Her
imagination turns restlessly from one image to another:

There then followed a quick Succession of different Scenes. A Play-house, a
Church, a Court, a Poppet-show, rose up one after another, till at last they
all of them gave Place to a Pair of new Shoes, which kept footing in the Heart

for a whole Hour. These were driven off at last by a Lap-dog, who was succeeded by a *Guiney* Pig, a Squirril and a Monky. I my self, to my no small Joy, brought up the Rear of these worthy Favourites. I was ravished at being so happily posted and in full Possession of the Heart: But . . . I found my Place taken up by an ill-bred awkward Puppy with a Mony-bag under each Arm. (Ault, pp. 131–2)

Aurelia is plainly a coquette: the Church takes her fancy, but so does a pair of new shoes. Nothing is valued for longer than it occupies her imagination. Her image-making faculty is working overtime, but the judgment has no place. Amid this confusion Pope struggles to turn his own transient image into a permanent occupant of her heart. Similarly, in the poem the Baron's billet-doux, carrying its confession of love, is trapped amid the brilliant paraphernalia upon Belinda's dressing-table, vainly asserting its message in competition with so many other rivals for her attention. To intrude a moral message about 'the values of society' at this point risks blurring the fine suggestive detail that Pope achieves at the psychological level of his drama.

The product of the toilette is a new Belinda proudly displaying her hair to the world. The twin curls sported at her neck are not the result of judgment, but are created by the imagination as the coquette's chief weapon. They are there to entrap her male admirers in fancy's maze: 'Love in these Labyrinths his Slaves detains, / And mighty Hearts are held in slender Chains' (ii, 23–4). The curl is literally a 'fancy', since it is the sylphs (once again representing the imagination) who 'divide the Hair' (i, 146). After all, their duties in tending 'the Fair' include

> To draw fresh Colours from the vernal Flow'rs,
> To steal from Rainbows ere they drop in Show'rs
> A brighter Wash; to curl their waving Hairs . . . (ii, 95–7)

The labours are not Betty's, but the sylphs' (though it is Betty who receives the praise 'for Labours not her own'). At the dressing-table art does all it can, but it is the imagination which presides and performs the decisive act.

During these 'sacred Rites of Pride' Belinda is confirmed as a girl dangerously reminiscent of Milton's fanciful Eve. In the first canto her slumbers bring a 'Morning-Dream' as Ariel appears to whisper at her ear. The dream, like Eve's, is a warning of her imminent fall, but one which should also inform and reassure her – if its advice is heeded. Here at her toilette we are again meant to recall Eve and the moment when shortly after her creation she is so taken with her own beauty that she gazes at the 'smooth watry image' (iv, 480) in the pool, a gesture which hints at her pride (here justifiable) and her want of that 'higher intellectual' (ix, 483) which Adam is meant to provide. Belinda likewise is fascinated by her own image, in a cameo which suggests how her pride and fancifulness will lead her into danger: 'A heav'nly Image in the Glass appears, / To that she bends, to that her Eyes she rears . . .' (I, 125–6).

Now transformed by the imagination, Belinda becomes its creature. Emphasis shifts from solid physical reality to the shifting and intangible, so that in this new context her identity (as a newly 'painted Vessel') merges with that of the boat carrying her to Hampton:

> But now secure the painted Vessel glides,
> The Sun-beams trembling on the floating Tydes,
> While melting Musick steals upon the Sky,
> And soften'd Sounds along the Waters die. (ii, 47–50)

The definition of the scene dissolves ('melting', 'soften'd'); the winds play gently around her and the whole picture slips into soft focus as the 'secondary' qualities of sound and colour take over. We are meant of course to recall here the magic of Cleopatra's barge as described by Enobarbus. Shakespeare's heroine, another exploiter of the imagination, lay on her cloth of gold 'O'er-picturing that Venus where we see / The fancy outwork nature' (II, ii, 200–1). The purple sails were 'so perfumed that / The winds were love-sick with them', and to the sound of flutes boy-cupids stood beside her waving 'divers-colour'd fans', so that 'from the barge / A strange invisible perfume hits the sense'.[30]

Thanks to the sylphs' transformation of her, Belinda is no longer the lazy girl hammering the floor with her slipper, but now resembles a 'goddess' in the powerful hold she has on the imaginations of those about her. Her function is well seen here in comparison with Swift, whose goddesses are clearly *not* celebrated by the imagination; they are regularly shattered by fact and reality, their abstract beauty dragged into a suicidal conjunction (and rhyme) with the concrete: 'Proceeding on, the lovely Goddess / Unlaces next her Steel-Rib'd Bodice . . .' ('A Beautiful Young Nymph Going to Bed', 23–4). The art lavished on Belinda at her dressing-table is raised far above this kind of thing by the mock-heroic direction of the poem (the inverse of Swift's movement towards travesty) which transforms the scene to a magic ritual. The phrase 'Repairs her Smiles' (i, 141) in a Swiftian context would destroy her, but as part of the 'mystic Order' the sting of the words is strangely lessened. Even the idea of 'toil' (powerfully felt in the 'Anguish, Toil, and Pain' of Corinna's daily self-assemblage)[31] gains a fastidiousness in Pope's lines: 'From each she nicely culls with curious Toil, / And decks the Goddess with the glitt'ring Spoil' (i, 131–2).

Like the imagination itself Belinda is brilliant, unstable, alluring, and independent of morality. Her curls may be her chief glory, but another object identified with her, and which she has power to transform, is the cross upon her breast. Enacting the imagination's power, she metamorphoses it from the symbol of Christian *truth* into a thing of *beauty* – a brilliant extension of herself sparkling in sympathy with her. Won from its responsibility within the world of Nature, it now annihilates creeds, and, uniting men rather than dividing them, becomes an image 'which *Jews* might kiss, and Infidels adore' (ii, 8). But in the gossipy world of the court where truth goes for nothing and reputations shatter in a moment (a world thriving on fiction and fancy) this 'painted Vessel' is precarious. Cleanth Brooks has usefully noted the recurrent references to the 'frail china jar' as an image of Belinda's *chastity*, 'like the fine porcelain, something brittle, precious, useless, and easily broken'.[32] But the jar represents the heroine even more closely than this suggests, for the fate that threatens it haunts Belinda also. The shattering of this jar would destroy its charm for the imagination. It would no longer be a thing for contemplation, whose wholeness and perfection lifts it above a physical existence, but instead a mere artifact, whose pieces betray the laborious effort put into its making, now exposed as 'painted Fragments' (iii, 160). Once cracked it would suddenly revert to its physical origins, revealing the 'important Hours'[33] that went into its making and which are now necessary for its repair:

> White lead was sent us to repair
> Two brightest, brittlest earthly Things
> A Lady's Face, and China ware.
>   (Swift, 'The Progress of Beauty', 50–2)

Once more Swift's goddess has to confront the nightmare: her face no longer casts a spell over her beholders, but has descended to the world of truth, where it is just another cracked object needing repair.

Long before Belinda is roused by the lap-dog and the Baron's letter (cunningly tied around the dog's neck?), the Baron himself has been engaged in serious business. Besides seeking a rendezvous with Belinda, he has constructed a sacrificial altar to Love, on which he has offered his whole collection of female frippery gathered from former idols ('three Garters, half a Pair of Gloves' (ii, 39) etc – his masculine version of the coquette's sword-knots). He has to this point lived within the fickle imagination of the lover (the twelve romances out of which he constructs the altar are evidence enough of this), but he symbolically abjures his career as a sexual philanderer for the one supreme prize. All the trophies which his imagination has fed on are consumed by the flames. One vision now haunts him, that of Belinda and her lock of hair: 'Th'Adventrous *Baron* the bright Locks admir'd, / He saw, he wish'd, and to the Prize aspir'd . . .' (ii, 29–30).

One critic has considered the Baron to be an unsympathetic philanderer, a man for whom the lock is merely the greatest of all trophies which he wants to acquire in order to increase his renown in society.[34] This harsh view is misleading, since it tends to ignore the extent to which the Baron's imagination has fallen a prey to Belinda – the 'slender Chains' of her beauty hold him transfixed, and the coquette's own aggressiveness is stressed at several points. Nor should we forget the figure of the foppish Sir Plume[35] who confronts him after the 'rape' – the Baron's dignified and self-possessed reply (iv, 131–40) shows the contrast between them, and his alliance with Clarissa also suggests that Pope does not see him as a mere 'philanderer'. No, his seizure of the lock is more the act of the adventurous lover as described by Spenser:

> [Her] image printing in his deepest wit,
> He thereon feeds his hungrie fantasy,
> Still full, yet never satisfyde with it . . .
> Thereon his mynd affixed wholly is,
> Ne thinks on ought, but how it to attain;
> His care, his joy, his hope is all on this . . .
> Then forth he casts in his unquiet thought,
> What he may do, her favour to obtaine;
> What brave exploit, what perill hardly wrought . . .
> (*An Hymne in Honour of Love*, 197–220)

The lock as we know is more than mere hair: it is the source of Belinda's power. It is up to the Baron, with Clarissa's help, to bring this goddess down to earth, to the solid ground where things stand and are known for what they really are.

In their encounter across the card-table at Hampton Court Belinda plays the aggressive game of love, and, though the final victory is hers, she loses the Queen of Hearts to the Baron. During the interval of the coffee-drinking ritual he is given his chance to issue a public challenge to her feelings for him. The sylphs, aware that a 'dire Event' is imminent, that Belinda's existence as a creature of the imagination is threatened, awake her consciousness of the cherished lock. But fancy's 'mazy Ringlets' (ii, 139) are drawing the Baron inexorably closer:

> A thousand Wings, by turns, blow back the Hair,
> And thrice they twitch'd the Diamond in her Ear,
> Thrice she look'd back, and thrice the Foe drew near.
> Just in that instant, anxious *Ariel* sought
> The close Recesses of the Virgin's Thought;
> As on the Nosegay in her Breast reclin'd,
> He watch'd th'Ideas rising in her Mind,
> Sudden he view'd, in spite of all her Art,
> An Earthly Lover lurking at her Heart. (iii, 136–44)

We are reminded of the busy imagery of Aurelia's heart in the *Guardian* essay. Here Ariel, through Momus' glass, watches the 'Ideas' within her, and he is disturbed by what he sees, because it threatens the *fancy-free* world in which Belinda has hitherto lived, and over which the sylphs preside. This is both the moment at which the virgin is to fall, and the moment when the imagination is challenged by truth. By loving the Baron (wearing his image in her heart) Belinda no longer 'rejects Mankind' (i, 68). Ariel does not abandon her out of pique[36] but because the sylphs, who like Pope's imagination have worshipped and cherished her, are rendered powerless the moment truth intervenes. And so inevitably Ariel retires from her with a sigh, 'his Pow'r expir'd (iii, 145). The mutual love of the Baron and Belinda is, literally, a moment of truth – that is why Clarissa supports it. She gives the scissors to the Baron in order finally to recall her from the world of girlish fancy. Aubrey Williams is right in seeing here that Belinda has been given the opportunity to make her 'Fall' a fortunate one.[37]

The sylphs and their lock are satanically involved in the events of the poem: they tempt Belinda to wrongful pride and ambition, and they tempt the Baron also. The fact that Pope stresses the curling quality of the lock suggests that we are meant to sense its intriguing satanic character: Milton's devil hid within the 'mazie foulds' (*PL*, ix, 161) of the serpent in order to lead Eve astray, and at the moment of temptation he appeared before her as a 'Fould above fould a surging Maze' (ix, 499) as he 'Curld many a wanton wreath in sight of *Eve*, / To lure her Eye' (ix, 517–18). We remember that Comus's domain is within 'the blind mazes of this tangl'd Wood' (*Maske*, 180), a place where it is important that the lady see clearly, undazzled by the fertile imagination of her tempter. To sport with 'the tangles of *Neaera*'s hair' (*Lycidas*, 69) is to delight in the fanciful world of love elegy rather than attempt the true vision of the divine poet. Such Miltonic entanglements usually involve the delighted imagination, revelling in its 'error' (a word whose etymology Milton consciously exploits).[38] Nor is it only Milton who explores this idea:

> The wanton lover in a curious strain
>   Can praise his fairest fair;
> And with quaint metaphors her curled hair
>   Curl o're again.
> (George Herbert, 'Dulnesse', 5–8)

In 'Jordan II' Herbert speaks of 'Curling with metaphors' (the self-delighting imagination is distracted from Heavenly truth) and Crashaw describes how music 'doth curle the aire / With flash of high-borne fancyes' ('Musicks Duell', 137–8). A sonnet from *The Phoenix Nest*, perhaps by Sir Walter Raleigh,[39] provides an even closer parallel, when it speaks of 'Those eies which set my fancie on a fire, / Those crisped haires, which hold my hart in chains . . .'. By linking Belinda's curls with the equally traditional idea of 'fancy's maze'[40] (and perhaps recalling a line of Cowley: '*Love* walks the pleasant Mazes of her Hair', 'The Change', 2) Pope is able to exploit the delightful falsehood implicit in the imagination. In the fanciful world which the sylphs represent, the maze is a beneficent idea, and it is human truth which threatens – the 'mystick Mazes' through which they guide young women are a protection against reality. But it is in the curls of Belinda's hair that the Miltonic idea has full force. The lock allures her worshippers by its 'mazy Ringlets' (ii, 139) which

> graceful hung behind
> In equal Curls, and well conspir'd to deck

> With shining Ringlets the smooth Iv'ry Neck.
> Love in these Labyrinths his Slaves detains . . . (ii, 20–3)

The dangerous *conspiracy* is confirmed when Pope remarks that
'Fair Tresses Man's Imperial Race insnare' (ii, 27). Once Clarissa's
clear beam of truth strikes through, however, curls become
irrelevant, a mere distraction from the unpalatable truth: 'Curl'd or
uncurl'd . . . Locks will turn to grey . . .' (v, 26). The curl is less a
'thing' than a temporary posture. The sylphs preside over it
because it is a fancy; hair is the true thing, the curl (as Herbert's
lines demonstrate) is a *metaphor*. No wonder that once the sylphs
have gone, the remaining lock loses its curl: 'The Sister-Lock now
sits uncouth, alone, / And in its Fellow's Fate foresees its own; /
Uncurl'd it hangs . . .' (iv, 171–3). The 'poor Remnant' has
surrendered its power as a thing of the imagination. The truth
about hair is that time will turn it grey, and, however alluring, a
curl is only a distracting temporary beauty.

The Baron's outrage is that he treats the lock as a thing rather than
an idea. With the help of Clarissa's scissors (the scissors being to
truth what the lock is to the imagination) the Baron snips off the
hypnotising curls, badge of coquettry, and thus challenges Belinda
to descend from the metaphorical to the realm of truth. He also
challenges her *pride*, that passion which her imagination has fostered
and cherished. The Baron's action and Clarissa's words combine in
an attempt to make reality dawn upon Belinda. The Baron may be
her foe, but Belinda should be grateful for the truth – even from her
enemy:

> If once right Reason drives *that Cloud* [Pride] away,
> *Truth* breaks upon us with *resistless Day*;
> Trust not your self; but your Defects to know,
> Make use of ev'ry *Friend* – and ev'ry *Foe*.
> (*An Essay on Criticism*, 211–14)

The Baron's initiative is given theoretical support by his ally
Clarissa, who steps forward as truth's representative to insist that
reality cannot be held at bay for long: 'Oh! if to dance all Night, and
dress all Day, / Charm'd the Small-pox, or chas'd old Age
away . . .' (v, 19–20). Clarissa knows that Belinda cannot exist as an
object of the imagination forever. If Belinda is sensible she will
preserve what her beauty has gained; she will surrender her merely
hypnotic 'charm' (the allure of the imagination) in favour of a deeper

and more genuine 'virtue' committed to, rather than denying, human values. While the sylphs embraced her she rejected mankind – that is, she cherished the imagination and shut out reality. Clarissa's scissors challenge her: the sharp cutting-edge of truth has met material hair, not angelic substance which can unite again. Ben Jonson expresses this same idea very trenchantly in his *Discoveries*. He is talking about the way the senses entangle the soul in error, and how the reason is able to deal with this: 'by those Organs [of sense], the *Soule workes*: She is a perpetuall Agent, prompt and subtile; but often flexible, and erring; intangling her selfe like a Silke-worme: But her *Reason* is a weapon with two edges, and cuts through.'[41] Clarissa's 'two-edg'd Weapon' (iii, 128) is therefore not just a humorous parody of the hero's sword, but the weapon of reason which cuts through the entanglements of imagination.

Belinda's chief error has been to mistake the aura for the reality, and therefore to lose the human scale of things. Her beauty has made her adored, but it has also fostered pride and selfishness, cutting her off from her fellow-men. Pope alerted us to this danger through Ariel's words in her dream: 'Know farther yet; Whoever fair and chaste / Rejects Mankind, is by some *Sylph* embrac'd . . . (i, 67–8). To reject mankind is to ignore the truth about herself as a woman ('the flesh-and-blood creature . . . who marries, breeds, ages, and wears, has all sorts of dire consequences – and eventually dust and the grave').[42] The cutting of the lock is a sad moment (the sylphs leave her for ever), but it is also, as Clarissa points out, her moment of opportunity.

Clarissa's speech at the opening of Canto v, which Pope added in 1717 'to open more clearly the MORAL of the Poem' (Pope's note), is an exercise in worldly realism. It is bringing the truth home to a fanciful girl, and so its tactics are common sense, good humour, and the knowingness and cunning born of experience. She acknowledges at once the power of beauty, but points out that without 'good Sense' everything which this power gains will be lost. She therefore tries to turn Belinda's eyes away from surfaces to the moral qualities within (from her 'Face' to her 'Virtue', from 'Charms' to 'Merit'). Clarissa's practicality shows in the stress she places upon learning something useful, and in her determination to confront Belinda with 'those foes to Fair ones, Time and Thought':

> But since, alas! frail Beauty must decay,
> Curl'd or uncurl'd, since Locks will turn to grey,
> Since painted, or not painted, all shall fade,
> And she who scorns a Man, must die a Maid;
> What then remains, but well our Pow'r to use,
> And keep good Humour still whate'er we lose? (v, 25–30)

Clarissa's tone supports the contrast she is trying to make, between the superficial things of life and its stark realities. 'Curl'd or uncurl'd', 'painted, or not painted' – the phrases chime hesitatingly alongside the laconic factual sentences ('Beauty must decay', 'Locks will turn to grey', 'all shall fade') which toll the truths Belinda must recognise.

J. S. Cunningham detects within Clarissa's speech some 'limitations in her range of vision' (rightly, perhaps, since she is asserting truth, not imagination) and he is troubled by her worldliness and opportunism.[43] But in this, as in other ways, Pope has judged his tone to perfection. Clarissa, expressing the moral of the poem, must obviously be cleared of any hint of prudishness: indeed, it is against this that she issues her warning. Her 'opportunism' is in fact an attempt to recall imagination back to reality, and though she fails to persuade Belinda, her words re-echo as we contemplate the heroine's fall.

The Baron acts, and Belinda reacts prudishly. In allegorical terms, the gnome Umbriel (a prude roaming the earth in search of mischief) descends into Belinda's spleen to give her a 'hypochondriack fit' or 'the vapours', a fashionable disease for distraught young ladies. The spleen itself is technically the seed-bed of the base imagination, the melancholy fancy which in woman can lead to self-delusions and hysteria. Bright's *Treatise of Melancholie* (1586) puts it pithily: 'darknes & cloudes of melancholie vapours rising from that pudle of the splene [pollute] both the substance, and spirits of the brayne, [and cause] it, without externall occasion, to forge monstrous fictions, and terrible to the conceite . . .'[44] The Cave of Spleen which Umbriel enters is therefore dark and misty, a place of grotesque hallucinations:

> A constant *Vapour* o'er the Palace flies;
> Strange Phantoms rising as the Mists arise;
> Dreadful, as Hermit's Dreams in haunted Shades,
> Or bright as Visions of expiring Maids. (iv, 39–42)

Umbriel, 'a dusky melancholy Spright', feels at home here, for the human body is the element of earth, and gnomes sink downward by nature (i, 63). If the sylphs inspire pleasurable dreams, then the gnomes bring the nightmares. Robert Burton describes this 'hypochondriacal melancholy' in these terms: 'windy vapours ascend up to the brain, which trouble the imagination, and cause fear, sorrow, dullness, heaviness, many terrible conceits and chimeras . . . and compel good, wise, honest, discreet men . . . to dote, speak and do that which becomes them not . . . (I, iii, 2, ii) And Thomas Walkington, in describing the dire effects of 'adust melancholy', describes how the sufferers 'are in bondage to many ridiculous passions': 'Ther was one possest with this humour, that tooke a strong conceit, that he was changed into an earthen vessell, who earnestly intreated his friends in any case not to come neare him . . .' (f. 69b). This nightmare breaks in upon the now distraught Belinda. Pope's version of the unpleasant melancholy fancies which haunt her is a playful one:

> Unnumber'd Throngs on ev'ry side are seen
> Of Bodies chang'd to various Forms by *Spleen*.
> Here living *Teapots* stand, one Arm held out,
> One bent; the Handle this, and that the Spout . . .
> Men prove with Child, as pow'rful Fancy works,
> And Maids turn'd Bottels, call aloud for Corks. (iv, 47–54)

The transforming 'pow'rful Fancy' has become a nightmare of sexual incongruity. Vessels have merged with the human form once again, but no longer to recall a china vase or Cleopatra's barge. Here they gesture mockingly, and like Comus's grotesque followers these metamorphosed figures warn against the lure of physical desire.

Belinda's fanciful reaction to the 'rape' takes the wrong, prudish form, failing to see the Baron's action as a social joke which relies for its deeper meaning on his dedication to his love. The joke-rape, nevertheless, is a perversion of what Belinda has been wanting, a gesture which to achieve womanhood she should have accepted calmly and rightly. The result of this inability to see clearly at the important moment is that Belinda turns at once from coquette to prude,[45] from a flighty and irresponsible girl towards a possible bleak future as an old maid. Clarissa's prophecy (laughed out of the coquettish world that surrounds Belinda) has struck the mark. Maturity *must* finally dispel imagination, here taking the form of the brilliant mythological world of the sylphs and gnomes. Belinda has freed herself from the coquettish fancy of the sylphs, but only to be reclaimed by the imagination in the shape of Umbriel, who after his successful trip into her fancy-breeding spleen exults over his new disciple: 'Triumphant *Umbriel* on a Sconce's Height / Clapt his glad Wings, and sate to view the Fight . . .' (v, 53–4). At the breaking of the gnome's vial Belinda yearns for a sad and solitary refuge:

> Oh had I rather un-admir'd remain'd
> In some lone Isle, or distant *Northern* Land . . .
> There kept my Charms conceal'd from mortal Eye,
> Like Roses that in Desarts bloom and die.
> What mov'd my Mind with youthful Lords to rome?
> O had I stay'd, and said my Pray'rs at home! (iv, 153–60)

Such an over-reaction is both false and fanciful, and is ominously reminiscent of Spleen's handmaid, *Ill-nature*,

>   like an *ancient Maid*,
> Her wrinkled Form in *Black* and *White* array'd;
> With store of Pray'rs, for Mornings, Nights, and Noons,
> Her Hand is fill'd . . . (iv, 27–30)

It also echoes the longing for solitude in Adam's cry of guilty hopelessness after the Fall:

>   O might I here
> In solitude live savage, in some glade
> Obscur'd, where highest Woods impenetrable
> To Starr or Sun-light, spread thir umbrage broad . . . (*PL*, ix, 1084–7)

The flattering sylphs have left her, to be replaced by the imaginative world of the guilt-ridden and prudish gnomes, the sad mental landscape of the melancholic. Umbriel's bag has its effect too, and as Thalestris 'fans the rising Fire' (iv, 94) Belinda's mind forms a horrific picture of what had previously been a delightful ritual:

> Was it for this you took such constant Care
> The *Bodkin*, *Comb*, and *Essence* to prepare;
> For this your Locks in Paper-Durance bound,
> For this with tort'ring Irons wreath'd around?
> For this with Fillets strain'd your tender Head,
> And bravely bore the double Loads of Lead? (iv, 97–102)

The imagination has again transformed the scene, and for the lighter-than-air fancy of the sylphs has substituted ideas of oppressive weight and constriction. The act of imagination which created her lock is now seen (equally wrongly) as a ritual of bondage. The dressing-table has become a torture-chamber. Belinda cannot break out of her imagination, only migrate from one image to another. Clarissa, the truly mature woman (like Martha Blount in the *Epistle to a Lady*) is not enwrapped in the imagination in this way, but occupies an area within the poem set apart from the dazzling female world around the heroine.[46] She stands before us on a pair of 'sublunary legs' (in Keats's phrase),[47] and her down-to-earth message, though it receives a chill reception, strikes the note of human truth.

But Clarissa's words are ignored as Belinda's world disintegrates into chaos and confusion. The lock, however, the cause of all this anarchy, has disappeared. Because all along it has been a fancy rather than a physical object, it is fitting that the lock should vanish during the struggle. It dissolves as all gestures of the imagination are bound to do. It would have 'died' anyway once it had become separate from Belinda; it would have become a pathetic relic, telling of nothing but dust and ashes:

> Dear dead women, with such hair, too – what's become
> of all the gold
> Used to hang and brush their bosoms? I feel chilly
> and grown old.
> (Browning, 'A Toccata of Galuppi's', 44–5)

But Browning's cold draught of truth is not the note on which Pope wishes to end. The lock began as an object of imagination and now it is to end as one, playfully transformed to the most exalted level of vision. Pope ends the poem with a fancy of his own, by which the lock is awarded its final metamorphosis:

> But trust the Muse – she saw it upward rise,
> Tho' mark'd by none but quick Poetic Eyes . . .
> A sudden Star, it shot thro' liquid Air,
> And drew behind a radiant *Trail of Hair*. (v, 123–8)

By a delightful compliment Pope rescues the imagination from the chaos of melancholy and frustration on which the dramatic action of the poem ends, and makes a playful gesture towards its divine character. The stellification of the lock is a parody of the release of the contemplative soul as sought by Il Penseroso and the Lady in the *Maske*, to be achieved by the divine imagination's guiding the intellect to knowledge of God. The 'quick Poetic Eyes' of imagination view the lock on its journey, and so do the sylphs who pursue it through the skies. In spite of truth's attack beauty has remained untouched, and, as with Pope's poem itself, the challenge to the imagination has brought about a glorious release. At the end of his work Pope suggests that the *Lock* will remain a vivid image for as long as men (whether beaux, lovers, star-gazers or prophets) have imaginations. Arabella Fermor will now be the representative not of earthly, but of 'Heavenly Beautie' like that celebrated by Spenser:

> By view whereof, it plainly may appeare,
> That still as every thing doth upward tend,
> And further is from earth, so still more cleare
> And faire it growes, till to his perfect end
> Of purest beautie, it at last ascend.
> (*An Hymne of Heavenly Beautie*, 43–7)

The Rape of the Lock explores so many aspects of the imagination: its kinship with beauty and pride; its opposition to judgment and truth; its insubstantiality, physicality, anarchy and self-deception; its functioning as dream, nightmare, madness and (finally) divine vision. The humorously transcendent ending, however, is a tactical flight from the challenge delivered to the imagination by the rest of the poem, and it is in this sense 'detachable' where the ending of *Eloisa to Abelard* is not. Whereas the drama of that poem comes from the conflict between one image and another (enacting 'the struggles of grace and nature, virtue and passion'), the drama of *The Rape of the Lock* pits image against reality, fancy against truth. *Eloisa to Abelard* is neoplatonic in the way it presents the soul's encounter with the flesh, in its concern with different levels of vision, and its acceptance of the imagination as a path to divine truth. *The Rape of the Lock* can be seen contrastingly as an empiricist poem, with its opposition of imagination and reality, and its location of truth in the worldly, unillusioning good-sense of Clarissa. The final stellification of Belinda's beauty is therefore best seen as a complimentary platonic postscript, flattering both to Arabella Fermor and to Pope's own art. By leaving his poem among the stars Pope certainly does not wish us to forget the many earthly issues which the story of Belinda's lock has raised. However, at this stage of his career he feels able to end in the realm of imagination rather than truth.

But Pope was soon given the opportunity to put matters in

perspective. In November 1714 he discovered to his surprise that Arabella Fermor had married (not, incidentally, the 'Baron'). In writing to congratulate her he completely avoided the fanciful compliment he had lavished on his Belinda. Approaching her now as a married woman about to take on many new responsibilities as friend, wife and parent, he stressed the 'better things' that she could expect from her future status, 'better' because these would be more firmly grounded. A poet's imagination had celebrated a girl's beauty and charm, but from now on Belinda the woman must strive for a more solid (though ironically less lasting) tribute:

It may be expected perhaps, that one who has the title of Poet, should say something more polite on this occasion: But I am really more a well-wisher to your felicity, than a celebrater of your beauty. Besides, you are now a married woman, and in a way to be a great many better things than a fine Lady . . . You ought now to hear nothing but that, which was all you ever desired to hear (whatever others may have spoken to you) I mean *Truth*.

FOUR

Women and the imagination:
Epistle to a Lady

I

The ending of *The Rape of the Lock* could almost be an illustration of
some lines from George Granville's 'Essay upon Unnatural Flights
in Poetry':

> But Poetry in Fiction takes Delight,
> And mounting in bold Figures out of Sight,
> Leaves Truth behind, in her audacious Flight . . .
> (*Poems upon Several Occasions*, 1712, p. 173)

Two decades later the Pope of the 1730s, translator of Homer, editor
of Shakespeare and successful literary figure with a European
reputation, could look back at the development of his poetic career
and view his early work as having been too generous in its treatment
of the imagination. The well-known couplet in his *Epistle to Dr
Arbuthnot* (1735) sees his maturing as a poet in terms of a movement
out of 'Fancy's Maze' towards the pursuit of 'Truth', and the rousing
close of *An Essay on Man* (1734) acknowledges the role which his
philosophic friend Bolingbroke had in this: '. . . urg'd by thee, I
turn'd the tuneful art / From sounds to things, from fancy to the
heart . . .' (iv, 391–2). This does not mean that after 1717 Pope was
less willing to explore the workings of imagination in his poetry (far
from it), but that the victories which it had won in *Eloisa to Abelard*
and *The Rape of the Lock* could not so easily be repeated. The mature
Pope wished to show how, rather than transcending the claims of the
world, the imagination should tether itself to them.

In the previous two chapters we examined how Pope presented
the heroine's dilemma in terms of her imaginative activity. In *Epistle
II. To a Lady. Of the Characters of Women* (1735) he returns to his
interest in female psychology, and it is not surprising to find that the
control and directing of the imagination is again an important
theme. This chapter will argue that in *Epistle to a Lady* Pope explores,

with as much fascination as sadness, why so many talented and lively-minded women lead negative and frustrated lives, and that he finds the answer in their essential fancifulness.[1] The very long tradition concerning the fickleness and instability of the female sex (Vergil's *varium et mutabile semper femina, Aeneid*, iv, 569–70) was by Pope's day being increasingly seen in terms of an undisciplined imagination, and when examined against the conventional images Pope's *Epistle* comes across as a subtle and sympathetic account of an issue usually handled with far less sensitivity. In this poem Pope goes beyond the simplistic label of 'fancifulness' to present what is in effect an anatomy of the self-destructive aspects of imaginative activity. He investigates how it can be implicated in a whole range of character defects: instability, hypocrisy, heartlessness, silliness, inconstancy, falseness, shallowness and superficiality (Pope understands this distinction), selfishness, restlessness, self-destructiveness, lack of priorities, cruelty, madness, folly and pride. He recognises that an undisciplined imagination is somehow at the heart of so much betrayal of human emotion.

This theme is reflected in his use of an imaginative 'sketchbook' style to exploit the imagination of his reader, and is set off by a related theme of *creativity* (the counterpart of the negative and self-destructive quality of the women he describes). Pope never finds it easy to divorce life and literature, and so it is fitting that he should try also to understand these women in literary terms: imagination, truth, art, nature, decorum, judgment, wit, the rules, correctness, poetic justice – these concepts provide the staple vocabulary for any eighteenth-century discussion of literature, and in Pope's *Epistle* they join to provide a subordinate theme of great interest as the poet sets out to explore Heaven's 'last best work'.

II

In associating women with an undisciplined imagination Pope was exploiting a theme which had been touched on by a number of writers over the previous century and a half. Of course, the changeableness of the female sex had long been proverbial. Since the days of Catullus, Vergil and Ovid, woman's supposed fickleness had provided poets with matter for humour, satire, polemic or tragedy, and it was only a short step to linking this with the unstable, protean nature of the imagination. Renaissance and seventeenth-century

attacks on women exploited the notion that the female's psychological make-up was fundamentally different from the male's, and it was
in such a context that women's susceptibility to fanciful delusions
was developed. The soul's being traditionally feminine (*anima*) did
allow certain female figures (such as Milton's Lady) to have divine
visions, and an active imagination could be a spiritual asset. Anthony
Gibson's *A Womans Woorth, defended against all the men in the world*
(1599) was able to use the notion to women's advantage: 'the vertue
feminine hath bin of greater efficacie then men . . . for it consisteth
much more of debating cases, and the facultie imaginative, which
indeed are the happiest functions of the soule . . .' (f. 4). And in the
later age of Pope an anonymous writer could assert the superiority of
women's brains by reference to their imaginations: 'their brain being
generally temper'd with heat and moisture, which renders the mind
quick and piercing, they have mostly an excellent imagination, a
ready invention, and an easy discernment. Their memory is for the
most part happy and their fancy sprightly . . .' (*Woman's Superior
Excellence over Man . . . By Sophia, a Person of Quality* (1740), p. 84).

But in a male-dominated society it is not surprising that emphasis
was also given to the baser elements of imaginative activity. J. L.
Vives, for example, stressed the aspect of instability: 'Womans
thought is swyfte and for ye most part unstable walkyng and
wandrynge out from home and sone wyl slyde by the reason of it
owne slypernes, I wote nat howe far' (*Instruction of a Christian Woman*
[?1540], sig. Ciiib). According to John Knox (himself not a model of
controlled reasonableness) such mental unsteadiness led them into a
whole range of vices: 'Nature I say, doth paynt them furthe to be
weake, fraile, impacient, feble and foolishe: and experience hath
declared them to be unconstant, variable, cruell and lacking the spirit
of counsel and regiment . . .' (*The First Blast of the Trumpet Against
the Monstruous regiment of women* (1558), f. 10). In the England of
Charles II the subject of woman still provided men with an
opportunity for name-calling as they searched for suitable images to
describe her as an offence against Nature. In this context she could be
seen as 'crooked' in that her mind was thought to be moved by
'fancy' rather than reason:

> Her crooked mind's a Metaphor of Hell,
> Her Tongue's an Engine which doth horror tell:
> Her perverse Will doth for her Reason stand,
> Her mad Passion does her Will command.

Her Prudence by her fancy moves apace . . .
(Female Excellence: or, Woman Display'd . . . By a
Person of Quality (1679), p. 4)

Much play was also made of the deceptiveness of woman's beauty, whose attractive surface could conceal unpleasant realities: 'Within a gawdy Case, a nasty Soul, / Like T—— of quality in a gilt Close-stool . . .' (John Oldham, 'A Satyr upon a Woman, Who by her Falshood and Scorn was the Death of my Friend' in his *Satyrs upon the Jesuits* (1681), p. 149). Each of these attacks on woman demonstrates how imaginative activity was thought appropriate for her, in that her supposed 'nature' shared the qualities traditionally associated with that faculty–lack of judgment ('the spirit of counsel and regiment'), lawlessness, deception, a concern with surfaces and colours, restless activity, and of course, changeableness: 'changeful as the Wind, / Which Rainbows on a Cloud their fickle Min[d] . . .' (C. Taylor, *The Scale, or, Woman weigh'd with Man* (c. 1715?), p. 6). And we are back again with the typical rainbow image. The maze also makes its inevitable appearance: 'Nothing but vain fantastick Woman's chang'd; / And through all Mischiefs various Mazes rang'd . . .' (Robert Gould, *Love given over* (1709 ed.), p. 8).

This association of woman with imagination[2] placed her in a naturally subservient position to the more masculine 'judgment',[3] just as Milton's Eve was created subordinate to the 'higher intellectual' of Adam (*PL*, ix, 483).[4] Society of course reinforced this by excluding women from organised education and from public careers, so that her role could easily be a merely ornamental one. The parallel with the imagination extended to her social position: she was conceded the empire of beauty, but was discouraged from shouldering responsibilities or making judgments. Lady Mary Wortley Montagu, as so often, puts the woman's viewpoint trenchantly: '. . . (contrary to all other Authors) I see with a favourable Eye the little vanitys with which they amuse themselves, and am glad they can find in the imaginary Empire of Beauty, a consolation for being excluded every part of Government in the State' (*The Nonsense of Common-Sense*, ii, 27 Dec. 1737). Woman had to work within the sphere of imagination ('the imaginary Empire of Beauty'): government and responsibility (in the mind as in the state) belonged to the judgment.

By far the most important literary precedent for the tradition within which Pope works is Milton's portrayal of the nature and fall of Eve. We saw in the previous chapter[5] how Pope is concerned to associate Belinda with the pride and fancifulness of the first woman, and how both Milton and Pope implicate the imagination in the 'fall' of their deluded heroines. *Paradise Lost* characterises Eve as a being whose imagination is dangerously active when functioning independently of Adam's rational authority. She is from the beginning taken with images: her own reflection in the pool, the dream aroused in her fancy by Satan, the alluring picture of the fruit which Satan's description creates in her, and finally her divine dream (to counterbalance her demonic one) which presages 'some great good' (xii, 612) and is her own version of the revelation which Michael unfolds to Adam while she sleeps. Adam's reassurance comes through direct intellectual converse with the Angel, but Eve's is conveyed through her imagination. This distinction between them is preserved to the end.

In the decades following the publication of Milton's epic (1667) there was renewed controversy over the nature and role of women, with both male and female authors making contributions to a debate which ranged from the good-humoured or philosophical, to the satirical and scurrilous. The biblical Eve naturally figured largely (as she had done in Renaissance attacks on women), but a new Miltonic emphasis also began to assert itself, based on Milton's analysis of the relationship between Eve and her husband. In John Dryden's dramatised version of *Paradise Lost, The State of Innocence* (1677), for example, Adam accuses his newly-fallen wife in all the familiar terms: 'Add, that she's proud, fantastick, apt to change; / Restless at home; and ever prone to range: / With shows delighted . . .' (V, i). The same theme appears in *The Great Birth of Man: Or, The Excellency of Man's Creation and Endowments Above the Original of Woman: a Poem* (1686) by 'M.S.' which re-tells the creation and fall of man in anti-feminist terms. Eve here has benefited from Milton's analysis of the fanciful tendencies of our first mother, so that she becomes a kind of Belinda in Paradise. She is an easy target for the serpent, and her kinship with Pope's heroine is clear from Satan's description of her obsession with her own image. She would (he believes)

> Seek fragrant Smells, and then she'd fall in Love
> With her own Face, whilst in some shady Grove,
> Making a Mirrour of a Fountain, where
> She'd kiss her Shade, and curl her Silver Hair . . . (p. 7)

Her temptation and fall involves a movement from her fantasising about being Queen of Heaven: 'Cherubins curl my Golden Locks, whilst I / Command Attendants, with my sparkling Eye' (p. 9) to her self-accusation after she has eaten the forbidden fruit:

> Away these Gilded, Airy Visions, pass . , .
> Ah Fool! What Happiness thou'st lost for Toyes,
> What solid Good, for visionary Joys? (p. 10)

This Eve, who seems to stand somewhere between Milton's Eve and Pope's Belinda, has clearly been the victim of her own imagination.

This aspect of female behaviour became one of the favourite topics for the periodical essayists of Queen Anne's reign. *The Tatler* (1709–11) and its counterpart *The Female Tatler* (1709) good-naturedly satirised fancifulness as one of the foibles of the modern woman. It had become something of a commonplace, to the extent that one serious defender of the status and rights of women, Lady Mary Chudleigh, took it for granted as a feminine weakness. Her *Essays upon Several Subjects* (1710) were specifically directed at a female audience, and she expressed the hope that women could overcome their impressionableness and unsteadiness of mind:

I know most People have false Idea's of Things; they think too superficially to think truly; they find it painful to carry on a Train of Thoughts; with this my own Sex are principally chargeable: We are apt to be misled by Appearances, to be govern'd by Fancy, and the impetuous Sallies of a sprightly Imagination, and we find it too laborious to fix them; we are too easily impos'd on, too credulous, too ready to hearken to every soothing Flatterer . . . ('Of Friendship', p. 173)

Again, the figure of Milton's Eve ('our credulous Mother', ix, 644) hovers over this passage, and in stressing the mastery of the passions, the importance of 'clear Ideas' and the necessity of distinguishing truth from falsehood, Lady Mary Chudleigh is handling the kind of Miltonic themes which would very soon be concerning Pope. She also had a practical reforming zeal, which led her to recommend ways of discouraging women's fancifulness: they should study Geometry (''Twill enable us to fix our Thoughts, and give a check to that quickness of Imagination, which is seldom consistent with solidity of Judgment' ('Of Knowledge', p. 10)) and they should beware of frittering away their leisure-time ('we shall have no idle Moments to throw away on Romances and Trifles of that Nature, which serve only to stuff the Memory, to fill it with extravagant Fancies' (p. 14)).

In the following year Joseph Addison treated the same subject in a satirical manner in *Spectator* 15 (17 March 1711), a paper which in its tone and theme is close both to *The Rape of the Lock* and *Epistle to a Lady*. Addison's subject is the 'light, fantastical Disposition' of women, and the 'numberless Evils' which befall them as a result. The essay records tragic examples of women betrayed by their fancies – the indecisive coquette who weds a beau because he has added 'a supernumerary Lace to his Liveries', and the melancholy Cleanthe who has married an invalid for his glittering coach. External decoration, colourful visual effects, and the play of light on shining surfaces – these are the terms in which Addison explores 'this unaccountable Humour in Woman-kind, of being smitten with every thing that is showy and superficial'.

Such self-destructive superficiality is seen as being a function of a restless imagination, which plays about the surface of things without understanding the solid truth beneath (in Addison's words, such women 'consider only the Drapery of the Species'). The association of truth with solidity and plainness, and of imagination with the shifting, dazzling, decorated, colourful and superficial, is at the root of the matter for authors of this period, particularly Pope and Swift. Reduced to its simplest, it becomes a contrast between beauty as *something seen* and truth as *something known*: beauty as located on the surface, therefore subject to all the vagaries and cheats of the imaginative faculty, and truth as established at the heart of things, to be understood through experience and judgment. This contrast between imagination and judgment is therefore interpreted as juxtaposing surface and substance, the shifting and the constant, decoration and plainness, colour and chiaroscuro, dazzle and illumination, beauty and truth. Addison sums up the matter in a sentence which could well serve as a gloss on either *The Rape of the Lock* or *Epistle to a Lady*: 'When Women are thus perpetually dazling one anothers Imaginations, and filling their Heads with nothing but Colours,[6] it is no Wonder that they are more attentive to the superficial Parts of Life, than the solid and substantial Blessings of it.' Like Pope and Swift, Addison believes that women's imaginations throw them into danger, and the most trivial of things can bring about their destruction: 'A Pair of fringed Gloves may be her Ruin . . . Lace and Ribbons, Silver and Gold Galloons, with the like glittering Gew-Gaws, are so many Lures to Women of weak Minds or low

Educations . . .', or, as John Gay expresses it in his poem *The Fan* (1714):

> Thus the raw Maid some tawdry Coat surveys,
> Where the Fop's Fancy in Embroidery plays;
> His snowy Feather edg'd with crimson Dyes,
> And his bright Sword-knot lure her wand'ring Eyes;
> Fring'd Gloves, and gold Brocade, conspire to move,
> 'Till the Nymph falls a Sacrifice to Love. (ii, 109–14)

The glittering folds of the serpent have become the fancy clothes of the fop.

When Pope came to write his *Epistle to a Lady*, therefore, he had available to him a tradition which tended to identify women with the imaginative faculty, and which viewed both in relation to a masculine 'judgment' which should be given authority over the more wayward and self-destructive quality. Early in his poetic career Pope showed himself interested in the 'marital' implications of the relationship between these faculties in his *To a Young Lady, With the Works of Voiture*, which appeared in Lintot's 1712 Miscellany.[7] The influence of Addison's essay is clear in the figure of Pamela (who marries a fool for his 'gilt Coach') and also in Pope's exploration of the tensions between a life devoted to wit and fancy, and the severer judgments of the critics:

> Let mine, like *Voiture*'s, a gay Farce appear,
> And more Diverting still than Regular,
> Have Humour, Wit, a native Ease and Grace;
> No matter for the Rules of Time and Place:
> Criticks in Wit, or Life, are hard to please,
> Few write to those, and none can live to these.
> 　Too much *your Sex* is by their Forms confin'd,
> Severe to all, but most to Womankind . . . (25–32)

The danger is that judgment will be a tyrant, and that for a woman ('by nature yielding') such a marriage may prove a terrible imprisonment:

> Well might you wish for Change, by those accurst,
> But the last Tyrant ever proves the worst.
> Still in Constraint your suff'ring Sex remains,
> Or bound in formal, or in real Chains . . . (39–42)

The confinement of a wit by the rule-obsessed critics is equated here with the tyranny of husband over wife, in a theme which will powerfully re-emerge in *Epistle to a Lady*, where the relationship between imagination and judgment is again seen in marital terms.

In his *Epistle to a Lady* Pope is therefore tackling a subject in which the use and abuse of the imagination offers itself as a theme, and is working within a tradition of thought whereby a woman's fancifulness could be seen, satirically or tragically, as influential in many areas of her experience. There was precedent for associating this with her proverbial instability and for expressing the relationship between imagination and judgment in terms of that between woman and man. It was Adam's role to support and direct Eve, and in a similar way judgment ought to support and direct imagination. *Epistle to a Lady* draws such themes together, and as a critique of womankind it manages to balance satire and tragedy through its awareness of the relationship between critical judgment and imaginative sympathy.

III

Being a poem expressly 'Of the Characters of Women' *Epistle to a Lady* will, if decorum is to be observed, demand a style which befits the nature of the female sex as Pope sees it. Not surprisingly, he finds that decorum in a kind of art which is predominantly imaginative in character. In two important passages strategically placed within the poem Pope espouses the techniques of painting; not the grand style demanded by a heroic subject, nor the style of a formal portrait, but one which brings into play those images traditionally associated with the imagination – colours, clouds, chameleons, the rainbow and secondary light-effects. This technique marries style and subject to the extent that his approach becomes not just a stylistic choice but a commitment to a belief: that these women are united by their capacity for fanciful delusion. The artistic principle which Pope employs in these pictures deserves to be examined in detail, since it holds the clue to the poem's integrity of style and structure.[8]

The two passages frame (if that is not too formal a word) the pictures of inconstancy which form the first half of the poem:

> Come then, the colours and the ground prepare!
> Dip in the Rainbow, trick her off in Air.
> Chuse a firm Cloud, before it fall, and in it
> Catch, ere she change, the Cynthia of this minute. (17–20)

> Pictures like these, dear Madam, to design,

> Asks no firm hand, and no unerring line;
> Some wand'ring touch, or some reflected light,
> Some flying stroke alone can hit 'em right:
> For how should equal Colours do the knack?
> Chameleons who can paint in white and black? (151–6)

Taking these passages into account, Martin Price regards the poem as concerned with 'bad art':

the very grotesqueness of bad art has a fascination, for in the failure or misdirection of intention the ambitions of art are made all the more conspicuous . . . Running through the poem is an implicit analogy between the variability and ostentation of vain women and the broken light and color of dazzling but superficial painting.

   (*To the Palace of Wisdom*, 1964, p. 162)

Professor Price's analogy between the nature of Pope's art in the poem and the characters of his women is perceptive,[9] but I believe that to talk of 'bad art' is to use too black-and-white a term in this context. The art of the *Epistle* cannot be 'bad' since the essence of these women is restlessness (sudden storms, strange flights, whimsy, vicissitude and swirling brains) and so it is appropriate that such figures require 'no firm hand, and no unerring line' (152). It is part of the poem's decorum that such a style is an instrument of the imagination. It is certainly a secondary level of artistic activity, concerned with surface brilliance and highlighted details, but Pope knows that this very elusiveness demands a kind of genius. In the *Epistle* he does not deliberately 'misdirect' his intention in order to elevate by contrast the achievements of great art; rather his aim is directed towards finding a suitable medium.

   The poet seems to delight artistically in the possibility his subject gives him for showing his skill at a style different from that expected in a moralising epistle. In 1718 Pope complimented Sir Godfrey Kneller on a similar artistic triumph: 'a Genius like yours never fails to Express itself well to all the world. And in the warmth with which it is agitated, let it but throw the Pen or Pencil with never so careless a dash, all people would see 'tis a noble Frenzy, a Vaghezza, like the *Foam* of a Great Master' (18 Feb. 1718). Pope was of course himself a painter and had watched Kneller at work in his studio. In his twenties he had taken lessons from his friend Charles Jervas, and one of his exercises was to copy portraits by his teacher. In 1713 he described to John Gay the delight this held for him:

I begin to discover Beauties that were till now imperceptible to me. Every Corner of an Eye, or Turn of a Nose or Ear, the smallest degree of Light or Shade on a Cheek, or in a dimple, have charms to distract me . . . [I] am in some danger even from the Ugly and Disagreeable, since they may have their retired beauties, in one Trait or other about 'em. (23 Aug. 1713)

Implicit in such fondness for shading and detail is a relationship of sympathy between painter and sitter, where the artist is able to discover redeeming features even in the ugly. On the other hand, this kind of art runs the risk of allowing disagreeables to evaporate: the imagination is in danger of playing about the surface and missing the heart, of delighting in the parts while falsifying the whole.[10]

The dilemma is briskly resolved by Sir Joshua Reynolds in his remarks on the grand style of painting: 'all trifling or artful play of little lights, or an attention to a variety of tints is to be avoided; a quietness and simplicity must reign over the whole work . . .' (*Discourse IV*, 1771). Grandeur is achieved, he says, by 'reducing the colours to little more than chiaro oscuro'. Pope, however, knows that stylistic black-and-white, just like moral black-and-white, is inappropriate for his poem, and that he has chosen a difficult course in attempting to capture subtle shades of meaning and varieties of tone. In giving himself this challenge in *Epistle to a Lady* Pope resembles the young Hazlitt trying to paint in Rembrandtesque style the face of an old woman. The painter, while aware of extremes of dark and light, strives to preserve soft gradations of colour and avoid too stark and simplistic a contrast:

there was a gorgeous effect of light and shade: but there was a delicacy as well as depth in the *chiaro-scuro*, which I was bound to follow into all its dim and scarce perceptible variety of tone and shadow. Then I had to make the transition from a strong light to as dark a shade, preserving the masses, but gradually softening off the intermediate parts . . .
    ('On the Pleasure of Painting', *Table Talk* (1821))

In the *Epistle* Pope allows delicacy of tone and nuance of suggestion to break down the severe contrasts. There are certainly dark areas of the irredeemable (in Sappho and Queen Caroline), and the moon spreads its ideal light over the poem's ending; but elsewhere there is a great deal of colour and 'variety of tone and shadow' in which the poet's attitude is less clear cut.

As we saw from his letter to Gay, Pope is conscious of the relationship between a decorous stylistic 'sympathy' and an emotional 'sympathy' ('I am in some danger . . .'). But elsewhere he is careful to distinguish aesthetic and emotional 'light and shade' from the clear *ethical* principles which remain understood throughout. Sympathy of such kinds does not mean that Pope's moral imperatives are weakened. In Epistle II of *An Essay on Man* he warns in remarkably similar terms against this assumption. He is discussing the 'light and darkness' combined within mankind:

> Tho' each by turns the other's bound invade,
> As, in some well-wrought picture, light and shade,
> And oft so mix, the diff'rence is too nice
> Where ends the Virtue, or begins the Vice.
>   Fools! who from hence into the notion fall,
> That Vice or Virtue there is none at all.
> If white and black blend, soften, and unite
> A thousand ways, is there no black or white? (ii, 207–14)

Through the association of imagination with colour, it becomes clear that Pope understands how it can complicate judgments and can render moral absolutes less distinct (as the sylphs do in *The Rape of the Lock*). The *chiaroscuro* of truth–falsehood and good–bad still exists, but Pope knows that the imagination is in an important sense capable of being a sympathetic medium by its ability to colour, transform, and break down boundaries. The age of sensibility was to explore and extend this aspect of the 'sympathetic imagination'. Laurence Sterne, for example, inherits the tradition when he explains his method of sketching the 'most whimsical character' of Uncle Toby: '–not the great contours of it, –that was impossible, –but some familiar strokes and faint designations of it, were here and there touched in, as we went along . . .' (I, xxii). The quixotic imagination of Uncle Toby, one of the most 'sympathetic' characters in English fiction, makes the procedure entirely fitting.

The degree of Pope's sympathy with women-in-general is evident in his generous treatment of three images which were frequently applied to the female sex, but had by 1735 become tarnished by satirical use – the moon, the cloud and the tulip – and his use of these indicates the 'sympathetic' tendency of the early part of his poem. The simile of woman as the moon, for example, had been dealt a severe blow by Swift in *The Progress of Beauty* (1719), where the parallel between Celia and the Moon goddess is sustained with great satiric verve. The changeableness of womankind is presented through images of grotesque decay:

> And this is fair Diana's Case
> For, all Astrologers maintain
> Each Night a Bit drops off her Face
> When Mortals say she's in her Wain. (69–72)

In comparison with this, Pope's 'Cynthia of this minute' is definitely untarnished.

A less obvious parallel, between woman and a cloud, had by the date of *Epistle to a Lady* also become a dubious one. Oldham's coruscating *Satyr upon a Woman* . . .(1681), quoted earlier in this chapter, had used the image less innocently than Pope: 'Such on a Cloud those flatt'ring colours are, / Which only serve to dress a Tempest fair.' For Oldham the cloud symbolises woman's changeability in terms of deceit and ill temper. Another less than flattering portrait is 'Miss Cloudy', one of the intriguing women whose activities are described in *The Mall: or, The Reigning Beauties* (1709). The issue of woman-as-cloud, however, became something of a *cause célèbre* in 1732 with a published poetical exchange between Thomas Sheridan and Swift. In a rather playful manner Sheridan's *A New Simile for the Ladies* offered the cloud as an image to fit 'ev'ry Circumstance' of womankind including her imagination and her delight in colour:

> The *Clouds* build Castles in the Air,
> A Thing peculiar to the Fair . . .
> The *Clouds* delight in gaudy Shew,
> For they like Ladies have their Bow . . .
> Observe the *Clouds* in Pomp array'd,
> What various Colours are display'd,
> The Pink, the Rose, the Vi'let's Dye,
> In that great Drawing-Room the Sky . . . (27–52)

Swift as usual enjoyed puncturing fancifulness, and he seized the opportunity to defend clouds against this libellous comparison. His *Answer To a late scandalous Poem* points out to Sheridan that clouds only give 'Claps aetherial', and that they are relatively stable:

> You'll see a Cloud in gentle weather
> Keep the same face an hour together,
> While Women, if it could be reckon'd
> Change ev'ry feature ev'ry second. (43–6)

Pope's 'firm Cloud' is a humorous oxymoron, but it lacks the satirical bite that had become associated with the image.

At line 41 Pope introduces another simile: 'Ladies, like variegated Tulips, show, / 'Tis to their Changes that their charms they owe . . .' A poem which anticipates in several interesting ways both *The Rape of the Lock* and *Epistle to a Lady*, namely *The Circus: or, British Olympicks: a Satyr on the Ring in Hide-Park* (1709), describes the ageing coquette on display, dazzling the eyes of her male admirers:

> . . . in the *Ring* she always will be seen
> In various Colours, Yellow, Red, and Green,
> And like her Horses, skinny, old, and lean.
> No gaudy Tulip in the Month of *May*,
> Smells half so rank, or dresses half so gay. (p. 10)

The final three lines give the idea a distasteful edge, highlighting by contrast how Pope allows the image to delight so that 'Changes' and 'charms' are interdependent. Typically, Swift in his turn used the tulip to point out that woman's beauty has its source in earth, and to earth it will return: his *The Lady's Dressing Room* (1730) ends with a stinging reference to 'gaudy Tulips rais'd from Dung'.

Pope must have been aware that as parallels for womankind the moon, the cloud and the tulip were tarnished images which had been turned, by his friend Swift and others, to ridicule and obscenity. With this point in mind we begin to see how Pope is once again avoiding Swiftian burlesque, and how at the opening of the *Epistle* he is deliberately reinstating the innocence of these similes, which reinforce the position of 'sympathy' we have been considering. Nevertheless, they also hint at a more severe satire, and represent in some ways a conscious naivety on the poet's part, by which he makes gestures of fascination and delight[11] in order to establish an attitude which will be placed under increasing strain as the poem progresses.

The characters of women do indeed fascinate him in all their brilliant detail; but as we move through the poem from portrait to portrait he allows us to see under the glittering surface to the many undercurrents of frustration and despair, so that our immediate imaginative engagement with these women (reflected in Pope's sketchbook art) is deepened into an understanding of the human tragedies they act out and their many failures to establish close, enduring relationships. We also begin to see how the imagination, when it is allowed merely to play about the surface of life, can encourage a wide range of follies and vices. Pope as writer, and we as

readers, are made to feel an increasing tension between our more
sympathetic imaginative responses[12] to these women and our sense
(as judges) of the moral issues involved.

IV

The keynote is struck in the opening lines of the poem, where Pope
immediately challenges the notion of stable categories with what
seems a rather dismissive generalisation:

> Nothing so true as what you once let fall,
> 'Most Women have no Characters at all'.
> Matter too soft a lasting mark to bear,
> And best distinguish'd by black, brown, or fair. (1–4)

At first glance these remarks seem to deny most women their
individuality, by suggesting that in a man's catalogue the only
memory they leave is of the colour of their hair. Much depends,
however, on how we interpret this reference to women's *softness* and
its consequent implication for a sense of their *character* (or lack of
character). Nowadays we tend to think of a person's character
primarily in terms of his or her individuality (and we allow for a
'character' to surprise or intrigue us – 'She's quite a character!'). But
Pope and his contemporaries placed emphasis more on the stability
of a person's nature, so that a man or woman's character was
something consistent and known. It was of course a commonplace
of the neoclassical criticism of the age that 'character' in its truest
sense was formed of an appropriate cluster of qualities fitting
naturally together and observing 'decorum'. Pope's interest in
human beings was more subtle than that, and in Cloe, for example,
he presents a 'character' with ruthless insight. But the unstable
women sketched in the opening half of the poem (1–156) are handled
differently. For Pope they are less 'characters' than bundles of
characteristics awkwardly and destructively lodged within the same
person. These women cannot be said to possess a 'character' in the
sense in which the age used the term.

An associated issue here concerns woman's *softness* ('Matter too
soft a lasting mark to bear'). Pope's phrasing shows that he is being
specific about the word's associations, and that it is not a case of
muscular weakness or a tendency to be pliant and yielding – Pope's
women are certainly not that. By 1735 'softness' could be used to

suggest a sensitivity to impressions, seen particularly in terms of the readiness with which a person reacted to images. 'Softness' of mind had therefore become linked to the traditional view of women as susceptible to impressions on their imagination. Defoe, for example, tells of the dangers facing a young girl at a masquerade, whose mind is 'so captivated and soften'd by the Gaiety of every Thing about her, that she is fit to receive any Impressions . . .'[13] The softness and impressionableness of Eve are insisted upon by Milton: 'soft' is used of her at important moments in the poem[14] and Satan is able to enter her more than once ('his words . . . / Into her heart too easie entrance won', ix, 733–4). Conversely, Comus believes that the Lady is for 'gentle usage, and soft delicacy', but her mind is resistant to his sensuous fancies by being 'clad in compleat steel' (*Maske*, 680, 420). To return to Pope's own time, the author of *The Prude, A Tale* (1722) discusses how prudes (unlike coquettes) are *un*impressionable; the tubes within their nerves are literally closed to all the pleasures which try to pour through them:

> The little Atoms that in Swarms
> Visit from Bodies of all Forms,
> A proper Pleasure to dispense
> To all and every sportive Sense;
> That buz about where Fancy dwells,
> With all their Sweetness from their Cells,
> The callous Nerve forbids . . .
> No soft Impression with its Charms
> Sports in the Arteries . . . (pp. 10–11)

In other words, the prude's lack of 'softness' is physiologically unnatural. It took a woman writer, Sarah Fige in *The Female Advocate* (1687),[15] to understand the virtue of this softness and to place it within a spiritual perspective:

> And as a Woman's composition is
> Most soft and gentle, she has happiness
> In that her soul is of that nature too,
> And yields to any thing that Heav'n will do;
> Takes an impression when 'tis seal'd in heav'n. (pp. 15–16)

Pope's 'soft' women, therefore, are impressionable people whose minds are easily played upon by things around them.

Being susceptible in this way, a woman's 'character' will take colour from her surroundings. Her identity will be altered by the

contexts in which she finds herself, so that the 'truth' about her will
be relevant only to her garments and gestures at any given moment,
and it will be difficult, if not impossible, to differentiate a temporary
posture from the continuum of 'reality' beneath it. This is the point
made in Pope's second paragraph:

> How many pictures of one Nymph we view,
> All how unlike each other, all how true!
> Arcadia's Countess, here, in ermin'd pride,
> Is there, Pastora by a fountain side . . . (5–8)

The question of a stable and objective 'truth' clearly concerns Pope at
the beginning of his poem, and his exclamation in line 6 points the
irony of a situation where 'truth' can only be a relative term. This
echoes the idea expressed in the poem's opening line, that a chance
remark can be the truest thing he has ever heard (in this context it
can). Through the course of the *Epistle* the notion of relative truth is
going to be strained and finally overthrown, but here truth follows
where imagination leads.

   The character-sketches open with four women who are in their
different ways elusive and contradictory. The first, Rufa, is an
extreme of indecorum, 'whose eye quick-glancing o'er the Park, /
Attracts each light gay meteor of a Spark' (21–2), an image
immediately replaced by one of 'Rufa studying Locke'. The
glittering public idol and the studious private woman are incongruous; her eyes range the park in search of something to take her
fancy, but at our next glance they are being directed and disciplined
in intellectual activity. The effect is not merely of contradiction,
however. The merging power of the imagination comes into play
here, so that the two images to some degree superimpose
themselves: Rufa's study of Locke cannot avoid being seen as yet
another posture, a whim pursued while the fancy takes her. Such a
merging is repeated in the succeeding analogy:

> As Sappho's diamonds with her dirty smock,
> Or Sappho at her toilet's greasy task,
> With Sappho fragrant at an ev'ning Mask . . . (24–6)

Here Pope skilfully allows 'fragrant' to develop distasteful nuances
from its proximity to the 'greasy task' which precedes it, and though
judgment tells us that Sappho's diamonds would be reserved for
more formal occasions, imagination cannot avoid superimposing

them on the 'dirty smock'. His art shows itself conscious at such moments of the interplay between imagination and judgment, and it is part of the stylistic decorum of the poem that it should use suggestiveness in this way. He exploits the merging power of the imagination in order to set in motion an undercurrent of uneasiness which will become more defined during the course of the poem.

The 'soft-natured'[16] Silia and Papillia exhibit fancifulness in different directions. Silia's eyes peer into the mirror:

> Sudden, she storms! she raves! You tip the wink,
> But spare your censure; Silia does not drink.
> All eyes may see from what the change arose,
> All eyes may see – a Pimple on her nose. (33–6)

The picture of the soft and fearful Silia erupts into incongruous violence, and Pope directs the reader's attention, just as he directs (through cruel repetition) the eyes of all around her, upon the anti-climactic pimple ('All eyes may see . . . All eyes may see'). Our judgments may tell us that the pimple is an anticlimax, but in our imaginations it grows in size and importance as the focus of so much attention.

If Silia's emotional outburst exhibits the imagination's false sense of priorities, Papillia's exemplifies how the reality can never match the fantasy:

> Papillia, wedded to her doating spark,
> Sighs for the shades – 'How charming is a Park!'
> A Park is purchas'd, but the Fair he sees
> All bath'd in tears – 'Oh odious, odious Trees!' (37–40)

As an 'idea' the *park* attracts her, but once provided, the all-too-actual *trees* seem odious in comparison. A fantasist, implies Pope, will inevitably feel frustrated by reality.

The description of Calypso ('picture' is here entirely unsuitable) is the most enigmatic of the whole epistle. While all the other pictures make powerful use of visual touches (whether the bathos of Silia's pimple or the symbolic collapsing temple of Atossa), Calypso remains a woman haunted by negatives and comparatives, her abstract qualities either denied or shifting place within the line, her presence made uneasy by the fact that hers is the only description given in the past tense:

> 'Twas thus Calypso once each heart alarm'd,
> Aw'd without Virtue, without Beauty charm'd;

> Her Tongue bewitch'd as odly as her Eyes,
> Less Wit than Mimic, more a Wit than wise:
> Strange graces still, and stranger flights she had,
> Was just not ugly, and was just not mad;
> Yet ne'er so sure our passion to create,
> As when she touch'd the brink of all we hate. (45-52)

Pope moves away from Homer's Calypso (the nymph who offered Odysseus immortality if he would stay on her island and be her husband) towards a woman who stirred powerful feelings in Pope and Martha. From the beginning actual qualities are absent: she is 'without Virtue, without Beauty', yet these are framed by their effects ('Aw'd . . . charm'd'); the response is there, but the cause is elusive. After the negatives come relatives: her wit, mimicry and wisdom float free – they have no attributive, absolute power, but only a relative existence. The following line emphasises this uncertainty with the repeated 'Strange . . . stranger', where these accidental, airy notions ('graces', 'flights') again play off each other in the comparison. (Pope's original, 'Sylvia, a Fragment', was more positive: 'But some odd Graces and fine Flights she had').[17] In this context 'still' develops irony: it would sit easier later in the line ('and still stranger flights') but would then lose the awkward emphasis it gains from straining against the 'flights'. The churlish negatives return in the next line, where 'just' could be either 'only just' or 'simply'; the fluidity of this passage makes us able to accept the ambiguity because there is ambiguity in Calypso herself. Pope insists on recording his irrational reactions to a powerful woman who is difficult to know. After this the sudden 'touch'd the brink' achieves power by being defined by sensuous contact but undefined by grammar ('Yet ne'er so sure . . . As when'); even 'sure' is made *un*sure by 'ne'er so', which leaves even this certainty relative. 'All we hate' is again unspecific, not merely because it is not elucidated ('all' does not clarify) but because Calypso touched 'the brink', not the thing itself which eludes us. 'Yet *ne'er so sure* our passion *to create*': the omission of the active verb relieves Pope of his commitment to the past tense, and 'to create' leaves open the possibility of future passion, just as the present tense 'we hate', on which the passage ends, remains active.

Throughout the description Pope emphasises what are in Locke's terms 'secondary' qualities (mimicry, wit, graces, flights), attributes which involve the imagination of the perceiver, superficial powers better defined through another's response than seen as qualities inherent in her. She does not possess qualities as such, and yet she can charm, bewitch, arouse passion, and awe. Pope is remarking on the irrational way we can register emotions without responding to qualities inherent in the object. Mariana in Ned Ward's dialogue *Female Grievances Debated* (2nd ed., 1707) offers a helpful gloss on this passage: 'I believe the *Ideas* that we form in our own Imaginations are oftner the cause of our *Passions*, especially that of *Love*, than any real *Force* or *Influence* that is deriv'd from the outward Object . . .' (p. 41). This is in part the mystery of Calypso. Her outstanding attribute is mimicry, a skill of playing with other identities, imposing one image upon another and thereby cheating us. Ned Ward's Eliza replies to her friend: 'I believe we are sometimes apt from the sight of one Object to form another in our Thoughts, and so Cheat our selves into a Passionate Desire of Substantially enjoying that which is but an imaginary Shadow, the mere Chimerical Off-spring of our own Teeming Fancy . . .' (p. 46). Calypso is in some ways such a cheat. As Pope says, there is something odd about her power to bewitch. He gives us no image of her, and she remains an unsettling abstract (the Greek *Kalypso* – 'she who conceals').

The subject of the next sketch (thematically and grammatically) is 'Narcissa's nature', and yet we are immediately confronted by a horrifyingly unnatural idea: 'Narcissa's nature, tolerably mild, / To make a wash, would hardly stew a child . . .' (53–4). In a context of tolerable mildness, the intolerable harshness of stewing a child registers in our imaginations, however much our judgments acknowledge the negative, and this image of the torturing of innocence unsettles us as we consider Narcissa's attitude to commitment and duty. She

> Has ev'n been prov'd to grant a Lover's pray'r,
> And paid a Tradesman once to make him stare,
> Gave alms at Easter, in a Christian trim,
> And made a Widow happy, for a whim. (55–8)

The danger of Narcissa's whimsicality (psychologically a function of her restless imagination) is that her 'moral' actions are only such in name: they are not performed out of any sense of duty or responsibility but merely when the fancy takes her. All this can be very harmless, but Pope's tone grows more serious as he contemplates her unsettling brand of religion:

> Now deep in Taylor and the Book of Martyrs,
> Now drinking citron with his Grace and Chartres.
> Now Conscience chills her, and now Passion burns;
> And Atheism and Religion take their turns;
> A very Heathen in the carnal part,
> Yet still a sad, good Christian at her heart. (63–8)

Because her character has no deep continuum of commitment, she swings between faith and disbelief, burning in passion then shivering in the cold draught of conscience. The image of the stewing child returns as we think about Narcissa's own martyrdom and how she is torturing herself. She does have a 'heart', but in public she scorns 'Good-nature'. She is unable to reconcile the various aspects of her personality, with the result that she puts herself and others under intolerable strain.

Philomedé is introduced with alliterative scorn:

> See Sin in State, majestically drunk,
> Proud as a Peeress, prouder as a Punk;
> Chaste to her Husband, frank to all beside,
> A teeming Mistress, but a barren Bride . . . (69–72)

She may be a peeress, or this may be a role she slips into. Is she proud of her status, or *as* proud as a peeress? Is she only majestic through drink? Once again, identity eludes us. She manages (and this is quite an achievement) to outrage nature, judgment, wit and taste: she is unnatural in her role as a wife; her judgment ('that noble Seat of Thought') is merely the doctrine of a day; her wit takes her like a sudden 'fit'; and her taste turns out to be a 'hearty meal'. At the root of the matter is the unsteady relationship between her mind and her body:

> What then? let Blood and Body bear the fault,
> Her Head's untouch'd, that noble Seat of Thought:
> Such this day's doctrine – in another fit
> She sins with Poets thro' pure Love of Wit. (736)

'Pure Love' merges into 'Love of Wit', and her judgment, which should be in a mutually co-operative relationship with her wit, is entirely overthrown by her fitful mind. Pope himself had summed up the matter in a well-known passage in *An Essay on Criticism* (1711): 'For *Wit* and *Judgment* often are at strife, / Tho' meant each other's Aid, like *Man* and *Wife*' (82–3). In Philomedé both relationships are unfruitful.

By Pope's day it had of course become a commonplace that wit without judgment was an unsteady and dangerous quality, but the relationship between the two terms varied. John Dennis, for example, maintained (against Pope) that judgment should actually *rule* the wit: 'Now cannot I for my Soul conceive the reciprocal *Aid* that there is between Wit and Judgment. For tho' I can easily conceive how Judgment may keep Wit in her Senses, yet cannot I possibly understand how Wit can controul, or redress, or be a help to Judgment' (*Reflections Critical and Satyrical Upon . . . An Essay Upon Criticism* (1711); Hooker, i, 405). Earlier in his career Dennis had given an interesting description of the man of wit as being a compound of 'Fancy and Judgment':

[By a Man of Wit, I mean] a Man like you, Sir, or our most Ingenious Friend, in whom Fancy and Judgment are like a well-match'd Pair; the first like an extraordinary Wife, that appears always Beautiful, and always Charming, yet is at all times Decent, and at all times Chast; the Second like a Prudent and well-bred Husband, whose very Sway shews his Complaisance, and whose very Indulgence shews his Authority.

(Letter to Wycherley, 30 Oct. 1695; Hooker, ii, 383)

In Dennis's simile of marriage between 'Fancy and Judgment' the former is seen as female, the latter as male exercising 'Sway', rather reminiscent once again of the perfect hierarchical relationship between Milton's unfallen Adam and Eve. The imagination is attractive, but the judgment should have a sensitively-operated authority. Dennis's view of their relationship is less one of equal co-operation than of control, and it places Pope's words in interesting relief. Pope's theme is mutual aid (between wit and judgment, wife and husband), Dennis's theme is mastery and correction. In the *Epistle* Philomedé does not rebel against her husband, she is merely chastely uncooperative, and Pope deplores such emptiness in a relationship, just as he deplores the dictatorship of one partner over the other, whether the wife's power-seeking (210–14) or the husband's tyranny (288). The ideal relationship between wit and judgment is reconciliation and co-operation, and this is projected into the ideal marriage described towards the poem's close (261–4).

The theme of imagination at its most delusive and destructive is exemplified in Flavia. She is a 'wit'; her mind is hyperactive and neurotic, fancy with no judgment to restrain it. It is symptomatic that she has been reading too many romances,[18] since her

imagination is full of the grand gestures of self-destructive passion
which such stories specialise in:

> Nor asks of God, but of her Stars to give
> The mighty blessing, 'while we live, to live.'
> Then all for Death, that Opiate of the soul!
> Lucretia's dagger, Rosamonda's bowl. (89–92)

Flavia is a would-be Eloisa who fancies her society flirtation to be a
heroic passion. Her vocabulary, which Pope presents as incongruous in an eighteenth-century woman-of-society, is drawn from
romantic fiction and is typically a perversion of religious language
('mighty blessing', 'the soul'). However, in Flavia's mental
landscape it is the stars which bless, and drugged release which
parodies the soul's flight at death. In this context transcendence
becomes a yearning for insensibility; the creative becomes merely
destructive; mental power becomes 'impotence of mind'. And all
this, says Pope, is built on a trivial, awkward irony: 'A Spark too
fickle, or a Spouse too kind' (94). The hyperactivity of her
imagination ends by destroying her:

> Wise Wretch! with Pleasures too refin'd to please,
> With too much Spirit to be e'er at ease,
> With too much Quickness ever to be taught,
> With too much Thinking to have common Thought:
> Who purchase Pain with all that Joy can give,
> And die of nothing but a Rage to live. (95–100)

Lady Mary Chudleigh, in a passage similar to Pope's, had described
this self-destructive tendency:

> In Fancy's flatt'ring Glass they gaze,
> And, fond of the transporting Sight,
> Give way to Raptures of Delight.
> Too fierce their Joys, too quick their Sense,
> They cannot bear what's so intense . . .
>   ('Of Pride', 1710)

Flavia's 'Quickness' is as much 'keen sensibility' (Johnson's
Dictionary, 'Quickness' 3) as celerity of mind, and it links up with her
'too refin'd' pleasures (Johnson, 'refine' v.n. 3: 'to affect nicety').
Her imagination is so sensitively alive to impressions, so minutely
responsive, that it is the mental equivalent of having too exquisite a
sense of touch: '. . . tremblingly alive all o'er, / To smart and

agonize at ev'ry pore . . .' (*Essay on Man*, i, 197–8). In this context the 'Opiate' of death comes as a release.

In his next paragraph Pope turns from wits to glance at a series of women who pass into the area of sheer folly, so that they are no longer fascinating paradoxes, but puzzling nonsensical blanks: 'Woman and Fool are two hard things to hit, / For true No-meaning puzzles more than Wit . . .' (113–14). 'True' is again heavily ironic, continuing the stress that the word undergoes during the course of the epistle. The 'opiate' theme is picked up here in the folly of the woman who

> in sweet vicissitude appears
> Of Mirth and Opium, Ratafie and Tears,
> The daily Anodyne, and nightly Draught,
> To kill those foes to Fair ones, Time and Thought. (109–12)

Drug-induced euphoria is a kind of imaginative self-arousal. Thought is the enemy because it is conscious and therefore too close to reality, and it reminds her of the responsibility of being human. Reality (The Clarissa-voice) is uncomfortable, unillusioning; like Time it is always there waiting, and it eventually has to be faced. The drug, ironically, does not kill Time, only *thoughts* of Time. The realist (such as Clarissa is) confronts Time – the fantasist tries to evade it.

The folly of the aged Atossa is on a grand scale ('The wisest Fool much Time has ever made', 124) and Pope characterises it once again in terms of restlessness of mind: 'No Thought advances but her Eddy Brain / Whisks it about, and down it goes again' (121–2). By her instability Atossa is 'Scarce once herself, by turns all Woman-kind!', a female equivalent of Dryden's Zimri ('Not one, but all Mankinds Epitome', 546). In *Absalom and Achitophel* Dryden had explored how the imagination, breeding-ground of wit, could swing over into lunatic folly. In his satire the Popish Plot becomes a fictional 'plot' created in the fancies of Corah, Achitophel, and Zimri himself, whose restless brain was full of 'ten thousand freaks that dy'd in thinking' (552). These powerful talents, suggests Dryden, will finally prove ineffectual because their mental instability will defeat them. By associating Atossa with Zimri, therefore, Pope brings Dryden's theme of thwarted ambition and wasted talents into his own poem. The eddying whirlpool of Atossa's brain suppresses conscious thought and becomes a self-destructive vortex because it turns the mind in on itself. It is not directed or focused, and the inevitable irony is that she is

> by the Means defeated of the Ends,
> By Spirit robb'd of Pow'r, by Warmth of Friends,
> By Wealth of Follow'rs! without one distress
> Sick of herself thro' very selfishness! (143–6)

This recalls Flavia's 'impotence of mind' (93). If they are unable to discipline and channel their minds, implies Pope, women are in danger of having no power to achieve anything. It is relevant to note here how Hobbes stresses the importance for human mental activity of having an *end*: 'Besides the Discretion of times, places, and persons, necessary to a good Fancy, there is required also an often application of his thoughts to their End; that is to say, to some use to be made of them' (*Leviathan*, I, viii). And we recall his warning that 'without Steddinesse, and Direction to some End, a great Fancy is one kind of Madnesse' (I, viii). From Pope's point of view the ending of a thing is the achievement of its purpose, and as he moves towards the end of his own work he will return to this theme in contemplating the end which awaits restless women when they grow old, 'Fair to no purpose, artful to no end' (245).

At this stage in the *Epistle* (lines 151–6) Pope pauses to look back at his collection of paintings and to remind us of the imaginative art he has used to capture these 'chameleons'. As he has moved from Rufa to Atossa, woman's fanciful nature has shifted to reveal a variety of aspects and colours. Her mental restlessness has shown itself in incongruity, inconsistency, hypocrisy, folly, madness, impotence and self-destruction, and Pope's art has attempted to fit itself to these elusive people. Now, as he enters the second half of his poem, he turns to two women who apparently are unmoved and unmoving.

Cloe stands apart from the other sketches in being a character-analysis. Unlike the previous women she is neither passionate nor unstable, but resembles a work of art which is correct but cold: she is Addison's *Cato* after Shakespeare's *Othello*: restrained, artful, decorous, moral, plays by the rules, but 'communicate[s] no vibrations to the heart'.[19] But Cloe too is marked by a fanciful nature. Here it is not silly or wildly self-destructive, but it robs her of that true friendship which the poem celebrates. Cloe's fancifulness manifests itself in her wrong priorities; it is a function of her superficiality:

She, while her Lover pants upon her breast,
Can mark the figures on an Indian chest;
And when she sees her Friend in deep despair,
Observes how much a Chintz exceeds Mohair. (167–70)

In this way, in spite of her chilling equanimity, Cloe observes the decorum of Pope's fanciful art. Jacob Bryant's description of an *Indian screen* reveals the nuance behind Pope's words: 'glaring with colours, and filled with groups of fantastic imagery, such as we see upon an Indian screen: where the eye is painfully amused; but whence little can be obtained, which is satisfactory, and of service' (*A New System, or, an Analysis of Ancient Mythology* (1774–6), I, xvii). Cloe in her turn exposes the dangers of imaginative art (hence her position in the poem immediately following Pope's mention of wand'ring touches and flying strokes, colours and reflected lights). Her picture opens the second half of the poem, where these purely imaginative principles are tested and found wanting. Fanciful women, said Addison, 'consider only the Drapery',[20] and here Pope exposes the coldness which results from superficiality. Sir Joshua Reynolds, in his *Discourse IV* (1771), moves on from the question of colour to the issue of priorities in a painting:

In the same manner as the historical Painter never enters into the detail of colours, so neither does he debase his conceptions with minute attention to the discriminations of Drapery. It is the inferior stile that marks the variety of stuffs. With him, the cloathing is neither woollen, nor linen, nor silk, sattin, or velvet: it is drapery; it is nothing more.

In considering 'only the Drapery' (as Addison said), her eye preferring chintz to mohair when her heart should have been responding to her friend's despair, Cloe allies herself with the superficial artist. Her imagination's engagement with the surface, not the heart, of things exemplifies the sketchbook art of the poem and now exposes its human failings.

The picture which follows is the only 'certain Portrait' in the poem, that of Queen Caroline, her unredeemed vices for ever set beneath a thick layer of varnish:

One certain Portrait may (I grant) be seen,
Which Heav'n has varnish'd out, and made a *Queen*:
The same for ever! and describ'd by all
With Truth and Goodness, as with Crown and Ball:

> Poets heap Virtues, Painters Gems at will,
> And show their zeal, and hide their want of skill. (181–6)

Here 'Truth and Goodness', in a poem which finds these qualities so elusive, have a mock certainty and solidity. She is not enigmatic (unlike Calypso), simply false. Poets have heaped virtues upon her, just as painters have covered her form with tasteless gems, and her 'Truth and Goodness' are merely the trappings of regal power, the poet's equivalent of 'Crown and Ball'. The cry of 'The same for ever!' completes the indictment and points the contrast with the other sketches in the poem.[21]

Pope now goes on to identify two ruling passions behind the female sex in an attempt to locate some stable principle behind their actions, and he finds this in 'The Love of Pleasure, and the Love of Sway' (210). In the course of the epistle each desire is exposed as finally self-defeating: the women he has been describing end up either powerless or pleasureless. Men have the possibility of public concerns and lives of business, but women are encouraged by society to conform to their pleasure-loving 'Nature': 'That, Nature gives; and where the lesson taught / Is but to please, can Pleasure seem a fault?' (211–12). The contrast is drawn during the poem between pleasure, seen as something elusive and fleeting, and the cheerfulness of Martha Blount which 'can make to morrow chearful as to-day' (258) and therefore endures through time. Pursuit of pleasure recalls a familiar image:

> Pleasures the sex, as children Birds, pursue,
> Still out of reach, yet never out of view,
> Sure, if they catch, to spoil the Toy at most,
> To covet flying, and regret when lost . . . (23–4)

They are toys of the mind which will never satisfy or endure, and we are back here in Belinda's toyshop-fancy filled with shifting images. In turning to generalise about the female sex Pope gives pleasure a temporal context, so that the women become as fleeting as the pastimes which preoccupy them. They are still direction-less, unreal, but now their beauty is merely a ghostly memory:

> As Hags hold Sabbaths, less for joy than spight,
> So these their merry, miserable Night;
> Still round and round the Ghosts of Beauty glide,
> And haunt the places where their Honour dy'd. (239–42)

Such pleasures are associated by Pope with the activity of the imagination because they share the characteristics of superficiality, restlessness and evanescence. They are imaginary delights because they have nothing deep, stable or lasting to give, and the aim in pursuing them is to escape from reality into the fashionable world of masquerades, balls, routs, pageants and gossipy card-parties. When Pope declares that 'ev'ry Woman is at heart a Rake' (216) he is suggesting that women's fancies easily draw them into such aimless activities.[22]

The theme of frustration is brought to a climax as Pope takes his leave of the old women:

> See how the World its Veterans rewards!
> A Youth of Frolicks, an old Age of Cards,
> Fair to no purpose, artful to no end,
> Young without Lovers, old without a Friend,
> A Fop their Passion, but their Prize a Sot,
> Alive, ridiculous, and dead, forgot! (243–8)

Under the eye of eternity beauty has left nothing behind it. Flirtations frustrated them in youth as genuine friendship eludes them in age. Their 'art' (a compound of their schemings *and* their paintings) has created nothing, because only truth withstands time:

> Ah Friend! to dazzle let the Vain design,
> To raise the Thought and touch the Heart, be thine!
> That Charm shall grow, while what fatigues the Ring[23]
> Flaunts and goes down, an unregarded thing. (249–52)

It is with a calculated effect of relief, therefore, that Martha Blount steps forward to be addressed by Pope on a level of stable friendship. She offers a softer light after the previous bright colours, and calm sobriety after the heady succession of sketch-book figures. No longer 'the Cynthia of this minute', the moon now appears as a chaste goddess to cast a steady, clear beam; the glitter of the imagination, implies Pope, may delight for a while, but dazzle will usually conceal the truth. We should see things steadily and see them whole:

> So when the Sun's broad beam has tir'd the sight,
> All mild ascends the Moon's more sober light,
> Serene in Virgin Modesty she shines,
> And unobserv'd the glaring Orb declines. (253–6)

In the final three paragraphs Pope draws together the various thematic strands of his poem. After creatures of the imagination (beautiful, fascinating, elusive, then seen as increasingly superficial, self-destructive, and finally tiresome) Pope turns to someone who will reconcile the delights of the imagination with a stable identity, such as will encourage commitment and be known and increasingly loved through time; someone whose art will not sacrifice the more solid virtue of truth, and who will combine sensitivity to experience with firmness of conviction. Martha Blount is eulogised as this reconciling figure:

> Reserve with Frankness, Art with Truth ally'd,
> Courage with Softness, Modesty with Pride,
> Fix'd Principles, with Fancy ever new;
> Shakes all together, and produces – You. (277–80)

The ideal woman is seen, aptly for the imagery of the poem, as representing Heaven's 'last best work' (272). She is like a living and perfectly-achieved work of literature, which can simultaneously 'raise the Thought and touch the Heart' (250), and who unlike Philomedé embodies the ideal co-operative relationship between 'Fancy' and 'Fix'd Principles', seen (to employ the now familiar image) in terms of a living, satisfying marriage:

> She, who ne'er answers till a Husband cools,
> Or, if she rules him, never shows she rules;
> Charms by accepting, by submitting sways,
> Yet has her humour most, when she obeys . . . (261–4)

Pope ends his poem, therefore, by returning to his opening theme. His imaginative style was a decorous choice for describing erratic, fanciful women: small things were magnified and Pope's chameleon-like art was able to highlight the trivial details; it could mimic romantic passion or the chill insincerity of the superficial; it could mirror mental perplexity and confusion of roles by exploiting ambiguities or allowing images to merge one with another; it could permit the heartless to be known and convey the mystifying power of the unknowable. Distortion, mimicry, ambiguity and mystery are employed by Pope in the course of a poem which presents a series of women who challenge those 'Fix'd Principles' upon which great art is usually built (truth, nature, judgment, taste, decorum) just as they challenge the notion of stable 'character'. The poet skilfully highlights them, and at times his imagination reaches out in a certain sympathy to them; but finally such notions of life and art seem to cry out for a constant element, for something known through experience, and the poem appears to chart such a movement 'from fancy to the heart'. But imagination cannot be dismissed: we do not face in *Epistle to a Lady* a choice between imagination and truth, but rather come to understand as the poem reaches its close that this boundless faculty needs to be tethered: 'Imagination has no limits, and that is a sphere in which you may move on to eternity; but where one is confined to Truth, (or to speak more like a human creature, to the appearances of Truth) we soon find the shortness of our Tether' (Pope–Swift, 19 Dec. 1734). If imagination ignores truth, then it can be delusive, destructive, and frustrating; but when art and truth are in alliance, 'ever new' imagination is there also. Pope finally believes that their relationship must be a living one which survives by reconciliation.

An important difference between the *Epistle* and *The Rape of the Lock* emerges here. Within her context Clarissa is less a reconciling figure than a chilling douche of reality. Martha Blount embodies Clarissa-like 'Good-humour', but her silent appeal lacks the undertones of cynicism and calculation present in Clarissa's speech, and her 'Frankness' is moderated by 'Reserve'. Her role in the *Epistle* is not to dispel fancy, but to tether it, and she draws towards herself those feelings of sympathy which Pope has explored in the course of the poem. The poet's initial sympathetic stance in relation to the female sex is strained and exhausted, but finally returns to become focussed on its ideal representative. The earlier poem's 'sympathy' (in the stylistic and emotional senses) with Belinda complicates that poem's satirical judgments throughout, and though Clarissa's speech points the moral clearly, the final metamorphosis of the heroine's beauty is a flattering gesture that trumps Clarissa's card. The *Epistle* works more consistently towards the *right use* of the imagination, by widening the investigation of its superficialities and wrong sense of priorities. The contrast here is not merely between external charming beauty and dark internal nightmare: the *Epistle* ends in the belief that the imagination should illuminate the inner life also. That light which can merely reflect off surfaces, which can deceive and dazzle, must be allowed to be more deeply *penetrating* – something like the activity of James Thomson's 'penetrative Sun, / His Force deep-darting' (*Spring*, 79–80) who creates precious stones in the caverns of the earth; or, in Pope's terms, the divine Phoebus Apollo, lord of the sun and of poetry, 'who Wit and Gold refines, / And ripens Spirits as he ripens Mines . . .' (289–90).

FIVE

The imagination as process:
The Dunciad Variorum

I

She is a goddess, but one not yet disimprisoned; one still half-imprisoned, – the articulate, lovely still encased in the inarticulate, chaotic. (*Past and Present*, 1843, ch. 2)

Thomas Carlyle's Sphinx (emblem of celestial order, beauty and wisdom, but also of infernal darkness, fatality and chaos) is the kind of paradoxical figure which lies close to the heart of *The Dunciad*. As a creative artist Pope understands how art makes articulate those things which may lie in the mind unclear and unformed, and we have seen how his interest in the workings of the imagination regularly extends into a consideration of its capacity for anarchy. In *Eloisa to Abelard* his heroine tries to articulate the chaos within her and polarise the elements of her merging vision; in *The Rape of the Lock* the Cave of Spleen episode reveals the inarticulate and chaotic fancies within Belinda; *Epistle to a Lady* again looks beneath the beauty of women, to the chaos of their lives and the self-destructive restlessness which drives them. But it is in *The Dunciad* that we encounter the goddess herself. Dulness, as Pope presents her, shows the dark, riddling nature of the Sphinx: her power of creativity brings things into being, but her productions remain 'encased in the inarticulate, chaotic'. She is the goddess of the imagination as process.

There are of course several 'Dunciads', and the development of the poem with this title, through its various manifestations between 1728 and 1743, is a complicated one. Unlike the enlargement of *The Rape of the Lock* between 1712 and 1717, the change from the three-book *Dunciad* with its hero Lewis Theobald, to the four-book *Dunciad* of 1743 and its hero Colley Cibber, is not part of a single artistic enterprise. The shift in emphasis that occurs with the introduction of the fourth book, as well as the new terms of reference which Cibber's presence as the hero imposes, means that the 1743

version is not the final achievement of the poem which Pope had set
out to write in the late 1720s. The culmination of that original
intention is *The Dunciad Variorum* of 1729.

This chapter will concentrate attention on the three-book *Dunciad
Variorum* for several reasons. This earlier version addresses more
closely the theme of imaginative anarchy; in the later poem Dulness
is more all-embracing, so that a psychological disorder afflicting the
literary world has become a universal social disease (the climactic
passage describing the encroachment of final darkness, for example,
is in 1743 an actual event overtaking the poet himself and not, as in
The Dunciad Variorum, the triumphant vision of the mad prophet
Settle, pronounced with relish as the apotheosis of his god). The
theme I want to isolate is certainly present in the later version, but the
issue has been widened in complex ways and the emphasis is less
securely placed. I also wish to consider some of Pope's possible
sources and the traditional images of chaos and mental anarchy
which he is employing, and *The Dunciad Variorum* develops these in a
consistent and interesting way. It is also a unified and effective poem
in its own right. Finally, and perhaps most importantly, I want to
discuss some of the work of Lewis Theobald (one aspect of which
seems to have intrigued and influenced Pope) and to examine the
nature of Theobald's inheritance from Elkanah Settle, a transfer of
trust and power which lies at the heart of the poem's action.
References will therefore be to the 1729 *Dunciad Variorum* unless
otherwise stated, and that title will be used throughout except when
considering a passage unique to the 1743 version. It should of course
be pointed out that many of the passages discussed occur unaltered in
the later text, and consequently much of what is said here does, I
believe, hold true for the final version of the poem.

Textual complication is not the only factor which makes *The
Dunciad* a difficult poem to discuss. The interrelation of its themes
and images, and the way in which the layers of suggestiveness
accumulate, means that to enter the poem at any point is to discover
tracks leading in many directions; it is necessary to sustain a clear line
of argument while at the same time doing justice to the
interconnectedness of every aspect of the poem.[1] At the centre of the
labyrinth is the figure of Dulness, the impresario for the poem's
activities, and so it may be helpful to begin by considering some of
the associations which she brings with her and how this affects our
understanding of the imaginative world she rules. This chapter will

therefore try first of all to investigate the neoplatonic nature of the imagery of mist and mud associated with her, and to show how such images tended to express the debasement of the soul in terms of irresponsible imaginative activity. From this vantage-point it will be possible to argue that Pope represents the goddess's malign powers as the skilful exploits of a fantasy-queen, a power who is the driving-force behind the modern indulgence in imaginative experience represented in the poem chiefly by the Settle–Theobald tradition of visual spectacle which Pope regards as so destructive of art and morality. Dulness is a fantasy-queen in both senses: she is herself a fantasy-figure drawing together into one concept many attributes of imaginative activity – her ability to conjure visions, to transform, to merge ideas, and to transcend time and space. But she also has the capacity for inspiring others to vision by encouraging them to indulge their own fantasies. Looked at in this way *The Dunciad Variorum* holds satisfyingly together as an exposé of many kinds of distorted imagination. In this poem Pope again turns to explore the relationship between imaginative disorder and moral disorder, and in doing so he takes many artistic risks in the service of his theme. Above all, he risks allowing his own art to sink back into the *process* of its making, just as his heavy 'variorum' volume risks being a 'work in progress' accumulating annotatory jetsam as it rolls on its way. It is the relationship between product and process[2] which concerns Pope in *The Dunciad Variorum*, and in particular he wishes to explore the results of making imaginative activity an end in itself, so that what should be a means to a finished artistic product has become its own justification. This is what 'fantasy' (in our modern term) implies for Pope: it is a pleasurable activity which leads nowhere and creates nothing (though the creative *process* is forever being enacted), existing merely as an experience which never achieves the artifact; it is (in images Pope would have appreciated) the muddy scree around Parnassus; the slimy nostoc,[3] not the star.

II

The Dunciad Variorum is an imaginative *tour de force*, but it is so in specific ways and for specific ends. In order to identify the nature of its presiding deity we must recall the characteristics of the 'base' imagination as discussed in chapter two. Dulness is a travesty of the divine,[4] and as such she inspires a satanic kind of imaginative spectacle. In being the 'directing soul' (i, 147) of the proceedings, the goddess parodies the way in which the soul should direct affairs – that is, by transcending the flesh, raising the mind, and inspiring lofty thoughts and actions. Dulness's reversal is manifest in the activity and imagery of the poem, whose movements are not upwards, but sidelong or downwards. Aspiration becomes abasement; vision manifests itself as mad delusion; divine light is replaced by mist and cloud; the baser elements of water and earth (combined as mud) overcome the higher elements; above all the dunces' physicality is insisted on: the tactile images accumulate and there is much stress on the products not of the spirit, but of the body, whose waste materials become a medium of expression.

In the course of *The Dunciad Variorum* two of these images gain especial power and are the source of some of its most memorable effects: those of mist/cloud and mud/slime. Pope did not choose these merely for the sake of the poem's atmosphere, as a kind of pathetic fallacy for its disreputable goings-on, but because they allowed him to draw upon a significant tradition of thought and a network of association within it. Each of these images had been regularly used to express the soul's estrangement from the divine (often seen in terms of undesirable imaginative activity) and it is partly through them that this powerful theme is established in *The Dunciad Variorum*.

The figure of the goddess Dulness is inseparable from the clouds and fogs which surround her. In a parody of the classical Jove, she is twice 'cloud-compelling', because when used in her service the minds of her followers cease to be clear and penetrative. The 'healing mist' (i, 152) for which Theobald prays is the comforting shroud which encloses the mind when it contemplates itself and feels no sense of adventure or responsibility to the world outside. Such clouds are not simply the emblem of ignorance and stupidity, but are the refracting medium through which the goddess always appears. Her fogs are also the mists of selfhood which distort reality:

> All these and more, the cloud-compelling Queen
> Beholds thro' fogs that magnify the scene:
> She, tinsel'd o'er in robes of varying hues,
> With self-applause her wild creation views . . . (i, 77–80)

The shifting colours of her tinsel garments as she watches the proceedings show that Dulness is a descendant of the sylphs, in that she encourages and presides over imaginative excess. The dazzling scene she watches is a projection of herself, her own 'wild creation' which she greets with 'self-applause'. The fogs which 'magnify the scene' recall how close this is to that murky breeding-ground of images, Belinda's spleen, where 'A constant *Vapour* o'er the Palace flies; / Strange Phantoms rising as the Mists arise . . .' (*Rape of the Lock*, iv, 39–40)[5] A 'veil of fogs' (i, 218) circulates around Dulness, making a link between her delusive nature and the traditional image of Satanic deception. We recall how Milton's Satan wanders through Paradise as a dark mist in which form he is able to enter the serpent's mouth, paralleling the way he can reach the organs of Eve's fancy. These mists and colours which Satan spreads across the mind are also mentioned by Daniel Defoe, whose description of the Devil is uncannily apt for Pope's goddess:

[He is] the *Calumniator* and Deceiver, that is, the Misrepresenter . . . he puts false Colours, and then mannages the Eye to see them with an imperfect View, raising Clouds and Fogs to intercept our Sight; in short, he deceives all our Senses, and imposes upon us in Things which otherwise would be the easiest to discern and judge of . . .

(*The Political History of the Devil*, 1726, p. 173)

Dulness practises the same deception: her mists and false colours substitute delusion for reality, thereby enervating the power of reason. The puritan Richard Sibbes uses very similar terms to remind his readers of the importance of seeing things as they really are: it is vital, he says, 'to awake the *soule*, and to stirre up *reason* cast asleepe by Sathans *charmes*, that so scattering the *clouds* through which things seeme otherwise then they are, wee may discerne and judge of things according to their true and constant nature . . .' (*The Soules Conflict with Itselfe*, 1635, p. 285). The mists of Dulness conceal the 'true and constant nature' of things. Everything about her is shifting, restless, deceitful and tantalising, and beneath her gaze things change, merge, or circle in a vortex.

Another interesting parallel is a passage from Book IV of Rowe's *Callipaedia* (1712), where he describes how easily mankind turns aside from reason only to be deceived by 'Show' and 'false Beauty':

     . . . huddled Images but slow ascend.
   From earthly Dregs the circling Fogs arise,

> And misty Vapours skim before our Eyes;
> The Soul is forc'd, while pent in darksome Clay,
> To grope in Shades, and guess the doubtful Way.

This extract illustrates how Dulness is closely related to neoplatonic imagery, where the soul is trapped within the body and having lost the guiding light of reason has only the mists of error through which to grope her way. Sir John Davies's poem about the soul, *Nosce Teipsum* (1599), expresses the same general idea and takes it a little further:

> When *Reasons* lampe which like the *Sunne* in skie,
>   Throughout *Mans* litle world her beams did spread,
>   Is now become a Sparkle, which doth lie
>   Under the Ashes, halfe extinct and dead:
>
> How can we hope, that through the Eye and Eare,
>   This dying Sparkle, in this cloudie place,
>   Can recollect those beames of knowledge cleare,
>   Which were enfus'd, in the first minds by grace? (61–8)

This sparkle of the divine light trapped within the mists of earth is the *synteresis*, 'a naturall power of the soule sette in the hyghest parte therof, movynge and sterrynge it to good, & abhorrynge evyll' (*OED*, date 1531). La Primaudaye remarks: 'Although sinne hath greatly troubled the minde . . . still there remayned in it some sparkles of that light of the knowledge of God, and of good and evil, which is naturally in men . . . This remnant that yet remayneth is commonly called by the Divines *Synteresis*' (*The French Academie*, 1594, ii, 576). Pope makes powerful use of this 'one dim Ray of Light' (iv, 1) in the fourth book of the 1743 *Dunciad*, where it is the last thing to disappear into universal darkness ('Nor *human* Spark is left, nor Glimpse *divine*!, iv, 652).[6]

The mists of Dulness, therefore, are related to the convention which represents heavenly truth in terms of a clear beam of light, and which uses mist and cloud to express man's distance from the divine. It is linked to the 'false colours' of satanic deception, and to the erratic movements (huddling, circling, groping) of a man lost in the fog of sin and unable to see his way clearly or direct himself to his proper end. The divine spark is within him, but these vapours all but extinguish it.

The other important image rooted in the language of neoplatonism is the clogging mud and slime which breeds the creations of

Dulness, and into which the dunces leap at the goddess's bidding (ii, 263). Like her mists and clouds, the mud is a medium of imaginative experience (Smedley's exciting visit to the 'Land of Dreams' ii, 316) and it is once again vision distorted and physicalised. Mud represents the elemental dregs, the earthly humidity which will be consumed by the ardour of divine love;[7] it is in part Spenser's 'fleshly slyme', and partly what Milton called 'the settl'd mudd of his Fancy'.[8] It is remarkable, in fact, how persistently the image of mud or slime is contrasted not with solid earth or images of cleanliness, but with images of light and references to true vision or divine imagination. In this way mud comes to be seen as the element of the visually handicapped, for those who traduce or outrage the divinely penetrative imagination. Abraham Cowley's handling of the superstition that falling stars turned to slime uses the idea to attack those men who allow 'Visions and inspirations' (rather than higher reason) to direct their minds:

> So *Stars appear* to drop to us from skie,
>   And gild the passage as they fly:
> But when they fall, and meet th'opposing ground,
>   What but a sordid *Slime* is found?
>   ('Reason: The use of it in *Divine* Matters', 13–16)

It is as though the stellified lock of our imaginations had sunk back to earth to be seen as the physical hair it really is. Donne uses the image in a literary context to contrast the 'slimy rimes bred in our vale below' with the perfection of Parnassus, where 'lame things thirst their perfection' ('To Mr E.G.'). Thomas Middleton (1600) remarks that without the goddess of light, the sun would falter and man would believe 'his lampe returnde to slime'.[9] Mud and slime are in these examples placed at the opposite pole from divine vision, and so it is fitting that John Marston should have recourse to the idea when he wishes to express disdain at false inspiration (in words which recall the later figure of Milton's Comus):

> My spirit is not puft up with fat fume
> Of slimy ale, nor Bacchus' heating grape.
> My mind disdains the dungy muddy scum
> Of abject thoughts . . .
>   ('To Detraction', *The Scourge of Villainy*, 1598)

The ale is 'slimy' not because it is badly brewed, but because it encourages the wrong kind of imaginative activity, bred by the

passions and the disturbed humours of the body. Marston strikes a
similar note in his play *What You Will* (1601), where Quadratus
defends the concept of 'fantasticness'. True *phantasia*, he declares, is a
'function . . . of the bright immortal part of man', and those who
misuse the term 'fantastic' to describe the fashionable fops of his day
are no better than 'the muddy spawn / Of slimy newts' (II, i, 188–9).
The perverting of the divine imagination is here seen as the activity
of mud-loving amphibious spawn.

The traditional opposition, therefore, is between mud/slime and
the aspiring divine imagination within man. It is no surprise in this
context to find that mud is regularly associated with glitter and
uncertain light-effects, since both traduce the true activity of the
imagination. Towards the opening of Satire VII of his *Scourge of
Villainy*, for example, John Marston voices his outrage at the way
muddy sensuality has overtaken intellect, and it is quite natural for
him to see this in terms of base fantasy, represented by misleading
glitter and glow:

> that same radiant shine –
> That lustre wherewith Nature's nature decked
> Our intellectual part – that gloss is soiled
> With staining spots of vile impiety,
> And muddy dirt of sensuality.
> These are no men, but apparitions,
> Ignes fatui, glowworms, fictions,
> Meteors, rats of Nilus, fantasies . . . (8–15)

Mud and glitter are here placed side by side, and the equation made
between meteors[10] and the equivocal generation of 'rats of Nilus'.[11]
The link is established by the *ignis fatuus* (or will o' the wisp), a
traditional image for the delusive aspects of imagination;[12] this
incandescent marsh-gas bred within a bog exemplifies how mud can
create misleading visions in the mind. We shall see how in the course
of the poem Pope works between these apparent polarities of
primordial slime and glittering show (mud and pantomime) to
suggest that the spectacles of Dulness remain embedded in the
primal matter of creation, and are debasing in their effect because
they have not pulled themselves free of the process which bred
them – like the 'nameless somethings' still asleep 'in their causes'
(i, 54).

Through the imagery of mist/cloud and mud/slime, therefore,
Pope presents his goddess Dulness as the enemy of the divine light,

because she deceives the mind with confusing shows and debases the imagination's divine potentialities. The choice of the name 'Dulness' (rather than 'Folly', for example) is significant here, since to be 'dull-sighted' was to suffer from a defect of vision.[13] What Dulness is not, of course, is conventionally dull: her world is a busy and glittering one, but marked by a failure of perspective or focus, and a consequent inability to produce clear ideas. Everything is done for temporary effect, and surface display replaces inner truth. Mental process substitutes for artistic achievement, and the anarchic imagination is allowed to overturn the understanding. Pope himself points out this aspect of Dulness in an explanatory note added in 1743:

Dulness here is not to be taken contractedly for mere Stupidity, but in the enlarged sense of the word, for all Slowness of Apprehension, Shortness of Sight, or imperfect Sense of things. It includes . . . Labour, Industry, and some degree of Activity and Boldness: a ruling principle not inert, but turning topsy-turvy the Understanding, and inducing an Anarchy or confused State of Mind. (Note to i, 15)

In the world presided over by Dulness, the hierarchy of the mind is reversed, 'turning topsy-turvy the Understanding'. The anarchy which for Pope has always accompanied imaginative activity when divorced from judgment becomes in this poem a major theme. Nowhere is Pope more concerned with the importance of seeing clearly.

John Sheffield, Duke of Buckingham, remarks in *An Essay upon Poetry* (1682) that 'all is dullness, when the Fancy's bad' (line 35). In *The Dunciad Variorum* Pope explores the 'bad' that can result from a misuse of the imagination, and his goddess is the false deity who apes the divinely creative mind and turns the soul to physical images and every kind of error. In this respect Pope's goddess is very close to the 'Dulness' described by Lady Mary Chudleigh in her essay 'Of Pride' (1710). She ends her piece with a moving prayer for 'eternal Wisdom' to illuminate her understanding, so that she may confront

the Dulness of my Apprehension, which, by its being too closely united to the Body, is fill'd with sensible Images, crowded with imaginary Appearances, like the first Matter, dark and full of Confusion, and hardly receptive of pure Idea's, of simple intellectual Truths; discover to me the Errors of my Judgment, the false Notions I have of Things . . . O that thou would'st be pleased to purifie and brighten my Imagination, make it strong and regular, fit to contemplate thy Divine Essence. (pp. 27–8)

It is something close to this concept of Dulness that I believe we should have in our minds as we read Pope's poem. *The Dunciad Variorum* makes powerful use of such ideas, and Dulness's world is indeed 'fill'd with sensible Images, crowded with imaginary Appearances, like the first Matter, dark and full of Confusion'; but although Pope's art draws him into this darker world, there remains throughout the implicit ideal of the imagination's comprehensiveness and clarity.

The contrast between these two kinds of vision (the clarifying and the confusing; one tending towards transcendence and revelation, the other towards darkness and chaos) is starkly seen if we compare two dream-visions, both published in 1715 – a comparison with particular significance for *The Dunciad Variorum*.

III

In 1715 Pope published an allegorical dream-vision, *The Temple of Fame*. The unearthly temple is a place of aspiration, and the poet gazes up in awe at the steep ascent. Before his inner eye the scene undergoes constant transformation, enacting the restless power of imagination:

> There might you see the length'ning Spires ascend,
> The Domes swell up, the widening Arches bend,
> The growing Tow'rs like Exhalations rise,
> And the huge Columns heave into the Skies. (89–92)

The towers seem lighter than air and the scene exhilarates the spirit. On Pope's part this is a conscious indulgence in the imagination, and he enters on his vision with a careful piece of scene-setting:

> (What Time the Mood mysterious Visions brings,
> While purer Slumbers spread their golden Wings)
> A Train of Phantoms in wild Order rose,
> And, join'd, this Intellectual Scene compose. (7–10)

Pope deliberately frames and prepares for his vision (the product of 'purer Slumbers') and the hint of anarchy is weakened by the phantoms joining to compose an 'Intellectual Scene'.

In the same year, another young poet (two months older than Pope) tried his hand at a similar fantasy; but this allegorical vision was closer to nightmare than dream, and the product of a troubled sleep. Whereas Pope's imagination creates a scene of aspiration and dedication set in the air above the created world, this fantasy explores a gloomy cave deep in the earth, reminiscent of Pope's own Cave of Spleen:

> In barren Soil, and damp unwholesome Air,
> Where weeping Clouds Eternal Dew distill'd;
> Where no gay Sun-shine did the Morning chear,
> Or Mid-day Fires the dark Meridian gild;
>   A Cave there stood; whose vaulted Sides were spread,
>   When Nature first rear'd her Created Head.

> Ten Thousand Doors, like Flaws in mouldring Earth,
> Led to the Center of the Gloomy Den;
> And each to streaky Gleams of Light gave Birth,
> That shot a-thwart the Dusk, and seem'd a-kin:
>   Pale as the Fire that on Night's Visage glows,
>   Serving alone her Horrors to disclose:

> Desart, yet populous, the Plains appear,
> Th'imperfect Image of a ghastly Dream;
> Here unknown Noises pierce the gallow'd Ear,
> There living Forms, like empty Phantoms, seem:
>   All was confus'd, yet all was of a piece;
>   Nature 'twas still, but Nature in Distress.

> A Hundred hideous Shapes the Cave surround,
> Th'Unlov'd Retinue of their Meagre Queen. . . . (i–iv)

This goddess is the presiding genius of Lewis Theobald's poem *The Cave of Poverty*, one of the literary creations but for which *The Dunciad* might not have existed. It is tempting to be unfair to the anti-hero of *The Dunciad Variorum*, and his poem is in some ways an agreeable parody with some successful imaginative effects. However, Theobald does allow his descriptive powers to dwell on the lurid and unusual, and *The Cave of Poverty* serves little purpose beyond being an entertaining and quirky indulgence in the imagination for its own sake. It certainly cannot be said to compose an 'Intellectual Scene'.

In stanza cxvii (it is a substantial poem) Theobald turns Poverty into a substitute for his muse:

> Ha'st thou not oft improv'd the Poet's Sense,
> Rais'd him to Fire, and made his Lays inchant?
>   Bards oft to Thee, more than the Muses, owe;
>   Thou giv'st the Theme, and mak'st the Numbers flow.

The claim that Poverty raises the poet to the 'Fire' of literary creation finds its parallel in *The Dunciad Variorum* when the heroic Theobald is made to declare: 'Me, Emptiness and Dulness could inspire, / And were my Elasticity and Fire' (i, 181–2). If 'Poverty', then why not 'Emptiness and Dulness'?

The flattery of Poverty, which so amused Pope, is one of two voices reaching the goddess within her gloomy cave. A pair of ingenious tubes delivers murmurs from the outside world to her attentive ear[14] – one tube curses, the other praises:

> These Sounds were thought their Murmurs to transfuse:
>   That little Elves behind, with Fans of Air,
>   Impell'd 'em to the Dusky Thorough-fare.
>
> Thither arriv'd, those Sounds, that in their Flight
> Only, like Winds, groan'd thro' the lab'ring Air,
> As thro' the Tubes their March they expedite,
> (Extravagance of Wonder to declare!)
>   Break into Words articulate and plain;
>   Coherent Words in one continued Strain. (lxvi–lxvii)

Such gradual emergence into coherence was something else that fascinated Pope. *The Dunciad Variorum* is full of emergings from nothingness, fusings of hints, groans of literary childbirth. Theobald is here exploring the 'Dusky Thorough-fare' of his own imagination, where vague and indistinct ideas take shape before utterance. It is such a moment, between the dark cave of fancy, and the daylight of sense and judgment, that Pope has chosen as the setting for his own nightmare vision.

Much of Theobald's *Cave of Poverty* describes the wealth of 'Imaginary Work' (xxvii) on the large tablets hung around the walls of the cave and representing the goddess's power. One of Poverty's victims, for example, is an ashen-faced debtor whom she mercilessly haunts; she 'Rides him in Dreams; and harrasses his Nights / With Tip-staves, and Imaginary Frights' (xxxii). In Theobald's poem the malign goddess assumes the role of nightmare impresario; she inspires and presides over the imaginings of her followers. Within her cave, however, there is no room for the ordering and rejecting role of the discriminating judgment. Reason does not belong in her cloudy internal world, but in the clear daylight of conscious rationality. Pope's *Dunciad Variorum* occupies a similar world, and his own goddess, Dulness, fulfils in several ways the identical function of presiding over a display of imaginative confusion and anarchy:

> Dulness o'er all possess'd her antient right,
> Daughter of Chaos and eternal Night:
> Fate in their dotage this fair idiot gave,
> Gross as her sire, and as her mother grave,
> Laborious, heavy, busy, bold, and blind,
> She rul'd, in native Anarchy, the mind. (i, 9–14)

As a 'fair idiot', Dulness will combine both the beauty and the madness of mental activity, adopting in the poem the kind of usurping role played by the figure of 'Fancy' in Sir Richard Blackmore's 'Hymn to the Light of the World': 'Fancy does fickle reign in Reason's Seat, / And Thy wild Empire, Anarchy, uphold . . .' (*Poems*, 1718).

At the beginning of Book I Pope takes us to Dulness's haunt, named (out of deference to his hero Theobald) the Cave of Poverty and Poetry,[15] where the very hollowness of the place emphasises the noise of the wind:

> Keen, hollow winds howl thro' the bleak recess,
> Emblem of Music caus'd by Emptiness:
> Here in one bed two shiv'ring sisters lye,
> The cave of Poverty and Poetry. (i, 29–32)

But the poem now begins playing its visual tricks; the draughty garret transforms as we read, and the grammar leads us outwards when the repeated 'Here . . .' moves to 'Hence . . . Hence . . .' and the 'cave' becomes the generator of literary activity which spreads out from this centre towards Tyburn, the Court, and the London churches. As our minds focus on this idea the scale starts to shift, the real garret dissolves and the poem's presiding deity appears, known not by her own features (she has no identity) but by her spirit within others. She stands at the entrance to her poem like a parody frontispiece, majestically swathed in cloud, supported by four virtues symbolic of her metamorphosing power:

> 'Twas here in clouded majesty she shone;
> Four guardian Virtues, round, support her Throne;
> Fierce champion Fortitude, that knows no fears
> Of hisses, blows, or want, or loss of ears:
> Calm Temperance, whose blessings those partake
> Who hunger, and who thirst, for scribling sake:
> Prudence, whose glass presents th'approaching jayl:
> Poetic Justice, with her lifted scale;

> Where in nice balance, truth with gold she weighs,
> And solid pudding against empty praise. (i, 43–52)

Under her influence these virtues have undergone a grotesque
change: Fortitude (who has become 'imperviousness to criticism'),
Temperance (here the enforced penury of the hack), Prudence
(gloomy apprehension of the debtors' prison), and Justice ('poetic'
justice weighing her outlay of flattery against her income of coin).
From this uneasy vantage-point Dulness gazes down through her
surrounding mists at the scene below, where her creatures
spontaneously stir out of the primal matter and a panorama of
ancient Chaos is surreptitiously transformed to a modern theatrical
spectacular:

> Here she beholds the Chaos dark and deep,
> Where nameless somethings in their causes sleep,
> 'Till genial Jacob, or a warm Third-day
> Call forth each mass, a poem or a play.
> How Hints, like spawn, scarce quick in embryo lie,
> How new-born Nonsense first is taught to cry,
> Maggots half-form'd, in rhyme exactly meet,
> And learn to crawl upon poetic feet.
> Here one poor Word a hundred clenches makes,
> And ductile dulness new meanders takes;
> There motley Images her fancy strike,
> Figures ill'pair'd, and Similes unlike.
> She sees a Mob of Metaphors advance,
> Pleas'd with the Madness of the mazy dance:
> How Tragedy and Comedy embrace;
> How Farce and Epic get a jumbled race;
> How Time himself stands still at her command,
> Realms shift their place, and Ocean turns to land.
> Here gay Description Ægypt glads with showers;
> Or gives to Zembla fruits, to Barca flowers;
> Glitt'ring with ice here hoary hills are seen,
> There painted vallies of eternal green,
> On cold December fragrant chaplets blow,
> And heavy harvests nod beneath the snow.
>   All these and more, the cloud-compelling Queen
> Beholds thro' fogs that magnify the scene:
> She, tinsel'd o'er in robes of varying hues,
> With self-applause her wild creation views,
> Sees momentary monsters rise and fall,
> And with her own fool's colours gilds them all. (i, 53–82)

This fine passage (which remains unaltered through the various versions of the poem) is a carefully modulated series of images tracing the emergence of a pantomime-like spectacle from the mud. This is the way dunce-art is made. The 'causes' in which the undefined 'somethings' sleep are the primordial slime before poetic creation, the chaos of the imagination at its first unconscious workings. In this dark seed-bed of images the literary *process* begins, 'Maggots half-form'd' encounter each other in rhyme ('maggots' here partly in its eighteenth-century sense of 'a whimsical or perverse fancy') and the 'hints' are hardly living, still in their embryonic state (Dulness is elastic and stretches or meanders at will). The goddess's fertile imagination is delighted by the 'motley Images', the confusion of metaphors which emerge in the mind without order or distinction, and the labyrinthine 'mazy dance' that is a sign of the fanciful madness inherent in this aimless activity. Definition is lost as the literary genres merge one into another to produce monstrous hybrids.[16] Gradually the spectacle works its way into the world of light, but it is the artificial light of the theatre where the backdrops superimpose on one another, and the resulting jumble of images becomes incongruous and disturbing. Dulness, however, is now transformed to a delighted spectator gazing from her theatre-box, and she applauds her very own 'wild creation'. She wears the tinselled garments of the rainbow, herself a glittering representation of the imagination at work, and 'her own fool's colours' play upon the scene before her, adding to the movement and light-effects as the 'momentary monsters' of her unruly imagination move aimlessly about.

Dulness's glittering spectacle emerges from the primordial slime, and in the earlier part of the above passage Pope is clearly alluding to the formlessness of the Biblical and Ovidian Chaos[17] and expects his readers to be reminded in particular of the well-known re-working of the idea in Milton's *Paradise Lost* ('the Womb as yet / Of Waters, Embryon immature involved' (vii, 276–7), the wild abyss where the four elements lie 'in thir pregnant causes mixt / Confus'dly' (ii, 913–14)). But the literary context of Pope's description links it also with Milton's Limbo of Vanity, in which

> All th'unaccomplisht works of Natures hand,
> Abortive, monstrous, or unkindly mixt,
> Dissolvd on Earth, fleet hither, and in vain,
> Till final dissolution, wander here . . . (*PL*, iii, 455–8)

Cowley's epic *Davideis* (1668) has been pointed out as a source for Pope's lines, in the passage from Book i where Cowley parallels God's creative activity with the workmanship of the poet labouring through early drafts to bring order to his 'fertile *Mind*'.[18] However, the role of the imagination in these first creative workings comes into clearer focus if we examine another likely source for Pope's lines. In 'A Letter from the Country to a Friend in Town, giving an Account of the Author's Inclinations to *Poetry*' John Oldham describes how the imagination brings ideas to birth:

> How, when the Fancy lab'ring for a Birth,
> With unfelt Throws brings its rude issue forth:
> How after, when imperfect shapeless Thought
> Is by the Judgment into Fashion wrought.
> When at first search I traverse o're my mind,
> Nought but a dark, and empty Void I find:
> Some little hints at length, like sparks break thence,
> And glimm'ring Thoughts just dawning into sence:
> Confus'd a while the mixt Idea's lie,
> With nought of mark to be discover'd by,
> Like colours undistinguisht in the night,
> Till the dusk images, mov'd to the light,
> Teach the discerning Faculty to chuse,
> Which it had best adopt, and which refuse.[19]

Here the 'Fancy' is a mother-figure giving birth to her 'rude issue' – thoughts which remain shapeless and 'glimm'ring' in the half-light, and images which are as yet merged confusedly together. The act of poetic creation is seen as the moving of these dusky forms out into the light, where the 'discerning Faculty' of Judgment sets to work discriminating and shaping the primal material. Oldham's 'Fancy' works within an area of darkness occasionally lit by uncertain light-effects as hints of ideas break out in sparks from the void and thoughts begin to glimmer with meaning. The parallels with the description in *The Dunciad Variorum* are striking, but Pope's Dulness does not allow the images to leave her twilight realm: the clear light of judgment is exiled from the world of her poem.

Oldham's lines appear to be a reworking of a passage from Dryden's preface to *The Rival Ladies* (1664) (the opening sentence, in fact, of his earliest critical essay).[20] In dedicating the play to The Earl of Orrery Dryden alludes to the primal stage of literary creation in words which must have impressed Oldham, and possibly Pope:

'This worthless present was designed to you long before it was a play; when it was only a confused mass of thoughts, tumbling over one another in the dark; when the fancy was yet in its first working, moving the sleeping images of things towards the light, there to be distinguished, and then either chosen or rejected by the judgment.' In *The Dunciad Variorum* passage the mists of Dulness prevent such a conscious sorting and re-working of the base imaginative matter, and the production which emerges in Pope's lines remains rooted in the muddy earth from which it grew. The dazzling incongruity of the pantomime-spectacle remains a jumble in the half-light of the imagination. The visionary world of *The Dunciad Variorum* is located in this kind of chaos. Images have not emerged into the light as fully created things – they are glittering and colourful, but are still being pushed around Dryden's dark lumber-room. They are tacky like the thread spun from the spider's body in Swift's *Battle of the Books*[21] (self-created and self-referential), and neither mature nor fully living and therefore not responsible. The childlike quality which critics find in the antics of the dunces in Book ii is expressive of the mental immaturity of Dulness's playful children who enjoy the easy indulgence in images, but also of the irresponsible energy of the imagination when it is left to its own work (we recall that the sylphs in *The Rape of the Lock* are privy to secrets which 'to maids alone and Children are revealed').[22] The dunces' antics have that restlessness which Dryden and Oldham describe – the twitchings, meanderings or convulsions of things still at birth within the imagination.

In no other of Pope's poems is the theme of merging, the loss of individual identity in the fluid mass, so powerfully sustained and endowed with such nightmarish possibilities. The merging tendency of imaginative activity has been present in the visions of Eloisa, the dark splenetic fancies of Belinda, and the 'merging of values'[23] over which the Sylphs preside; but it is in *The Dunciad* that Pope works out most fully the moral implications of losing an awareness of distinction and individuality. Pat Rogers generalises brilliantly on this very point: 'For the Augustans, the primal fear was not that things would fall apart, but that everything would somehow merge.'[24] The aspect of imagination which Pope satirises in *The Dunciad Variorum* is its capacity, in Hobbes's terms, 'pleasingly [to] confound dissimilar objects',[25] a tendency which encourages a regressive, childlike mentality that is content to surrender itself to the maternal element, to confuse reality and fantasy, and to wallow in the subjective – a realm which can never be challenged and which removes the individual from outside responsibilities. In our post-Romantic world we tend to associate the subjective with the individual. Not so for Pope. *The Dunciad Variorum* is a study of how, by indulging his private fantasies, a man surrenders his individuality and becomes (literally) part of a mass. It gives a paradoxical twist to the argument that the imagination tends to divide men, while the reason is able to unite them.[26] Pope would understand the import of that idea, and yet, while the dunces squabble and compete with childlike selfishness one with another they diminish as individuals and join into a happy band; a man thinks he is doing his 'own thing', while he swirls about in the vortex of Dulness.

This insidious merging of identities extends to the literary works of the goddess ('Prose swell'd to verse, Verse loitring into prose', i, 228), the theatrical landscapes which superimpose themselves (i, 70–76), the many references to undistinguished, unopened books, to shapelessness and loss of clarity as the mists encroach, and, most powerfully perhaps, in the insistent *plurality* of the poem – so many nouns are pluralised on every page. There is a sense of living things tumbling over themselves to gain entry to the poem, and in doing so ceasing to be alive in anything other than the most primal sense.

The nightmare of Dulness is that things merge as we read, just as the goddess herself is always in process. We may receive many images of her during the poem, but they blur in our minds, so that we finally retain no clear picture of her identity. She represents, after all, lack of clarity, distinction and individual significance, and Pope's aim in several of the poem's visually-crowded passages[27] appears to be to avoid 'composing' a scene, and instead to convey a flux of images so that the picture is forever shifting as we read. This tendency is reinforced by Pope's use of erratic movements, some of which are listed by Alvin Kernan: 'Dulness in the many forms and shapes it assumes, pours, spreads, sluices, creeps, drawls on, stretches, spawns, crawls, meanders, ekes out, flounders on, slips, rolls, extends, waddles, involves, gushes, swells, loiters, decays, slides, wafts, lumbers, blots, o'erflows, trickles.' It is, says Kernan, 'heavy, formless, and directionless, a vague slipping, oozing movement, like a sliding sea of mud going in any and all directions'.[28] At this point we need to recall Hobbes yet again: 'without Steddinesse, and Direction to some End, a great Fancy is one kind of Madnesse'. For all the apparent imaginative 'life' of

Dulness's creatures, they betray and misuse the faculty in the most irresponsible way. Instead of being a force of penetration, an ennobling power capable of lifting the spirit and directing it to a proper aspiration, a means of achieving great and lasting works of literature, it becomes in their hands self-pleasuring and sordid, turning energies inward, and either yoking man to the muddy earth, or merely amusing him with glittering toys. Both aspects betray what for Pope was the truly creative within man.

In *The Dunciad Variorum* mud and glitter represent two aspects of the imagination – the one of murky fertility, formlessness and lack of clarity; the other of the dazzle of mere beauty, of surface unrelated to structure, the world of Locke's secondary qualities. One image is of prenatal thoughtlessness, the other of the thoughtlessness of adolescence. Both these worlds exist of course in *The Rape of the Lock*, presided over by the prudish gnomes (internal spirits whose element is earth) and the coquettish sylphs (external spirits of the air). The gnomes encourage Belinda's internal anarchy to find expression in social chaos, whereas the sylphs delight in external surfaces and wish to preserve society's superficial rituals. In *The Dunciad Variorum* these two principles are brought together. Pope explores the relationship between the superficial shows (pageant, pantomime, opera – the glittering world of theatrical machinery) and the dark, internal world of the unconscious (mud, fogs, chaos and madness). He allows us glimpses beneath the surface spectacle to the chaos of process behind it, so that we recognise how the glitter has been bred by disturbed mental activity, and how it will encourage in its adherents those delusions which brought it into being.

He furthermore exposes the show itself as incomplete creation whereby the *medium* of experience has replaced the shaped independence of the work of art, and he conveys an uneasy distaste for the way an audience participates in the process of 'becoming', without its being able to understand (or value) the created 'being' which an achieved work should be. Pageant, pantomime and opera are, for Pope, media–events, repeated *processes* of creation which involve the audience in participatory imaginative activity, and whose spectacle and extravagant imagery supply a rapid progression of images to register entertainingly in the mind yet leave the judgment untouched. The judgment needs something stable and identifiable in order to exercise the faculty of discrimination and

evaluation, and unless art emerges from the insubstantial world of
mere experience and achieves something independent of the creative
process, implies Pope, then judgment will remain unexercised, and
the fascinating images will flow through the mind leaving nothing of
value behind. The experience will have been experienced, and that is
all. The theatrical events Pope satirises in *The Dunciad Variorum* are
in this way media experiences or processes, and have in one sense no
objective existence. He sees them as pandering to the subjective
responses of those imaginations which participate in them. In this
poem, therefore, Pope is exploring how the imagination can
preclude judgment and fall to contemplating its own activities – like
tinselled Dulness applauding her 'wild creation'.

In *The Dunciad Variorum* this idea is expressed in a striking passage
which merges the images of labyrinth and vortex:[29]

> As man's maeanders to the vital spring
> Roll all their tydes, then back their circles bring;
> Or whirligigs, twirl'd round by skilful swain,
> Suck the thread in, then yield it out again:
> All nonsense thus, of old or modern date,
> Shall in thee centre, from thee circulate.
> For this, our Queen unfolds to vision true
> Thy mental eye . . . (iii, 47–54)

The self-referential subjectivity[30] of Dulness means that her followers
have no vantage-point from which to direct their judgments. Her
activities are entirely self-justifying and submit to no external
objective criteria. Once the process of imagination has taken over,
implies Pope, the author and his audience co-operate in the enterprise
together, shutting out any kind of validation from outside. The
fantasist plays with us on his sticky thread of subjectivity and though
we seem to be moving somewhere, this is mere illusion.

The ramifications of this theme extend throughout the poem. The
picture of Theobald at his desk, for example, is that of a man with no
foothold; he has no objective standard to support him, no concepts
of value or proportion, so that he sinks lower and lower into the
infinite morass, in lines which echo the imagery of Pope's *Peri
Bathous; or, The Art of Sinking in Poetry* (1728):

> Sinking from thought to thought, a vast profound!
> Plung'd for his sense, but found no bottom there;
> Then writ, and flounder'd on, in mere despair. (i, 112–14)

Once again Lady Mary Chudleigh (1703) places the idea in its
spiritual perspective, combining (as Pope does) the images of
labyrinth, mud, mists and drowning:

> Thro' Labyrinths we go without a Clue,
> Till in the dang'rous Maze our selves we lose,
> And neither know which Path t'avoid, or which to chuse.
> From Thought to Thought, our restless Minds are tost,
> Like Ship-wreck'd Mariners we seek the Land,
> And in a Sea of Doubts are almost lost.
> The *Phoenix* Truth wrapt up in Mists does lie,
> Not to be clearly seen before we die;
> Not till our Souls free from confining Clay,
> Open their Eyes in everlasting Day.
>   ('On the Vanities of this Life')

Part of the power of *The Dunciad Variorum* is the way in which it
draws upon this traditional imagery of spiritual crisis. Such a frame
of reference prevents the poem from being a mere enactment of
imaginative excess and judgmental impotence; it also ensures that
Pope's attack on literary ineptitude will uncover a deeper malaise.

Dulness gazes with some satisfaction into the heart of Theobald
and sees the kind of images which mark him out as her
vicegerent-to-be:

> In each she marks her image full exprest,
> But chief, in Tibbald's monster-breeding breast;
> Sees Gods with Daemons in strange league ingage,
> And earth, and heav'n, and hell her battles wage. (i, 105–8)

Scriblerus comments: 'this alludes to the extravagancies of the Farces
of that author; in which he alone could properly be represented as
successor to *Settle*'. Prompted by his lunatic mental pantomime,
Theobald recognises the goddess as 'nearest at my heart' (i, 144) and
proceeds to offer up a sacrifice, addressing her as the patroness of
perplexity. She comforts her followers with the assurance that
artistic achievement is easy, and that the combination of busy
activity and a spontaneous response to the bias within one's own
mind will attain the desired end:

> O thou, of business the directing soul,
> To human heads like byass to the bowl,
> Which as more pond'rous makes their aim more true,
> Obliquely wadling to the mark in view.

> O ever gracious to perplex'd mankind!
> Who spread a healing mist before the mind,
> And, lest we err by Wit's wild, dancing light,
> Secure us kindly in our native night. (i, 147–54)

This is of course a grotesque parody of 'the directing soul' in which mere busy-ness substitutes for genuine creativity. George Puttenham provides the clearest exposition of Theobald's mental confusion:

> For as the evill and vicious disposition of the braine hinders the sounde judgement and discourse of man with busie & disordered phantasies, for which cause the Greekes call him *phantastikos*, so is that part being well affected, not onely nothing disorderly or confused with any monstruous imaginations or conceits, but very formall . . . and so passing cleare, that by it as by a glasse or mirrour, are represented unto the soule all maner of bewtifull visions . . .
>
> (*The Arte of English Poesie*, 1589, I, viii)

Theobald exemplifies the unsound brain: his mind is busy, disordered, 'monster-breeding'[31] and far from clear, so there is a certain irony in the way he shuns 'Wit's wild, dancing light' – he sees it as a will o'the wisp which will lure him astray, rather than as a means of directing the power of the imagination. Thin partitions may divide the great wit from the madman, but Theobald's madness lies in his obsession with a private fantasy rather than a public risk-taking with words. It is an easy, comforting madness, not misplaced genius.

Theobald's mental mists begin to take shape around him, and the goddess herself appears, distorted and undefined:

> Her ample presence fills up all the place;
> A veil of fogs dilates her awful face;
> Great in her charms! as when on Shrieves and May'rs
> She looks, and breathes her self into their airs. (i, 217–20)

Dulness is never objectified or clear. She is both a foggy *inspiration* (literally 'breathing in') but also a *projection* of confused minds, and thus she exists as an endlessly circular process: what her followers believe to be inspiration is just the return of their own ideas from her distorting mirror (she draws them in and recycles them). Similarly, her devotees may feel they are communicating with their audience, but they are in fact only supplying material for others' subjective fantasies.[32] It is an infinite cycle, sucking the thread in and yielding it out again. She inevitably sees Theobald as the embodiment of her ideals ('inevitably', because she is a projection of his imagination anyway):

> 'I see a King! who leads my chosen sons
> To lands, that flow with clenches and with puns . . .
> I see! I see! –' Then rapt, she spoke no more. (i, 251–5)

Her words break off and hang objectless in the air, an ecstasy of self-contemplation.

With Theobald enthroned as King of the dunces Dulness summons her followers and proclaims the Games, and throughout Book ii, like a true pantomime-producer, she shows her skill at creating visions. She is a parody of true aspiration, a fantasy which drives people to artistic activity by conjuring up an imagined prize:

> A Poet's form she plac'd before their eyes,
> And bad the nimblest racer seize the prize . . .
> All as a partridge plump, full-fed, and fair,
> She form'd this image of well-bodied air,
> With pert flat eyes she window'd well its head,
> A brain of feathers, and a heart of lead,
> And empty words she gave, and sounding strain,
> But senseless, lifeless! Idol void and vain! (ii, 31–42)

The publishers Lintot and Curll compete for this vision, and after much slithering in the slime Curll reaches for his fantastic prize, only to face frustration and disillusionment:

> And now the Victor stretch'd his eager hand
> Where the tall Nothing stood, or seem'd to stand;
> A shapeless shade! it melted from his sight,
> Like forms in clouds, or visions of the night! (ii, 101–4)

His prize has been only an idol ('like those various Figures in the gilded Clouds'),[33] a dream which fades as he attempts to embrace it. Lady Mary Chudleigh points the moral of Curll's situation in words which are recalled by Pope's passage:

> Each gaudy nothing which we view,
> We fancy is the wish'd for Prize,
> Its painted Glories captivate our Eyes;
> Blinded by Pride, we hug our own Mistake,
> And foolishly adore that Idol which we make.
> ('On the Vanities of this Life')

The theme of illusion continues through the rest of Book ii. Pope turns from the cheats and lies of gutter publishing to the matter of literary forgeries and pretences:

> Curl stretches after Gay, but Gay is gone,
> He grasps an empty Joseph for a John!
> So Proteus, hunted in a nobler shape,
> Became when seiz'd, a Puppy, or an Ape.
>   To him the Goddess. 'Son! thy grief lay down,
> And turn this whole illusion on the town.' (ii, 119–24)

These phantom-poets of the protean imagination are succeeded by the public image of Eliza Haywood which appears 'as before her works' a parody of fertility and maternal love:

> ˙ See in the circle next, Eliza plac'd;
> Two babes of love close clinging to her waste . . .
> The Goddess then: 'Who best can send on high
> The salient spout, far-streaming to the sky;
> His be yon Juno of majestic size,
> With cow-like udders, and with ox-like eyes. (ii, 149–56)

With such visions hovering before them the dunces all participate in Dulness's illusory games, which travesty in various ways the power of imagination and the images associated with it. There is the rainbow that Chetwood's urine makes: 'So Jove's bright bow displays its watry round, / (Sure sign, that no spectator shall be drown'd)' (ii, 165–6), an achievement transcended by Curll's effort which soars heavenward and brings from Pope a good-humoured parody of the divine flight of Belinda's lock ('Swift as it mounts, all follow with their eyes . . .' (ii, 177)). The next game alludes specifically to the tickling of the patron's fancy as the competitors play their feathers around him: 'Now at his head the dext'rous task commence, / And instant, fancy feels th'imputed sense . . .' (ii, 191–2). All this activity soon becomes exhausting, and so a tired imagination readily takes refuge in mere noise and distraction to achieve easy effects and conceal lack of invention: 'Such happy arts attention can command, / When fancy flags, and sense is at a stand' (ii, 221–2). In the fifth game, with energy renewed, the competitors explore the mud. Welsted thrashes aimlessly about in the murky whirlpools, but it is Smedley, heroically surviving a lengthy immersion, who returns to the surface to tell of his fantastic voyage to the land of forgetfulness where rivers flow, 'wafting vapours from the Land of Dreams' (ii, 316) (lines which, remarks Scriblerus, 'allegorically represent the *Stupefaction* and *visionary Madness* of Poets equally dull and extravagant').

Smedley's slimy vision is (entirely appropriately) a sexual, cosy and beautiful one:

> First he relates, how sinking to the chin,
> Smit with his mien, the Mud-nymphs suck'd him in:
> How young Lutetia, softer than the down,
> Nigrina black, and Merdamante brown,
> Vy'd for his love in jetty bow'rs below;
> As Hylas fair was ravish'd long ago. (ii, 307–12)

The unashamed beauty of such passages, in which 'base' matter is absorbed into 'forms pleasurable to contemplate', has been remarked upon by several critics.[34] This imaginative transmutation has been seen as Pope's 'undoubtedly very strange' sensibility allowing him to achieve 'an unusual degree of creative release' and 'to indulge intense feelings of an infantile nature by taking advantage of the permissive decorum of mock-heroic'. Emrys Jones (from whom these quotations come)[35] goes on to speak of 'a quality of complicity in the writing' in which 'what Pope as a deliberate satirist rejects as dully lifeless his imagination communicates as obscurely energetic'. Another critic, Traugott Lawler, comments on the mud-nymphs passage: 'The vileness of *lutum* and *merde* is absorbed in the lovely-sounding names; 'black' and 'jetty' do not fill the mind with images of murk and filth but of the luminously reflective surface of ebony or black marble.'[36] The perceptions of Jones and Lawler are entirely justified: the beauty of the passage is strange and transforming. What I believe is not justified, however, is a conclusion that at such moments Pope's conscious intention is being undermined by his imagination (Jones's 'complicity'). One of the aims of this book has been to show how consciously Pope exploits the imagination in his poems, and how aware he is of paradoxical responses. In *The Dunciad Variorum* the relationship I have tried to establish between Dulness and the world of fantasy makes Pope's intentions here a little clearer. We have seen how mud/slime is traditionally the antithesis of true vision, and Pope associates it in the mud-nymphs passage with 'vapours from the Land of Dreams' as the distorting medium of Dulness–a powerful emblem of the misuse of the imagination. In these lines Smedley does indeed create an attractive fantasy out of turds. For him, and partly for us as we read, Merdamante and Lutetia undergo an imaginative mutation, but their beauty (well caught in Lawler's phrase 'luminously reflective') is at the same time satirically controlled by Pope. The point is that Smedley fails to realise he has been embracing faeces. In this dark burlesque of pastoral beauty the transformation has, for the reader, *almost* been made. The 'almost' is important: Pope is here exploiting an awareness of subjective fantasy as 'process' (or the excretion of a disturbed brain),[37] a metamorphosis not entirely achieved. Here is a dunce passing base materials to us as objects of beauty. Pope makes sure we are reminded of the primal matter in which Smedley has been immersed, and which still clings to the 'black marble' of his poetry. Critics who ignore the *uneasiness* of such beauty do not do justice to the complexity of feeling which Pope is striving for at such moments in his poem.[38]

In reading Pope's poetry we may find that our own imaginative responses awkwardly complicate the moral issue; but at such moments we should beware of concluding that the poem's 'meaning' must either exclude such a response, or be compromised as a result. It is wrong to assert too readily that there is a 'complicity' in the writing of which Pope himself is not fully aware. His letters show how conscious he is of contradictory responses – and indeed how he can use them for literary effect. Likewise in his poetry, if we as readers find ourselves responding warmly to the antics of the dunces, or having uneasy, divided reactions to Pope's women, then this should not automatically be seen as compromising the satire. A reader who is drawn to love the imaginative profusion of the sylph-world should not be told he is 'wrong', that it is all extremely trivial and ought to be dismissed as such. On the contrary, any reading of (say) *The Rape of the Lock* or *The Dunciad* which does not take into account the imaginative appeal of the poem's world is not doing justice to Pope's art and the way it courts and exploits ambiguous responses. Pope still suffers from the label of 'satirist', which tends to oversimplify our expectations of his art and outlaw the more complex play of sympathies which we value in literature generally.

The theme of dreams and madness is continued into the final activity (if such it may be called) of Theobald's day of triumph, when a public reading of the works of 'Orator' Henley and Sir Richard Blackmore (the latter's epics *Prince Arthur* and *King Arthur*) causes all-conquering sleep[39] to spread in successive circular waves from Dulness across the 'sea of heads' (ii, 378) and the dunces are granted their dreams of lust or pride. It is a fitting conclusion to the day's events and completes the picture of Dulness as the inspirer of imaginative activity. Indeed, Hildebrand Jacob's invocation at the opening of his poem *Bedlam* (1723) could have been addressed to her:

> You who, like *Proteus*, in all Shapes appear,
> And every Hue, like the Camelion wear,
> Phantasia, airy Pow'r! . . .
> A thousand restless Forms around you sport,
> A thousand busy Dreams your Throne support.[40]

During the course of the poem these two worlds of sleep and madness are never far away, and they are of course closely linked by being two manifestations of imaginative anarchy.[41] Because the dunces' mental processes are those of imagination without the direction of reason, they are, by the terms of the age, insane. As Lord Shaftesbury rather disarmingly remarked: "Tis by means . . . of a controller and correcter of fancy that I am saved from being mad.'[42] There is no such corrector in Pope's poem, and the goddess (whose whimsicality creates a wild parody of judgment) has quite the reverse effect, tantalising her worshippers and urging them on to a succession of aimless activities. Their erratic locomotion parallels their mental perplexity: they combine obsession with obliquity, and they soar or sink as their minds aspire or slide.

The Dunciad Variorum is peopled with such a madness, with a furious energy which issues only in Bathos; there is a natural tendency for the dunces to sink into a state of imaginative chaos, returning to the element from which they briefly, if brilliantly, emerged. *Peri Bathous* (1728) describes the *Flying Fishes* in similar terms: 'these are Writers who now and then *rise* upon their *Fins*, and fly out of the *Profund*; but their Wings are soon *dry*, and they drop down to the *Bottom*' (ch. vi). The *Frogs*, seventh in Pope's characterisation of authors with a natural aptitude for the Bathos, 'neither *walk* nor *fly*, but can *leap* and *bound* to admiration: They live generally in the *Bottom of a Ditch*, and make a *great Noise* whenever they thrust their *Heads above Water* (ch. vi).

Scholars have seen that *The Dunciad* has links with this treatise of *The Art of Sinking in Poetry*, a Scriblerian production issued only a few months before the first publication of Pope's poem.[43] *Peri Bathous* after all concerns itself with bad writing and with exposing the incompetence of a number of authors (such as Blackmore,

Theobald and Ambrose Philips) who figure prominently in *The Dunciad*. But the correspondence is closer than that. The identification-mark of the Bathos which Pope's parody-treatise explores is the misuse of the poetic imagination, and the images through which the treatise conveys this reappear prominently in the poem.

In chapter v Pope gives the recipe. The writer who strives for the *Bathos* 'is to mingle Bits of the most various, or discordant kinds . . . as it shall please his Imagination, and contribute to his principal End, which is to glare by strong Oppositions of Colours, and surprize by Contrariety of Images . . . His Design ought to be like a Labyrinth, out of which no body can get you clear but himself.' This kind of sinking involves, therefore, a misuse of the imagination (seen here as glaring colours and confusing images). The initiate is to follow his own pleasure and create a Comus-like labyrinth, a maze of fancy into which a reader or spectator will be hypnotically drawn.

Such a world is alien to notions of proportion and clarity, as Pope explains in chapter xi: 'A genuine Writer of the Profound will take Care never to *magnify* any Object without *clouding* it at the same time; His Thought will appear in a true *Mist*, and very unlike what it is in Nature.' In *The Dunciad Variorum* Dulness accomplishes this to perfection, and some of Scriblerus' footnotes to the text point out this theme. The passage in Book i, for example, describing incongruous scene-painting ('Here gay Description Ægypt glads with showers . . .', i, 71) has the note: 'These six verses represent the inconsistencies in the description of Poets, who heap together all glittering and gawdy Images, tho' incompatible in one season, or in one scene.' It is important not to forget that Dulness is glitter seen through mist. She is a fusion of the Attendant Spirit and Comus, having the tinselled rainbow garments of the one, but also the other's 'power to cheat the eye with blear illusion' (155). Her labyrinth, like that of the enchanter Comus, is a delusive trap.

In its chapters on tropes and figures *Peri Bathous* gives particular examples of how bad writing can involve an undisciplined imagination. In chapter x, for example, we learn that

Under the Article of the *Confusing*, we rank the MIXTURE OF FIGURES, which raises so many Images, as to give you no Image at all. But its principal Beauty is when it gives an Idea just opposite to what it seem'd meant to describe. Thus an ingenious Artist painting the *Spring*, talks of a *Snow* of Blossoms, and thereby raises an unexpected Picture of *Winter*. Of this Sort is the following:

> *The gaping Clouds pour Lakes of Sulphur down,*
> *Whose livid flashes sickning Sunbeams drown.*

What a noble Confusion? Clouds, Lakes, Brimstone, Flames, Sun-beams, gaping, pouring, sickning, drowning! all in two Lines.

The writer of the Bathos regularly falls down in his attempts to be sublime, and he is unable to make constructive use of his active imagination. Instead of raising the mind to higher things, his mental pyrotechnics have the childish sparkle of fireworks which put on a brave show only to sink back to earth like falling stars. The unfortunate Blackmore had infected his imagination with too many such displays, so that when he came to describe the sublime moment of the Creation his plummeting, says Pope, was complete: 'The *Triumphs* and *Acclamations* of the *Angels*, at the Creation of the Universe, present to his Imagination the *Rejoicings of the Lord Mayor's Day*; and he beholds those glorious Beings celebrating the Creator, by Huzzaing, making Illuminations, and flinging Squibbs, Crackers and Sky-rockets' (ch. v).

With this image Pope has brought us back to one of the spectacles in which Dulness is involved – the Lord Mayor's Day Pageant in Book i:

> 'Twas on the day, when Thorold, rich and grave,
> Like Cimon triumph'd, both on land and wave:
> (Pomps without guilt, of bloodless swords and maces,
> Glad chains, warm furs, broad banners, and broad faces)
> Now Night descending, the proud scene was o'er,
> But liv'd, in Settle's numbers, one day more.
> Now May'rs and Shrieves all hush'd and satiate lay,
> Yet eat in dreams the custard of the day;
> While pensive Poets painful vigils keep,
> Sleepless themselves to give their readers sleep. (i, 83–92)

These beaming officials marching in one of Settle's London pageants are innocently happy playing their role in the imaginative spectacle, swathed in the fripperies of office, decorated, splendid and content – 'Pomps without guilt' indeed. This play on words suggests not just the innocence, but also the gilded-ness of the scene: the pageant delights by mere external decoration, and the swords are there for symbolic display, not use. The costumed dignitaries are glad to be enchained. Similarly, the succeeding lines uneasily suggest how they are reminded of their over-indulgence in the day's pleasure. A slight suggestion of the flatulence of Settle's verses ('But lived in Settle's

numbers one day more') is confirmed by the dreams of the mayors
and sheriffs as they relive the flummery of the day's proceedings.

Elkanah Settle is of course the poem's prophet-figure, whose
mantle (as Dulness's vicegerent) descends upon the shoulders of the
aspiring Theobald. The hero's inheritance from his illustrious
forbear is a central theme in *The Dunciad Variorum*, and so it is
important to understand the nature of Settle's bequest.[44] The answer
is to be found in the media-events and stage spectaculars of which he
was the acknowledged master – a role which to some extent
Theobald assumed with his own creations for the London theatre.

Settle's London pageants were pretentious spectacles of pride, and
popular occasions for the crowd to take part in some colourful
ceremonial.[45] Paid for by the wealthy city companies, the floats
glittered excessively as they made their way through the (presum-
ably on occasions) muddy streets. 'Glory's Resurrection' (the 1698
pageant financed by the Goldsmiths) had for its third float 'A
Triumphant Chariot of Gold' whose central figure was Astraea, the
Goddess of Justice, 'in a long Robe of Silver, a Crimson Mantle
fringed with Silver, a Veil of Silver fringed with Gold'. She held 'in
her Right Hand a Touchstone; in her Left a Golden Ballance with
Silver scales' (reminiscent of Dulness's 'lifted Scale'). Around the
central figure were grouped Charity, Concord and Truth (who
guided the chariot). Two unicorns drew the car, on the backs of
which were seated 'two beautiful Young Princes, one a Barbarian,
the other an European, sounding the Fame of the Company'. For
such things 'Mr Settle the poet' was paid £11 1s 6d.[46]

This kind of elaborate emblematic pageant, with its symbolic
figures caught in suitable gestures, seems to lie behind some of the
visual effects in *The Dunciad Variorum*, particularly the pictures of
Dulness enthroned (i, 43–52), the poet-idol with its sword-knot and
embroidered suit (ii, 31–48), and the statuesque Eliza Haywood (ii,
149–56). With the additional customary Lord Mayor's day fireworks
and the atmosphere of holiday revelry, the suggestion of mindless
celebration behind the dunce-antics of Pope's poem comes into
sharper focus. Such antics are evident in Settle's *Pope-Burning Pageant*
of 1680 (a nice thought), celebrated at a time of strong anti-Catholic
feeling in the wake of the Popish Plot. The procession of nine
allegorical floats (of various degrees of comprehensibility) 'was
attended by hundreds of *Flamboes* and *Torches*', and during the
burning of the Pope 'abundance of Fuzes, like falling Stars, and

artificial Fires'. Attention was centred on the statue of the great Eliza (not Eliza Haywood on this occasion, but Elizabeth the First) who was 'adorn'd with a Crown of Laurel, and a Shield, on which was inscrib'd Protestant Religion and *Magna Charta*'. The crowd's euphoria can only have been increased by the 'great store of Wine and other Liquors . . . profusely poured out to the Multitude'. As a climax to the celebration a 'Protestant', who had been bound upon the ninth float, was 'discharged from the *Inquisition*' and addressed the statue:

> Behold the Genius of our Land!
> England's Palladium! may this Shrine
> Be honour'd still, and ever stand,
> Than Palos Statue more Divine.[47]

Such empty revelry culminating in the adoration of a symbolic female divinity belongs to the same imaginative world as *The Dunciad Variorum*, and it exemplifies the dubious inheritance which Elkanah Settle hands on to his successor Lewis Theobald.

   This apostolic succession occurs in Book iii, where Theobald is granted his prophetic dream and the ghost of his illustrious forbear makes his appearance. It is Dulness who, as ever, is in charge of this imaginative flight. Theobald falls asleep in her lap and she sets him off on his visionary journey, once again showing herself the Queen of fantasy:

> But in her Temple's last recess inclos'd,
> On Dulness lap th'Anointed head repos'd.
> Him close she curtain'd round with vapors blue,
> And soft besprinkled with Cimmerian dew.
> Then raptures high the seat of sense o'erflow,
> Which only heads, refin'd from reason, know.
> Hence, from the straw where Bedlam's Prophet nods,
> He hears loud Oracles, and talks with Gods.
> Hence the Fool's paradise, the Statesman's scheme,
> The air-built Castle, and the golden Dream,
> The Maid's romantic wish, the Chymist's flame,
> And Poet's vision of eternal fame. (iii, 1–12)

As the 'seat of sense' is overcome Theobald loses the last vestige of reason and enters the world of fantasy, where divine pretensions have their source in madness. It is a realm where a fool is granted his desire and where an ambitious statesman can build castles in the air; it even includes the 'golden Dream' which we recall from *Eloisa to Abelard*, the young girl's romantic fantasising, the poet's aspirations, and the subliming flame of the alchemist attempting to transform base matter into gold. It is a world of hope and beauty which is finally self-deceiving.

Dulness encourages this deception, and her beloved Theobald floats off 'on Fancy's easy wing convey'd (iii, 13) to the vale of forgetfulness. It is in this dubious region that Settle makes his appearance in the form of a 'sage', broad-shouldered, long-eared and dressed in Settle's clothes. The vision addresses the aspiring Theobald, assuring him that his imagination will be granted sights denied to his waking senses: 'Oh born to see what none can see awake! / Behold the wonders of th'Oblivious Lake' (iii, 35–6). Settle describes for him the mysterious circles of the goddess's labyrinth[48] and reveals that she intends to present a feast of visions to his 'mental eye' (iii, 54). In a parody of Michael's revelations to the repentant Adam, Settle leads him to an appropriate hill which, because this is the vantage-point of Dulness, displays a scene of brilliance shrouded in mist:

> Ascend this hill, whose cloudy point commands
> Her boundless Empire over seas and lands.
> See round the Poles where keener spangles shine,
> Where spices smoke beneath the burning Line,
> (Earth's wide extreams) her sable flag display'd;
> And all the nations cover'd in her shade! (iii, 59–64)

From this cloudy hill Theobald surveys the encroachment of Gothic horrors upon classical civilisation and the outrages committed against the heritage of Greece and Rome. Moving to Britain Settle prophesies that his native land will be brought under Dulness's sway as the hour of her triumph approaches, and he describes how Gothic barbarity is gaining a foothold among critics, scholars and hacks. They are all in their various ways 'dim in clouds' (iii, 187), using their energies in every area except the truly creative, from the dusty Wormius to the insipid Welsted. Suddenly Settle's mind clears, as he urges the dunces to leave one thing sacred and not to scorn God Himself. But this is only a temporary lucid interval which confirms Settle in his madness:

> Thus he, for then a ray of Reason stole
> Half thro' the solid darkness of his soul;

But soon the Cloud return'd – and thus the Sire:
'See now, what Dulness and her sons admire . . .' (iii, 223–6)

With these words[49] Settle gleefully introduces what are apparently
the favourite works of Dulness and her followers – the pantomimes
and harlequinades of the 1720s which had become enormously
successful at the London theatres, the special-effects movies of their
day:

> He look'd, and saw a sable Sorc'rer rise,
> Swift to whose hand a winged volume flies:
> All sudden, Gorgons hiss, and Dragons glare,
> And ten-horn'd fiends and Giants rush to war.
> Hell rises, Heav'n descends, and dance on Earth,
> Gods, imps, and monsters, music, rage, and mirth,
> A fire, a jig, a battle, and a ball,
> Till one wide Conflagration swallows all.
>
> Thence a new world, to Nature's laws unknown,
> Breaks out refulgent, with a heav'n its own:
> Another Cynthia her new journey runs,
> And other planets circle other suns:
> The forests dance, the rivers upward rise,
> Whales sport in woods, and dolphins in the skies,
> And last, to give the whole creation grace,
> Lo! one vast Egg produces human race. (iii, 229–44)

But where has this spectacle come from? We remember the
passage in Book i (53–82, discussed above, pp. 126–7) where the
pantomime grows insidiously out of the primordial slime and
images madly superimpose themselves. Here, in the anarchy and
anachronism of the theatrical event, Pope intends us to recall the
earlier parallel passage. The feverish chaos described here (elemental
warfare of a grotesque kind) has, he implies, been bred in the
imagination of a sick man. The result is very close to the nightmares
described by Thomas Nashe:

And even as slime and durt in a standing puddle, engender toads and frogs
and many other unsightly creatures, so this slimie melancholy humor still
still [sic] thickning as it stands still, engendreth many mishapen objects in our
imaginations. Sundry times wee behold whole Armies of men skirmishing
in the Ayre, Dragons, wilde beasts, bloody streamers, blasing Comets, firie
strakes, with other apparitions innumerable . . .[50]

Once again, out of the slime grows the fantasy. The crazy excesses of
the pantomime (which the dreams resemble) are the products of

unhealthy minds and over-excited imaginations – this was the reaction of an admirer of Pope's, James Miller, who attacked the modern taste for pantomime in his *Harlequin-Horace: or, the Art*of Modern Poetry* (1731).[51] In his preface (directed at the producer, John Rich) Miller discusses their effect on theatre audiences: 'You are convinc'd . . . that the utmost Satisfaction they receive, is from being palpably play'd the Fool with. That their Judgments have got the *Palsy*, and their Imaginations the St. *Vitus's Dance*; the *first*, being benumb'd insensible, and unactive; the *last*, convuls'd, ridiculous, and unnatural . . .' In the poem (addressed to Pope) Miller declares that public taste is now for mere 'sick men's dreams' (Horace's 'aegri somnia', *Ars Poetica*, 7), grotesque fantasies which lack all the virtues of Pope's own works:

> Such Treatment, *Pope*, you must expect to find,
> Whilst Wit and Judgment in your Works are join'd;
> 'Tis not to Think with Strength, and Write with Ease,
> No – 'tis the *Aegri Somnia* now must please;
> Things without Head, or Tail, or Form, or Grace,
> A wild, forc'd, glaring, unconnected Mass. (15–20)

Miller is clearly recalling the world of theatrical excess which Pope had satirised in *The Dunciad Variorum* two years earlier. Not surprisingly, John Rich (manager of the Lincoln's-Inn-Fields theatre who took the lead in staging these media-events) has his own special place in Theobald's vision.[52] Settle points to the skies at Dulness's dazzling angel, who, like the false enchanter Comus, is seen scattering his magic dust of illusion and challenging the sun and stars:

> In yonder cloud, behold!
> Whose sarcenet skirts are edg'd with flamy gold,
> A matchless youth: His nod these worlds controuls,
> Wings the red lightning, and the thunder rolls.
> Angel of Dulness, sent to scatter round
> Her magic charms o'er all unclassic ground:
> Yon stars, yon suns, he rears at pleasure higher,
> Illumes their light, and sets their flames on fire.
> Immortal Rich! . . . (iii, 249–57)

In the parody-universe of pantomime John Rich did indeed have divine power. The imaginative confusion of the pantomime spectacle, as Pope describes it is total. The world has returned to

Chaos: the elements merge together, hell rises up to earth, and every image whirls confusedly about. At these sights Theobald is deeply impressed and joyous, and Settle points out that the cataclysmic scene is in fact a projection of his own mind:

> 'Son! what thou seek'st is in thee. Look, and find
> Each monster meets his likeness in thy mind . . .' (iii, 247–8)

> . . . 'And are these wonders, Son, to thee unknown?
> Unknown to thee? These wonders are thy own . . .' (iii, 269–70)

And indeed they were; in the field of pantomime, harlequinade and masque Lewis Theobald was the true successor to Elkanah Settle.

The imaginative world of *The Dunciad Variorum* is, as we have partly seen, that of the theatrical and processional extravagancies of the years 1680–1728. To examine some of the pantomimes, masques, harlequinades, operas and pageants of the time is to enter a world which Pope's poem clearly recalls. Seen in this context the inheritance that Settle bequeathes to Theobald becomes obvious, and indeed much of the point of *The Dunciad Variorum* is missed without the knowledge that in Settle's last years Theobald collaborated with him, and that Theobald's stage efforts could justly be seen as following directly in the Settle tradition of tasteless display.

Little that Settle touched did not blossom into extravagance. We have already glimpsed some of the flummery of his pageants, and this imaginative skill was put to use in his work for the London theatre. Act Four of the opera *The Fairy Queen* (performed in 1692 to the music of Henry Purcell)[53] has exactly the kind of display which Dulness views from her theatre box in Book i and which Theobald has just been admiring:

A Sonata plays while the Sun rises, it appears red through the Mist, as it ascends it dissipates the Vapours, and is seen in its full Lustre; then the Scene is perfectly discovered, the Fountains enrich'd with gilding, and adorn'd with Statues . . . Before the Trees stand rows of Marble Columns, which support many Walks which rise by Stairs to the top of the House; the Stairs are adorn'd with Figures on Pedestals, and Rails . . . Near the top, vast Quantities of Water break out of the Hills, and fall in mighty Cascade's to the bottom of the Scene, to feed the Fountains which are on each side. In the middle of the Stage is a very large Fountain, where the Water rises about twelve Foot.[54]

In such a scene the sublime teeters on the brink of the ridiculous. Light-effects and cloud-work are recurrent motifs in these shows,

and Pope's use of both in *The Dunciad Variorum* makes a telling
satirical point. These decadent grandchildren of the royal masques
still exploited the imagery and machinery of sun and moon,
clouds and stars, but without the deeper social and political
meanings. The glitter was still there, but little else. An even more
glaring example, which merges farce and the heroic in intriguing
fashion, is Settle's *The World in the Moon* (performed with the
music of Daniel Purcell and Jeremiah Clarke at the Dorset Garden
theatre in 1697).[55] Wildblood and his friend Stanmore take the
clownish Tom Dawkins to see a rehearsal of *The New World in the
Moon*, handing him over to Jo Hayns, operator of the
machines – with farcical results. In this jumbled creation, scenes of
domestic comedy alternate with rehearsal scenes in which the
machines take over:

The Flat-Scene draws, and discovers three grand Arches of Clouds
extending to the Roof of the House terminated with a Prospect of
Cloud-work, all fill'd with the Figures of Fawnes and Cupids; a Circular
part of the back Clouds rolls softly away, and gradually discovers a Silver
Moon, near Fourteen Foot Diameter; After which, Silver Moon wanes
off by degrees, and discovers the World within, consisting of Four grand
Circles of Clouds, illustrated with Cupids, &c. Twelve golden Chariots
are seen riding in the Clouds, fill'd with Twelve Children, representing
the Twelve Celestial Signs. The Third Arch entirely rolling away, leaves
the full Prospect terminating with a large Landscape of Woods, Waters,
Towns, &c.[56]

It is the kind of imaginative hotch-potch of which Elkanah Settle
was the master. The open-mouthed audience would applaud
wildly, and Pope's Dulness is there, applauding with them.

In *The Dunciad Variorum* it is upon Lewis Theobald's shoulders
that Settle's mantle descends, and indeed in the flamboyant art of
theatrical fantasy he was an obvious successor. In 1718 he furnished
songs and other verses for Settle's *The Lady's Triumph*, and also the
masque of *Decius and Paulina* for the last act.[57] There is much raw
material here for satire: much imagery of clouds, lightning, snow,
sun and eery flame; much flummery on the part of the characters.
Some regularly feel divinity rising within, or descending upon them;
some invoke the realms of night; some battle with chaos; some turn
into stars; some spread plague through the universe; and some fly
through the fog to their nocturnal caves.

For instance, Mr Leveridge (a popular performer in pantomime at this period) declares in Act II of *The Lady's Triumph* (a scene, it should be noted, set in Bedlam):

> My Soul's on fire – Oh, that I could ascend
> The Realms of Light, and sit enthron'd on Clouds!
> Thence hurl the Thunder, drive the fleecy Snow,
> And make the Skies blush with uncommon Lightnings![58]

(This is followed by the song 'Great Ambition! Pow'r Divine'.) It is as though Theobald and Settle were volunteering for Dulness's service – the only trouble being that Dulness is enthron'd *in* clouds rather than *on* them. Not to be outdone, Mrs Barbier enters, for a song whose refrain is 'O Realms of Night! O gloomy Pow'rs! / Receive me to your peaceful Bow'rs . . .' In choosing the hero for his first *Dunciad* it must have occurred to Pope that he was simply granting Theobald's desire.

Mr Leveridge reappears as Simo in Theobald's masque of *Decius and Paulina*, where he is once again filled with divine ambitions:

> I'm fill'd with Thoughts of sudden State;
> 'Tis *Jove* inspires
> These big Desires,
> This strange Ambition to be great.[59]

This draws an apt reply from his 'beloved Ida':

> Ah! *Simo*, if thy Wits remain,
> If no bad Star has hurt thy Brain;
> Let such vain Whimsies stand confin'd,
> And to thy Fortunes fit thy Mind:
> These Raptures would more welcome be,
> If right employ'd on Love, and Me.

This production, an example of collaboration between Settle and Theobald, plunges us appropriately into the world of *The Dunciad Variorum*; such things gleefully exploit the imagery of darkness, madness and ambition, but they use it indulgently for mere effect. They show verve and daring, and the audiences who thronged to them in the 1720s were undoubtedly swept up into the experience, but what was left, Pope suggests, when the thrill ended? Were men and women wiser or better?

The year 1725 saw Lewis Theobald triumph in the London theatre with his two extremely popular pantomimes, *Harlequin Sorcerer, with the Loves of Pluto and Proserpine* and *The Rape of Proserpine*. These

are the 'miserable Farces' alluded to in Pope's note (to iii, 307) as
Settle describes the triumphant progress of Dulness 'from Booths to
Theatre, to Court' (iii, 301).[60] Thanks to his efforts, Settle tells
Theobald, Hell itself will be the ally of their goddess:

> To aid her cause, if heav'n thou can'st not bend,
> Hell thou shalt move; for Faustus is thy friend:
> Pluto with Cato thou for her shalt join,
> And link the Mourning-Bride to Proserpine.
> Grubstreet! thy fall should men and Gods conspire,
> Thy stage shall stand, ensure it but from Fire . . .
> In flames, like Semeles, be brought to bed,
> While opening Hell spouts wild-fire at your head. (iii, 305–14)

This directly recalls the stage-directions in scene iv of his *Rape of
Proserpine*: 'An Earthquake is felt, and part of the Building falls; and
through the Ruins of the fall'n Palace Mount *Ætna* appears, and
emits Flames. Beneath, a Giant is seen to rise, but is dash'd to pieces
by a Thunder-bolt hurld from *Jupiter*.'[61] Pluto seizes Proserpine and
carries her off in his chariot. The stricken Ceres then descends in her
own chariot to bewail the loss of her daughter, and in her grief and
anger she sets fire to a field of corn (see Pope's own note to 310). Her
lament is interrupted by an infernal voice from beneath the stage,
crying: 'Let universal Order die, / And Nature sink into the Grave of
Ruin' (p. 14). This is the slogan of the followers of Dulness, whose
reign promises to overturn the order of nature and to usher in a
world which will be one great theatre. The establishment of her
empire will award private fantasies a public stage, and a creative,
co-operative community will become a passive audience for whom
'activity' is a swirl of the brain. Communal mindlessness is the key to
the antics of Pope's dunces, as it is the manifestation of Theobald's
theatrical activities.

In such ways the world of pantomime is central to an
understanding of *The Dunciad Variorum*. It provides Pope with the
image of a universe ruled by fantasy, where the imagination has been
totally severed from truth, to become an 'inarticulate, chaotic' world
of its own, a vortex of experience which draws the minds of the
faithful into an endless process of creation that has no product.
Reading Theobald's stage-directions today is a sobering experience:
what must have lived so brilliantly in the minds of his audiences has
perished with them.

'Let universal Order die', Theobald wrote, and at the climax of

Pope's poem this cry is brought to fulfilment. We have seen from the beginning how Dulness is a travesty of true creation, and this idea is now followed through to its inevitable outcome – at least within the imaginations of Settle and Theobald. *The Dunciad Variorum* began with primeval chaos, with half-formed, amphibious things emerging from the slime, and now the cycle has come round again:

> See! the dull stars roll round and re-appear.
> She comes! the Cloud-compelling Pow'r, behold!
> With Night Primaeval, and with Chaos old. (iii, 336–8)

In his moment of triumphant vision Settle presents Dulness as a parody of the *Logos*; she is the 'uncreating word' (iii, 340), and all human aspirations and achievements enter the undistinguished darkness, the medium where nothing has individual form or significance. Such a darkness is the enemy of both empirical and transcendental truth; sense experience is extinguished, and so is divine revelation; science is destroyed as well as faith:

> See sculking Truth in her old cavern lye,
> Secur'd by mountains of heap'd casuistry:
> Philosophy, that touch'd the Heavens before,
> Shrinks to her hidden cause, and is no more:
> See Physic beg the Stagyrite's defence!
> See Metaphysic call for aid on Sence!
> See Mystery to Mathematicks fly!
> In vain! they gaze, turn giddy, rave, and die. (iii, 347–54)

In a final swirl of movement every avenue to the truth is closed. It is no longer to be found in the ancients (Aristotle the Stagyrite), nor in heavenly light, nor in scientific knowledge. Gone is Eloisa's divine vision, Clarissa's pragmatism and Martha Blount's good sense. Dulness, that great enemy of the truth, has conquered, and all is brought to an end (appropriately) in the manner of a theatrical performance, with the goddess once again taking the role of producer: ' "Thy hand great Dulness! lets the curtain fall, / And universal Darkness covers all" ' (iii, 355–6). As Settle ends his speech (taking a metaphor from the world he loves) Theobald cries out in ecstasy and the spell is broken: ' "Enough! enough!" the raptur'd Monarch cries; / And thro' the Ivory Gate the Vision flies' (iii, 357–8).

Thus *The Dunciad Variorum* ends (unlike the 1743 version) with a reassuring reminder that we have been living within the imaginations of Settle and Theobald. The joke is finally Pope's, as Scriblerus points out in a footnote: 'By causing all this Vision to pass thro' the *Ivory Gate*, he expressly in the language of poesy declares all such imaginations to be wild, ungrounded, and fictitious.' Dulness's inspirations are certainly 'wild, ungrounded, and fictitious', but Pope's own vision cannot be so easily dismissed. At this stage of his career he may have believed that what defied the truth could never finally conquer; however, the danger posed for a society preferring fantasy to reality is clear enough, and Dulness has shown her hand. The poem's images haunt the mind, and the activities of the dunces become less trivial once we understand the nature of Dulness's threat. Unless we exercise *all* the faculties of our mind, and not just one at the expense of the others, then our love of fanciful childish games will move us imperceptibly towards the precipice. We shall have betrayed our imaginations, and the 'bright Intelligences' above our world will look down on us with scorn and pity:

It moves them to Compassion to see poor wretched Mortals chusing Servitude, and hugging Chains; proud of Toys, and fond of Bubbles; drawing Fairy-Rounds, and courting Shaddows; boasting of Sight, yet blindly stumbling on, and tumbling headlong down from Precipice to Precipice, till they are lost in a retrieveless Depth; they, and their vain Designs, forever hid in endless Night. Such is the Farce of Life, and such is the last concluding Scene.[62]

The stakes are perhaps higher than we think.

Postscript

Pope felt very strongly the extent to which humanity lives within the imagination, and how much a person's emotional involvement with experience is coloured by his imaginative activity. He knew this from observing human life around him, but also from his own experience as friend, lover and poet. He did not, however, theorise about the imagination, and to search for a label or a single theory to characterise Pope's views is to risk oversimplifying. At times he is exploring neoplatonic imagery, with its polarities of transcendent and fleshly vision; he is occasionally close to Richard Sibbes's puritan internal iconoclasm, to Lady Mary Chudleigh's urgent neo-stoicism, or to the empiricism of Hobbes and Locke. Furthermore, in sharing Milton's concern with the right and wrong ways of seeing he preserves his predecessor's understanding of the tension that can exist between the divine, the misleading and the chaotic within imaginative activity, and such cross-currents are turned to creative effect in his own work.

The most helpful concept is perhaps that of 'paradox', which may seem a dubious refuge from uncertainty, but it appears to be truest to the experience of reading him. Pope found his sense of man's paradoxical nature artistically fruitful, and at its best his poetry risks the uncertainties which come from exploiting that ambiguous medium where beauty shocks and energy may be akin to emptiness. Pope's poetry regularly acknowledges that it is working within a potentially deceptive medium, that life itself is an art (of creativity and relationship) and that the poet's artistry is life enacted in print on a page. When he confronts creativity, perception, deceit or selfishness in his poetry, it is always with an awareness of energies released and directed, and a sense of the morality which this combination involves. Just as life is a series of individual creative acts lived within a community, so art is for him hedged about with human responsibilities placing a moral pressure on creativity.

The vitality of his art lies in the way it exploits the tensions between a stable and a free element (judgment and sympathy, truth and imagination, order and chaos, structure and fluidity, confinement and flight, clarity and elusiveness, impersonal and personal, authority and anarchy, thought and passion). Pope's poetry works within a kind of gravitational field of emotions and responsibilities, and this often finds expression in movement between polarities: in Eloisa mounting up and yet being pulled back by the pulse of her erotic dreams, alternating between bliss and damnation until they might almost be interchangeable; in Belinda caught between air and earth, sylph and gnome, coquettry and prudery, dream and nightmare; in the women of *Epistle to a Lady* swinging restlessly between extremes – fever and chill, pride and humiliation, love and hate – so that relief is welcomed in terms of poise and reconciliation; perhaps it appears most strikingly in the gravitational fantasy of Dulness, where the mind (travestied as 'strong impulsive gravity of Head') is drawn into her vortex, and the only stable element amid all the meanderings is the true light which such activity outrages. The power with which Pope uses these tensions is inseparable from his understanding of the paradoxical human imagination, and as a poet he recognises that he is employing that same faculty himself.

Pope's imagination is expressed in terms of movement, whether soaring, sinking or sidling. If he does have the poet's prerogative of a more comprehensive vision than his characters, then that does not remove him from their struggle; on the contrary, his imagination enters it, and whether the poems end in sympathy (Eloisa), compliment (Belinda), reconciliation (Martha Blount) or apocalypse (Dulness), it is the paradoxical nature of humanity, and Pope's engagement with it, that generates the drama and provides the elements for a poetic solution.

A final note of paradox is struck by the fact that during his last illness in May 1744 Pope's eyesight began to play tricks on him. The result of this visual disturbance in the final weeks of his life was a strange mixture of images which (appropriately for this book) exemplified the range of imaginative activity that Pope's poetry had explored: surreal fantasy, superficial light-effects, and delightful vision.[1] A visitor remembered tearfully how the poet asked him as he sat by the bed: 'What great arm is that I see coming out of the wall?'; on a second occasion Joseph Spence recorded that Pope recognised something was wrong, complaining of 'that odd phenomenon (as he called it) of seeing everything in the room as through a curtain' and of 'seeing false colours on objects'. A few days before the end, however, Spence jotted down another cameo which struck a very different note: ' "What's that?" asked Pope pointing up in the air with a very steady regard, and then looking down on me, he said with a smile of pleasure and with the greatest sweetness and complacency, '"Twas a vision." '

For Lord Byron, the attitude which an age took towards Pope's work was a touchstone of its moral and artistic health.[2] The tributes he paid to his fellow-poet are warmer and more deeply felt than his praise of any other writer, and it is significant that two aspects of Pope's art called forth his particular admiration: imagination and morality. 'I will show more *imagery* in twenty lines of Pope than in any equal length of quotation in English poesy', he wrote to Murray in March 1821, and proceeded excitedly to itemise the images of the Sporus-passage from *Epistle to Arbuthnot*, concluding: 'Now is there a line of all the passage without the most *forcible* imagery? . . . look at the *variety* at the *poetry* – of the passage – at the *imagination* – there is hardly a line – from which a *painting* might not be made – and *is*.'[3] That final 'and *is*' clinches Byron's point as it moves imagination into the context of Pope's *artistry* (fulfilled potential). For Byron the potency of Pope's writings was also a *moral* one (he is 'the moral poet of all civilisation')[4] – not, it must be stressed, morality laid upon the surface (that, for Byron, was *cant*) but a function of his poetry's engagement with truth – its acceptance of the responsibility which art has to engage with the uncomfortably real and to deliver a challenge to humanity's infinite capacity for pride and self-deception. Pope's imagination is the meeting-point of his art and his morality – it is the point where vision recognises the claims of truth, where self encounters other. The fanciful characters who fill his poems recognise no such claim and remain shut within the self, so that the beams of imagination begin to shift, twist and circulate. Pope fervently believed that imagination should not be self-enclosed and self-referential. It is this conviction which gives an urgency to his satire, and which makes him a necessary poet for his own age and for ours.

Whether the period 1975–2000 will become known as the 'video age' or the 'age of fantasy', it is a period during which the function of the image in our culture will become a matter of growing concern. Literature will come under increasing pressure to examine the relationship between the image and the word. Will video itself become the touchstone, so that an image is judged by its power to affect an 'audience' rather than by its function within an artistic whole? Will the meaning of a written text reside solely in a reader's response to imagery? Will the Latin verb *to see* remain a burlesque of true vision? Poetry itself cannot remain untouched by this problem. One easy recourse will be for it to ape the tricks of video itself, and be a means of casting strange lights over the real world. But another important choice may be for poetry to bring the image (literally) to book, and to use that power within the written word to challenge the imagery it employs. Pope's poetry issues such a challenge, not merely to writers, but to all who value human relationships. It forces us to think about the links between illusion and self-delusion, and the complex role that imagination plays in our lives. It is a kind of poetry whose very unpopularity within an age (as Byron recognised in 1821) may be an indicator of its importance for that age.

Notes

INTRODUCTION

1 Emrys Jones, 'Pope and Dulness', *PBA* liv (1968), 231–63, p. 239.
2 To gain some idea of how the imagination can be involved with these four passions we need perhaps to take literally several modern phrases which commemorate this involvement: (i) to *fancy oneself* (i.e. to suffer the delusions of pride), (ii) *fancy ideas* (i.e. pleasing illusions often of an ambitious nature), (iii) to *fancy a horse* or a team (i.e. to believe, seldom on rational grounds, in the fulfilment of one's hopes or expectations), (iv) to *fancy someone* (i.e. to have one's imagination taken by external appearance).
3 'This *decaying sense*, when wee would express the thing it self, (I mean *fancy* it selfe,) wee call *Imagination* . . .' (Thomas Hobbes, *Leviathan* (London, 1651), I, ii). Quotations from *Leviathan* are taken from the edition by C. B. Macpherson (Harmondsworth, 1968). See Chapter Three, note 2.
4 John M. Aden, 'Dryden and the Imagination: The First Phase', *PMLA* lxxiv (1959), 28–40.
5 Robert D. Hume, 'Dryden on Creation: "Imagination" in the Later Criticism', *RES* xxi (1970), 295–314, p. 308.
6 John Bullitt and W. Jackson Bate, 'Distinctions Between Fancy and Imagination in Eighteenth-Century English Criticism', *MLN* lx (1945), 8–15.
7 Hester Lynch Piozzi, *British Synonymy; or, an Attempt at Regulating the Choice of Words in Familiar Conversation* 2 vols (London, 1794), i, 220–3.
8 James Beattie, *Dissertations Moral and Critical* (London, 1783), p. 72. James Engell (*The Creative Imagination* (Cambridge, Mass., and London, 1981)) quotes this passage, but significantly omits the final sentence.
9 *Spectator* 411 (21 June 1712).
10 The following is a selection of examples:
   (i) 'Their Fancy rose with a Refinement as much above that of their Masters, as the *Greek* imagination was superior to that of the *Ægyptians* . . .' (*An Essay on Homer*, Twickenham ed., vii, 29).
   (ii) 'In pensive thought recall the fancy'd scene,
        See Coronations rise on ev'ry green;

Before you pass th'imaginary sights . . .'
('Epistle to Miss Blount, on her leaving the Town, after the
Coronation', 33–5).

    (iii) 'I have been lying in wait for my own imagination this week and
more, and watching what thoughts of mine came up in the whirl of
fancy that were worth communicating to you . . .' (Pope–Caryll, 14
Aug. 1713).

11   Introduction to *The Iliad of Homer*, Twickenham ed., vii, xlvii.

12   Twickenham ed., vii, 4.

13   'So then, the first happiness of the Poet's imagination is properly
Invention, or finding of the thought; the second is Fancy, or the
variation, driving or moulding of that thought, as the judgment
represents it proper to the subject; the third is Elocution, or the Art of
clothing and adorning that thought so found and varied, in apt,
significant and sounding words: the quickness of the Imagination is
seen in the Invention, the fertility in the Fancy, and the accuracy in the
Expression' ('An account of the ensuing Poem, in a Letter to the
Honorable, Sir Robert Howard', *Annus Mirabilis*, 1667).

14   Twickenham ed., vii, 9, 13.

15   Twickenham ed, vii, 5.

16   Unless otherwise stated, quotations from Pope's poems are taken from
the one-volume edition of the Twickenham text, ed. John Butt (1965
ed.).

17   Quotations from Engell are *The Creative Imagination*, pp. 3–4. On his
selective quotation of Beattie, see note 8 above. See also Chapter Two,
note 18 and Chapter Four, note 12. My disagreement with Engell's
account of Hobbes is detailed in Chapter Three, note 2.

18   On Pope's extensive use of the *cloud* image in a context of imagination,
see below, pp. 17, 49, 63–4, 74, 76–7, 90, 93–4, 116–18, 123, 126, 135,
140–1, 144–5, 147–9. Shifting clouds have traditionally been associated
with imagination. One passage which probably influenced Pope is
Antony's speech in *Antony and Cleopatra*, IV, xiv, 2–11:

    Sometime we see a cloud that's dragonish,
      A vapour sometime, like a bear, or lion,
      A tower'd citadel, a pendent rock,
      A forked mountain, or blue promontory
      With trees upon't, that nod unto the world,
      And mock our eyes with air. Thou hast seen these signs,
      They are black vesper's pageants . . .
      That which is now a horse, even with a thought
      The rack dislimns, and makes it indistinct
      As water is in water.

In Pope's edition of *Antony and Cleopatra* (1725 *Shakespeare*) these are the
first lines in the play to be given approving asterisks (after 92 pages).

The fancifulness of Bridget Tipkin in Steele's *The Tender Husband* (1705) is indicated by her seeing a 'flying Dragon' in a cloud ('I look upon it to be a Prodigy . . .'), II, ii, 65.

19 'A visible revolution succeeded in the general cast and character of the national composition. Our versification contracted a new colouring, a new structure and phraseology; and the school of Milton rose in emulation of the school of Pope' (*Poems upon Several Occasions . . . by John Milton*, ed. Thomas Warton (London, 1785), pp. x–xi).

20 See, for example, Barbara Kiefer Lewalski, 'On Looking into Pope's Milton', *Études Anglaises* xxvii (1974), 481–500. The best account of the Miltonic allusions in *The Rape of the Lock* is by Kent Beyette, 'Milton and Pope's *The Rape of the Lock*', *SEL* xvi (1976), 421–36. Beyette shows well how the Miltonic references throughout the poem (to the *Maske* and *Paradise Lost*) suggest 'a struggle between true values and false values' (p. 431).

CHAPTER ONE

1 Quotations from Pope's correspondence are taken from *The Correspondence of Alexander Pope*, ed. George Sherburn, 5 vols (Oxford, 1956), hereafter cited as Sherburn. Dates are given in the form in which they appear in that edition.

2 An excellent discussion of the interrelationship of imagination and madness in the Eighteenth Century is Michael V. DePorte's chapter, 'Abnormal Psychology in England 1660–1760', in his *Nightmares and Hobbyhorses: Swift, Sterne, and Augustan Ideas of Madness* (San Marino, Cal., 1974), pp. 3–53. See also p. 139 below and note 41.

3 Joseph Spence, *Observations, Anecdotes, and Characters of Books and Men*, ed. James M. Osborn, 2 vols (Oxford, 1966), entry 28. Hereafter cited as Spence, *Anecdotes*.

4 In February 1728 Pope wrote in a similar vein to Swift: 'I shall be at Dublin in three days. I cannot help adding a word, to desire you to expect my soul there with you by that time; but as for the jade of a body that is tack'd to it, I fear there will be no dragging it after.'

5 Spence, *Anecdotes*, entry 340.

6 See Sherburn, i, 393 n. 1.

7 *Rasselas*, ch. 1.

8 Unless otherwise stated, quotations from Pope's prose works are taken from Norman Ault (ed.), *The Prose Works of Alexander Pope: The Earlier Works 1711–1720* (Oxford, 1936), hereafter cited as Ault.

9 'Her own statement, however, was this; that at some ill-chosen time, when she least expected what romances call a *declaration*, he made such passionate love to her, as, in spite of her utmost endeavours to be angry and look grave, provoked an immoderate fit of laughter; from which

moment he became her implacable enemy' ('Biographical Anecdotes of Lady M. W. Montagu', printed in *Lady Mary Wortley Montagu: Essays and Poems, and Simplicity, A Comedy*, ed. Robert Halsband and Isobel Grundy (Oxford, 1977), 6–54, p. 37). Lady Louisa Stuart (1757–1851) was Lady Mary's grandchild. See Halsband and Grundy, p. 6.

10 Pope alludes to Othello's predicament at the chaotic climax of *The Rape of the Lock*: 'Not fierce *Othello* in so loud a Strain / Roar'd for the Handkerchief that caus'd his Pain' (v, 105–6). This passage similarly charts a movement of fancy>passion>chaos. It is interesting to note that in Pope's edition of *Shakespeare* (1725), Othello's outburst: 'Excellent wretch, perdition catch my soul, / But I do love thee; and when I love thee not, / Chaos is come again' (III, iii, 91–3) is the first passage in that play to carry approving asterisks (after 53 pages of text). On Eloisa's echo of 'perdition catch my soul', see below, pp. 50.

11 See below, Chapter Two, note 33.

12 'Your serpent of Egypt is bred now of your mud by the operation of your sun' (*Antony and Cleopatra*, II, vii, 26–7). Quotations from Shakespeare are taken from the Arden edition. See below, Chapter Five, note 11.

13 In his edition of *Antony and Cleopatra* (1725 *Shakespeare*) Pope places approving asterisks (rather surprisingly) against the clown's prose speeches in Act V scene ii, 244–78, describing the worm of Nilus (twenty-four lines in all). Only a further twenty-three lines are asterisked throughout the whole play.

14   that handkerchief
      Did an Egyptian to my mother give,
      . . . she told her, while she kept it
      'Twould make her amiable, and subdue my father
      Entirely to her love: but if she lost it,
      Or made a gift of it, my father's eye
      Should hold her loathly, and his spirits should hunt
      After new fancies . . .
      The worms were hallow'd that did breed the silk . . .
                    (*Othello*, III, iv, 53–71)

CHAPTER TWO

1 Joseph Warton, *An Essay on the Writings and Genius of Pope* (London, 1756), p. 333.

2 Joseph Warton himself suggests of lines 307–12: 'This scene would make a fine subject for the pencil; and is worthy a capital painter. He might place Eloisa in the long ile of a great Gothic church; a lamp should hang over her head, whose dim and dismal ray should afford only light enough to make darkness visible. She herself should be represented in

the *instant*, when she first hears this aërial voice, and in the attitude of *starting round* with astonishment and fear' (*Essay*, p. 328). See also the description of Eloisa reclining against a tomb in his brother Thomas Warton's *The Pleasures of Melancholy*, lines 96–102 (*Poetical Works*, ed. Richard Mant (Oxford, 1802), i, 76–7).

3 W. B. Carnochan, *Confinement and Flight: an Essay on English Literature of the Eighteenth Century* (Berkeley and Los Angeles, 1977), p. 81.

4 Murray Krieger speaks of 'this failure of single intention, by Pope's being drawn into character, situation, and language even as he wishes to stand free of them to retain an a priori, unthreatened control over them' (' "Eloisa to Abelard": The Escape from Body or the Embrace of Body', *ECS* iii (1969–70), 28–47, p. 45); Thomas R. Edwards, Jr. argues that 'we miss the significant shifts of tone made possible by the superimposition upon the event of a detached speaking voice' (*This Dark Estate: a Reading of Pope* (Berkeley and Los Angeles, 1963), p. 25); and Patricia Meyer Spacks identifies 'the uncharacteristic lack of "placing" in this poem' (*An Argument of Images: the Poetry of Alexander Pope* (Cambridge, Mass., 1971), p. 237). I believe that the parallel which Pope maintains between Eloisa and Milton's Lady does help to 'place' the heroine, by providing a detached vantage-point from which Eloisa's visions may be assessed.

5 The phrases are from Pat Rogers, *An Introduction to Pope* (London, 1975), p. 47; and Edward E. Foster, 'Rhetorical Control in Pope's *Eloisa to Abelard*', *Tennessee Studies in Literature* xiii (1968), 63–74, p. 73. Krieger traces well the 'rhetorical structure' of the poem.

6 Jean H. Hagstrum, *The Sister Arts: The Tradition of Literary Pictorialism and English Poetry from Dryden to Gray* (Chicago, 1958), p. 213.

7 In interpreting Eloisa's struggle as taking place within her imagination, I oppose the view of David B. Morris: 'The entire poem varies between her excursions into fantasy and her vivid recollections of the past, both played upon a consciousness wholly alive to the controlling presence of reason. Although her understanding may seem to veer with each new image, in fact the shifts occur because, while allowing free play to the imagery of past and possibility, she never allows memory and imagination to overwhelm her perception of the actual state of things' (' "The Visionary Maid": Tragic Passion and Redemptive Sympathy in Pope's "Eloisa to Abelard" ', *MLQ* xxxiv (1973), p. 261. I concur with Spacks that 'all of the action in the poem takes place in Eloisa's memory or imagination, or is formed by a mixture of the two', p. 234).

8 The partition of the 'internal senses' seems to derive ultimately from Aristotle's *De Anima*, though Galen (second century A.D.) established their association with ventricles of the brain. See E. Ruth Harvey, *The Inward Wits: Psychological Theory in the Middle Ages and the Renaissance* (Warburg Institute, London, 1975), pp. 35, 60. See also H. A. Wolfson,

'The Internal Senses in Latin, Arabic, and Hebrew Philosophic Texts', *Harvard Theological Review* xxviii (1935), 69–133.

9   See Raymond Klibansky, Erwin Panofsky and Fritz Saxl, *Saturn and Melancholy* (London, 1964), pp. 68–9.

10   On faculty psychology, see Lawrence Babb, *The Elizabethan Malady: A Study of Melancholia in English Literature from 1580 to 1642* (East Lansing, 1951), pp. 2–5. See also Baxter Hathaway, *The Age of Criticism: The Late Renaissance in Italy* (Ithaca, N.Y., 1962), p. 340. The seventeenth-century physiological background to Augustanism is explored by DePorte, pp. 3–105.

11   Quotations from Burton are taken from *The Anatomy of Melancholy*, introd. Holbrook Jackson, 3 vols (London, 1932).

12   The quotations below are: IV, i, 121–2; V, i, 275; II, ii, 118; V, i, 295.

13   Gianfrancesco Pico della Mirandola, *On the Imagination*, trans. Harry Caplan, Cornell Studies in English, xvi (New Haven, Conn., 1930), p. 43. Further page references in the text will be to this edition.

14   Augustine, *De Genesi ad Litteram*, XII, xi, 22. *Patrologia Latina*, xxxiv col. 462 (dilectio autem nec per substantiam suam potest oculis corporis cerni, nec per imaginem corporis similem spiritu cogitari; sed sola mente, id est intellectu, cognosci et percipi).

15   Aquinas, for example, maintained that intellect could not operate without *phantasmata* provided by the senses. See Harvey, pp. 54, 61.

16   Philo, *On the Creation*, xxiii, trans. F. H. Colson and G. H. Whitaker (Loeb), i, 55–7.

17   *Brief Lives*, ed. Andrew Clark (Oxford, 1898), i, 292.

18   The terminology of 'divine' and 'base' imagination is my own; by it I intend to point up a distinction in Renaissance theory which is usually ignored. This can result in misleading generalisations about a 'Renaissance attitude' towards the imagination. Donald F. Bond, for example (in 'The Neo-classical Psychology of the Imagination', *ELH* iv (1937), 245–64) emphasises the platonists' denigration of the imagination (its 'inferior, distrusted position', p. 264) and sees the rise of empiricist psychology as enhancing the prestige of the faculty. James Engell takes a similar line in *The Creative Imagination* (1981); his rare references to Renaissance theory are marred by a Romantic terminology (e.g. he equates Sir Philip Sidney's 'golden' world of poetry with the ability of the imagination 'to shape a new universe of experience' (p. 106) – a phrase which misrepresents the notion of the platonic ideal pattern). Engell does not take into account Isabel G. MacCaffrey's important study, *Spenser's Allegory: the Anatomy of Imagination* (Princeton, 1976), which considers the favourable aspects of the medieval/Renaissance imagination and its relationship to artistic creativity (and especially allegory). MacCaffrey notes (p. 242)

the 'inherent duplicity' of the faculty in Spenser's description of Phantastes' chamber (see above, p. 27).

19 *Leviathan*, I, ii.

20 Burton (see p. 28 above). Andreas Laurentius declares: 'All melancho-like persons have their imagination troubled, for that they devise with themselves a thousand fantasticall inventions and objects, which in deede are not at all: they have also verie oft their reason corrupted . . .' (*A Discourse of the Preservation of the Sight*, trans. Richard Surphlet (London, 1599), p. 87).

21 See Lawrence Babb, 'The Background of "Il Penseroso" ', *SP* xxxvii (1940), 257–73; William J. Grace, 'Notes on Robert Burton and John Milton', *SP* lii (1955), 578–91; Klibansky etc., pp. 67–9. Pope makes a distinction between melancholies when he writes to Fortescue (21 Sept. 1736): '[Bevis Mount] is a place that always made me Contemplative, & now Melancholy; but tis a Melancholy of that sort which becomes a rational Creature, & an Immortal Soul.'

22 Levinus Lemnius, *The Touchstone of Complexions*, trans. Thomas Newton (London, 1576), f. 138b. Further references are to this edition, and will appear in the text.

23 Bovillus, *Proverbia vulgaria*. Quoted by Klibansky etc., p. 253. In 'The Author's Abstract of Melancholy' (prefixed to the *Anatomy*) Burton contrasted the delightful and the dismal images between which the mind of the melancholy man alternated – the 'phantasms sweet' against the 'fearful sights'.

24 'Melancholye therefore and Drunkennesse, are in condition alike. For Drunkards are ledde with many affections and phansies . . .' (Lemnius, f. 149b).

25 See the stimulating discussion of this theme in Paul Fussell, *The Rhetorical World of Augustan Humanism* (Oxford, 1965), 110–35 ('The Paradox of Man').

26 'The Background of "Il Penseroso" ' (see note 21 above).

27 Quotations from Milton's poems are taken from *The Poems of John Milton*, ed. Helen Darbishire (Oxford, 1961).

28 *The Dialogues of Plato*, trans. B. Jowett, 4th ed. (Oxford, 1953), i, 108.

29 Nashe says that melancholy 'sinketh downe to the bottome like the lees of the wine, and that corrupteth all the blood, and is the causer of lunacie' (*The Works of Thomas Nashe*, ed. Ronald B. McKerrow (Oxford, 1966), i, 357).

30 Sir Philip Sidney, *An Apology for Poetry*, ed. Geoffrey Shepherd (London, 1965), p. 100.

31 'We remember what we knew before when we existed outside the prison of the body. The soul is fired by this memory, and, shaking its wings, by degrees purges itself from contact with the body and its filth and becomes wholly possessed by divine frenzy.' Marsilio Ficino,

Letter 7, 'De divino furore', in *The Letters of Marsilio Ficino*, trans.
members of the Language Department of the School of Economic
Science (London, 1975), i, 44. The Ficinian neoplatonism of the *Maske*
is examined by Sears Jayne, 'The Subject of Milton's Ludlow *Mask*',
PMLA lxxiv (1959), 533–43.

32 See *The Poems of John Milton*, ed. John Carey and Alastair Fowler
(London, 1968), pp. 227–8n.

33 This interpretation opposes the view of David B. Morris, who speaks
of Eloisa's 'determination not to lapse into a stonelike fixity,
contraction, and cold, forgetting state of self-denial' (p. 263). Pope's
earlier poem 'On the Statue of Cleopatra' (*c.* 1710) gives an ironic gloss
to Eloisa's words. In this poem (translated from Castiglione) Cleopatra
speaks *as a statue*, pleading to be able to express her passion:
> Nor is it much to give me back my tears;
> Release my eyes, and let them freely flow;
> 'Tis all the comfort fate has left me now!
> The haughty *Niobe* whose impious pride
> Scorn'd Heaven it self, and durst the Gods deride,
> Still, tho' a rock, can thus relieve her woe,
> And tears eternal from the marble flow.
> No guilt of mine the rage of Heav'n cou'd move;
> I knew no crime, if 'tis no crime to love.
> Then as a lover give me leave to weep . . . (53–62)

Pope, as editor, printed this poem for the first time in *Poems on Several
Occasions* (1717) – the same year as the publication of *Eloisa*.

34 'The apprehensive faculty is subdivided into two parts, inward or
outward. Outward, as the five senses, of touching, hearing, seeing,
smelling, tasting . . . Inward are three – common sense, phantasy,
memory' (Burton, *Anatomy*, I, i, 2, vi. 'Imagination' is discussed in
subsection vii ('Of the Inward Senses'). See also note 8 above.

35 My interpretation of lines 69–70 differs from that of Geoffrey Tillotson,
who paraphrases thus: 'At first I thought you an angel, but when you
taught me that loving was no sin, I retreated from my misconception and
ran back happily through those paths of pleasing sense that I had first
traversed in the opposite direction' (*Pope and Human Nature* (Oxford,
1958), p. 30n. I see the movement as retrogression, not a return.

36 See *The Poems of Sir John Davies*, ed. Robert Krueger (Oxford, 1975), p.
344.

37 Trans. C. T. Wood etc., in *Man and Citizen. Thomas Hobbes's De
Homine and De Cive*, ed. Bernard Gert (New York, 1972), pp. 63–4.

38 Locke asks of the origin of Ideas: 'Whence comes [the mind] by that vast
store which the busy and boundless fancy of man has painted on it with
an almost endless variety?' (*An Essay Concerning Human Understanding*
(1690), II, i, 2). Quotations from Locke are taken from *An Essay*

Concerning Human Understanding, ed. A. D. Woozley (1964).

39   Critics have noted this merging. See Brendan O Hehir, ' "Virtue and Passion": The Dialectic of *Eloisa to Abelard*', *Texas Studies In Literature and Language*, ii (1960), 219–32; reprinted in *Essential Articles*, ed. Mack (Hamden, Conn., 1964), pp. 310–26. The discussion is taken further by Krieger, pp. 36–40.

40   O Hehir sees an opposite movement through the poem, with Eloisa's 'postulated antitheses' drawing closer together (pp. 222–9). Rebecca Price Parkin writes: 'There is nothing but the pattern of constant tossing to and fro and the recognition that only exhaustion (death) can bring it to an end – an end, not a solution' (*The Poetic Workmanship of Alexander Pope* (New York, 1966), p. 73). My own interpretation is closer to Spacks: 'one becomes absorbed in the operations of a sensibility incapable of making real distinctions, yet torn by the sense that the making of distinctions is crucial' (p. 238).

41   This parallel is explored interestingly by James E. Wellington (ed.), *Eloisa to Abelard*, University of Miami Critical Studies, No. 5 (Coral Gables, Fla., 1965), pp. 35–9. See also Reuben A. Brower, *Alexander Pope. The Poetry of Allusion* (Oxford, 1959), p. 75.

42   *The Works of Sir Thomas Browne*, ed. Geoffrey Keynes, 4 vols (London, 1964), iii, 230.

43   O Hehir, pp. 219–21; Krieger, pp. 43–4; and Spacks, p. 235.

44   The 'roseate bow'rs' pick up 'th'unfading rose of *Eden*' (217). Thomas R. Edwards, Jr., remarks of these lines: 'the language leaves little doubt that Pope sees the pitiful tenuousness of this fantasy' (*This Dark Estate*, p. 24). But it is wrong to assume that Pope is here condemning 'fantasy' itself, when Eloisa's struggle throughout has been fought within her imagination.

45   See above, Chapter One, note 10.

46   Girolamo Savonarola, *De Simplicitate Christianae Vitae* (Strassburg, 1615), liber ii, conclusio 7. Quoted by Louis L. Martz, *The Poetry of Meditation*, rev. ed. (New Haven, Conn., 1962), pp. 282–3.

47   Critics who argue the opposite case include Wellington: 'her spiritual commitment remains feeble to the last' (p. 45); and Edwards: 'her final acceptance of her lot seems more an exhausted toleration of what she has than a positive spiritual achievement' (p. 24). I have tried to argue that the disciplining of her imagination is a degree of spiritual achievement. In a persuasive article, Stephen J. Ackerman argues that Eloisa makes positive spiritual progress during the course of the poem; he places her repeated use of 'come' within the context of the 'Veni Creator Spiritus' hymn, showing how 'Pope's allusions to the Holy Spirit suggest that Eloisa's religious fervour at the end is no arbitrarily imposed solution . . .' ('The Vocation of Pope's Eloisa', *SEL* xix (1979), 445–57, p. 455).

CHAPTER THREE

1   'When a man *Reasoneth*, hee does nothing else but conceive a summe totall, from *Addition* of parcels; or conceive a Remainder, from *Substraction* of one summe from another . . . For REASON, in this sense, is nothing but *Reckoning* (that is, Adding and Substracting) of the Consequences of generall names agreed upon, for the *marking* and *signifying* of our thoughts . . .' (*Leviathan*, I, v.).

2   'For after the object is removed, or the eye shut, wee still retain an image of the thing seen, though more obscure than when we see it. And this is it, the Latines call *Imagination*, from the image made in seeing; and apply the same, though improperly, to all the other senses. But the Greeks call it *Fancy*; which signifies *apparence*, and is as proper to one sense, as to another. IMAGINATION therefore is nothing but *decaying sense* . . .' (*Leviathan*, I, ii).

My brief account of Hobbes seriously differs from that of Engell (see p. 6 above) who, I believe, misreads Hobbes's views in making them fit his thesis. My disagreement centres on four points:

(1) Engell's phraseology suggests that Hobbes's 'differentiation' between *imaginatio* and *phantasia* is much more than etymological ('despite his initial care in differentiating *imaginatio* from *phantasia* . . . he uses imagination and fancy as synonyms', p. 14). This implies that Hobbes's equation of the two terms in his own work is careless.

(2) In wishing to enlist Hobbes for 'the creative imagination' Engell uses the terms 'create' and 'creativity' loosely. ('On a "higher" second level, [imagination] produces new pictures and ideas, it fashions new experiences; it adorns and creates; it is the force behind art', p. 15). This seems to be a serious misreading, which introduces Engell's own term 'higher' and uses the words 'new' and 'creates' misleadingly.

(3) Hobbes's description of imagination as 'decaying' and 'weakening' sense is explained away by Engell ('A manner of speech, they mean only that the objects of sense are no longer present. Actually, imagination can produce sharper, more fortified effects than sense impressions, p. 14). What Hobbes says, however, is: 'the longer the time is, after the sight, or Sense, of any object, the weaker is the Imagination'. Hobbes's words are not mere 'manner of speech', and few writers took more care over 'manner of speech' than Hobbes.

(4) Engell appears to ignore Hobbes's repeated distinction between imagination and judgment (see above, p. 44). This leads him to say: 'Hobbes . . . claims that reason itself is a kind of imagination, refined with judgment and the desire for a specific end' (p. 16). Engell's repeated shift of emphasis is subtle, but falsifying. It finally allows him to move into the fanciful himself, so that imagination for Hobbes

becomes 'the driving force of man's intellectual, moral, and emotional being, the dynamo of creative energies and wisdom' (p. 17). By smuggling his own terms into the discussion Engell manages to distort Hobbes's meticulous emphases. Imagination *was* vitally important to him, but not in the ways Engell implies.

3 *Answer to Davenant* (1650), in *Critical Essays of the Seventeenth Century*, vol. ii [1650–1685], ed. J. E. Spingarn (Oxford, 1908), p. 60.

4 See p. 44 above.

5 'Fancy, without the help of Judgement, is not commended as a Vertue: but the later which is Judgement, and Discretion, is commendable for it selfe, without the help of Fancy' (*Leviathan*, I, viii). Seventeenth- and eighteenth-century discussions of the relationship between imagination and judgment are examined by Donald F. Bond, ' "Distrust" of Imagination in English Neo-classicism', *PQ* xiv (1935), 54–69.

6 'Some say the Senses receive the Species of things, and deliver them to the Common-sense; and the Common Sense delivers them over to the Fancy, and the Fancy to the Memory, and the Memory to the Judgement, like handing of things from one to another, with many words making nothing understood' (*Leviathan*, I, ii).

7 DePorte (pp. 6–12) discusses examples of 'modern' mechanistic theories of the brain (concerning animal spirits, nerve fibres, 'Medulary matter' etc.). In *Peri Bathous* (1728) Pope mocks mechanistic notions of poetic creation, and Lawrence Babb has demonstrated the close links between the Cave of Spleen episode (iv, 17–88) and Renaissance and seventeenth-century medical theory ('The Cave of Spleen', *RES* xii (1936), 165–76). See also Swift's 'Digression on Madness' (*A Tale of a Tub*, ch. ix) and *The Mechanical Operation of the Spirit*. Modern mechanistic physiology was ridiculed by their fellow-Scriblerian Dr John Arbuthnot (see *The Memoirs of Martinus Scriblerus*, ed. Charles Kerby-Miller (New Haven, Conn., 1950), pp. 137–41, 280–93). Arbuthnot defended ancient humoral pathology in his *Essay Concerning the Nature of Aliments* (1731), p. 200. On the aversion of Augustan writers to man-as-mechanism, see Fussell, pp. 84–109. The various 'modern' scientific theories of imagination, and their influence on literature, are discussed by G. S. Rousseau, 'Science and the Discovery of the Imagination in Enlightened England', *ECS* iii (1969–70), 108–35.

8 See DePorte, pp. 12–13.

9 See W. B. Hunter, Jr., 'Eve's Demonic Dream', *ELH* xiii (1946), 255–65. Hunter (pp. 262–3) quotes John Smith (*Select Discourses*, 1673) as maintaining that evil spirits can only touch the reason *indirectly*, through the medium of the imagination. Burton (*Anatomy*, I, 2, i, 2) remarks that Satan 'begins first with the phantasy, & moves that so strongly, that no reason is able to resist'.

10 On the *ignis fatuus* as an image of the delusive imagination, see Chapter Five, note 12 below.

11 Dennis H. Burden says of Satan's address: 'It is a poetry of beautiful unreason. The stars of night do not shine out of their joy in Eve's beauty and it was in order to show up this irrationality that Milton had arranged for Adam to talk with Eve on the previous evening about precisely why they do shine (iv, 660–75). Satan is speaking the satanic poetry that has charm but no sense' (*The Logical Epic* (London, 1967), p. 130).

12 See Burden, pp. 126–39.

13 Bernardo Tomitano, *Quattro libri della lingua thoscana* (3rd ed., Padova, 1570), p. 419; quoted by Hathaway, p. 312.

14 *Timber: Or, Discoveries* (*Works*, ed. Herford and Simpson, viii (Oxford, 1947), 564).

15 'I think that tastes, odors, colors, and so on are no more than mere names so far as the objects in which we place them are concerned, and that they reside only in the consciousness. Hence if the living creature were removed, all these qualities would be wiped away' (Galileo, *The Assayer* (Rome, 1623), trans. Stillman Drake, *Discoveries and Opinions of Galileo* (New York, 1957), p. 274).

16 D. J. Gordon, 'Poet and Architect: The Intellectual Setting of the Quarrel Between Ben Jonson and Inigo Jones', *JWCI* xii (1949), 152–78, considers the quarrel in terms of Jonson's distinction between the *soul* and the *body* of a masque; the *soul* lies in the controlling conception ('invention') addressed to the understanding; the mere *body* is the glittering outer show addressed to the senses.

17 The effect of Pope's introduction of the sylphs into the poem is very perceptively discussed by Robin Grove, 'Uniting Airy Substance: *The Rape of the Lock* 1712–1736', in *The Art of Alexander Pope*, ed. Howard Erskine-Hill and Anne Smith (London, 1979) (Hereafter cited as Erskine-Hill and Smith), pp. 52–88.

18 J. P. Hardy, *Reinterpretations* (London, 1971), p. 66.

19 John Dennis, *Remarks on Mr Pope's Rape of the Lock* (1728). See *Pope: the Critical Heritage*, ed. John Barnard (1973), p. 103.

20 Brower, p. 155.

21 Twickenham ed., ii, 122.

22 See Thomas R. Edwards, Jr., 'The Colors of Fancy: An Image Cluster in Pope', *MLN* lxxiii (1958), 485–9.

23 See p. 17 above.

24 This advertisement is printed in *The Rape Observ'd*, ed. Clarence Tracy (Toronto and Buffalo, 1974), p. 14.

25 Frederick Bracher, 'Pope's Grotto: the Maze of Fancy', *HLQ* xii (1948–9), 141–62, considers the grotto as 'a continuing expression of Pope's old delight in wandering in the maze of fancy' (p. 161). Pope's

own description of his grotto in 1725 gives it a similar character: 'When you shut the Doors of this Grotto, it becomes on the instant, from a luminous Room, a *Camera obscura*; on the Walls of which all the objects of the River, Hills, Woods, and Boats, are forming a moving Picture in their visible Radiations: And when you have a mind to light it up, it affords you a very different Scene: it is finished with Shells interspersed with Pieces of Looking-glass in angular forms; and in the Cieling is a Star of the same Material, at which when a Lamp (of an orbicular Figure of thin Alabaster) is hung in the Middle, a thousand pointed Rays glitter and are reflected over the Place' (Pope to Edward Blount, 2 June 1725).

26 Quoted by Bracher, p. 147.

27 See Twickenham ed., ii, 121; and Maynard Mack, 'Mock-heroic in *The Rape of the Lock*' (1950), in *Pope: 'The Rape of the Lock': a Casebook*, ed. John Dixon Hunt (1968), pp. 154–7, p. 156.

28 This interpretation is close to Robin Grove: 'the poetry seems to gain strength from recognizing just how elusive the moral order it creates from moment to moment is. No solidified morality could do justice to Belinda's world; and strict justice anyway is the last thing the Sylphs would want' (Erskine-Hill and Smith, p. 73). I wish to link this elusiveness with the 'amorality' of the imagination.

29 The evidence for its attribution to Pope is given in full by Ault, pp. lxv–lxvii.

30 *Antony and Cleopatra*, II, ii, 193–4, 203, 211–12.

31 'The Nymph, tho' in this mangled Plight,
Must ev'ry Morn her Limbs unite.
But how shall I describe her Arts
To recollect the scatter'd Parts?
Or shew the Anguish, Toil, and Pain,
Of gath'ring up herself again?'
  ('A Beautiful Young Nymph Going to Bed', 65–70).

32 Cleanth Brooks, 'The Case of Miss Arabella Fermor: a Re-Examination', *Sewanee Review* li (1943), 505–24. Reprinted in *The Well Wrought Urn* (1968 ed.), 65–84, p. 77.

33 'Thus after four important Hours / Celia's the Wonder of her Sex . . .' ('The Progress of Beauty', 41–2).

34 Hugo Reichard, 'The Love Affair in Pope's *Rape of the Lock*', *PMLA* lxix (1954), 887–902. J. S. Cunningham also follows this line (*Pope: 'The Rape of the Lock'*, p. 55).

35 '(*Sir Plume*, of *Amber Snuff-box* justly vain, / And the nice Conduct of a *clouded Cane*)' (iv, 123–4). Sir Plume is Thalestris' beau and Belinda's ally. There are suggestions in his name and accoutrements that he is part of Belinda's fanciful world: we recall the 'plumes' in which Spenser's *Fancy* was clothed (p. 60 above) and which relate Sir Plume to the airy sylphs; it should also be noted that his snuffbox is a 'fancy', and his

attitude reminiscent of the foppish Mr Novel, satirised in *The Female Tatler* 27 (5–7 Sept. 1709): 'Novel changes his *Snuff-box* very often, saying, he admired how he came to have such a plaguy dull Fancy . . . He cannot pass by a *Milliners* Shop, without going in and getting a new *Ribbon* for his Cane.' The relationship between *coquettes* and *plumes* is alluded to by Leonard Welsted in his poem 'To the Countess of Warwick, On her Marriage with Mr Addison, Aug. 2, 1716' (in what may be a humorous allusion to Pope's poem):

> Thy bright Example shall instruct the Fair,
> And future Nymphs shall make Renown their Care;
> Embroid'ry less shall charm the Virgin's Eye,
> And kind Coquets, for Plumes, less frequent die'
>   (*Epistles, Odes, &c.* (1724), p. 21).

36 '[Ariel] would not like to have Belinda "lose her heart" to any one beau . . . and when he presently detects "an earthly lover lurking at her heart," he abandons the girl . . . because she no longer meets his high standards of purity, levity, and honor' (Reichard, pp. 897–8). It is important to understand, rather, that the sylphs do not have 'standards'.

37 Aubrey Williams, 'The "Fall" of China and *The Rape of the Lock*', *PQ* xli (1962), 412–25, p. 420.

38 See, for example, Arnold Stein's note on 'mazie error' (iv, 239) in his *Answerable Style: Essays on Paradise Lost* (Seattle and London, 1967), pp. 66–7. In sonnet 38 of *Astrophil and Stella* Sidney speaks of 'my fancie's error' (line 5). Pope's *Odyssey* (tr. Fenton) has 'the serpent-mazes of deceit' (*Odyssey*, iv, 342), a phrase which draws these conventional associations together.

39 See *The Poems of Sir Walter Ralegh*, ed. Agnes M. C. Latham (London, 1951), pp. xlv–liii, and p. 78.

40 See also the opening of Prior's 'To the Honourable Charles Montagu, Esq.' (1692):

> 'Howe'er, 'tis well, that whilst Mankind
>   Thro' Fate's Fantastick Mazes errs,
> He can Imagin'd Pleasures find,
>   To combat against Real Cares.
>
> Fancies and Notions we pursue,
>   Which ne'er had Being but in Thought:
> And like the doting Artist, woo,
>   The Image we our selves have wrought.'

41 *Works*, ed. Herford and Simpson, viii (Oxford, 1947), 588.

42 Murray Krieger, 'The "Frail China Jar" and the Rude Hand of Chaos', *Centennial Review of Arts and Sciences* (1961). Reprinted in *Pope: 'The Rape of the Lock', a Casebook*, ed. John Dixon Hunt (1968), 201–19, p. 210.

43 J. S. Cunningham, *Pope: 'The Rape of the Lock'* (1961), pp. 44–5.

44 Quoted by Babb, *RES* xii (1936), p. 167. Thomas Nashe notes that '[the melancholy humour] with his thicke steaming fennie vapours casteth a mist over the spirit, and cleane bemasketh the phantasie' (*The Terrors of the Night* (1594). *Works*, ed. Ronald B. McKerrow (Oxford, 1966), i, 354).

45 'The central action in the poem is Belinda's descent from coquette to prude, from the dazzling rival of the sun . . . to the rancorous Amazon who shrieks in self-righteous anger' (Martin Price, *To the Palace of Wisdom* (1970 ed.), p. 151).

46 This is not to suggest that Clarissa's speech does not show Pope's imagination at work. John Butt has rightly pointed out that 'the many-layered richness' of the passage fuses his three inspirations 'drawn from fancy, morality, and books' ('The Inspiration of Pope's Poetry', in *Essays in the Eighteenth Century. Presented to David Nichol Smith* (Oxford, 1945), pp. 65–79). Clarissa shows how the 'fancy' can *serve* truth. By incorporating her speech for the 1717 edition of his *Works*, Pope clearly felt the need to make the claims of truth explicit.

47 'I make use of my Judgment more deliberately than I yet have done . . . I have of late been moulting: not for fresh feathers and wings: they are gone, and in their stead I hope to have a pair of patient sublunary legs' (Keats–Reynolds, 11 July 1819).

CHAPTER FOUR

1 Felicity A. Nussbaum, 'Pope's "To a Lady" and the Eighteenth-Century Woman', *PQ* liv (1975), 444–56, offers a reading of the poem set against typical expressions of contemporary views of women. In doing so, she touches on the theme I wish to follow through: 'The light images show the ephemeral nature of their flickering light, as well as the affected falseness of fanciful women . . . Governed by fancy and imagination, the women allow inconsequential occurrences to disconcert them' (p. 449). Thomas R. Edwards, Jr., remarks that the women in Pope's poem 'enact their fantasies as though they were experiences. Whether they feel too little, like Cloe, or too much, like Atossa, they are isolated from every reality except death' (*This Dark Estate*, pp. 73–4).

2 Edmund Waller gave a witty turn to the theme in 'To the Mutable Fair', a poem which finds an echo in Pope's *Epistle to a Lady*:
> Now will I wander through the air,
> Mount, make a stoop at every fair,
> And with a fancy unconfin'd
> (As lawless as the Sea or wind)
> Pursue you whereso'er you flie,
> And with your various thoughts comply. (1645 *Poems*, p. 65)

Here woman's changeableness is understood in terms of the unconfined imagination, and the poet resolves to transform himself as often as her fancy shifts its object. Waller remarks with a mixture of delight and frustration: 'never were the clouds reduc'd / To any Art'. In a similar way Pope declares at the beginning of his *Epistle* that his style will attempt to adapt itself to the variable nature of his subject ('Chuse a firm Cloud'). Pope, however, manages to combine Waller's witty gesture on behalf of his art with a certain moral toughness which comprehends many more aspects of female behaviour.

3   Female beauty, by taking the man's 'fancy', caused him naturally to associate woman with the imaginative faculty, and man's treatment of both was strikingly similar. Just as imagination could overthrow the judgment, so a woman's beauty could strike a male as irrational: 'an agreeableness that charms us without correctness, like a mistress whose faults we see, but love her with them all' (Pope–Cromwell, 20 July 1710). Pope is here talking about Ovid's elegies, but his choice of the mistress image illustrates how judgment and correctness could be thought to be suspended by woman's charm.

4   Adam acknowledges to Raphael that he has a proper sense of Eve's inferior mental powers:

'in outward shew
Elaborate, of inward less exact.
For well I understand in the prime end
Of Nature her th'inferiour, in the mind
And inward Faculties . . .' (*PL*, viii, 538–42)

5   See pp. 68–9 above.

6   By 1735 there had developed a close association between the female mind and the variety of colours; women were considered to excel at *fancy work*, and their skill at embroidery was usually attributed in part to their expertise in mingling the colours: (i) *Woman's Superior Excellence over Man . . . By Sophia* (1740) points out that women are supreme in 'works of fancy' and explains that in embroidery great skill is required 'to distribute the threads, to mingle the colours, to diversify the shades' (p. 79); (ii) In his poem 'On a Brede of Divers Colours, Woven by Four Ladies' Waller explores the analogy between the varied colours in the embroidery (which outdo the peacock and rainbow) and the minds of the ladies, 'where all their fancies shine'; (iii) *Darius's Feast: or, The Force of Truth* (1734) juxtaposes the 'native Lustre' of Truth against 'tinsel Vanities':

'Skill'd in the various Loom, the *female Race*
Weave curious Garments, silver'd o'er, or wrought
With gay Embroidery; the blended Colours
Red, azure, purple, green, are taught to shine
In bright Confusion . . .' (p. 10).

7   See Norman Ault, *New Light on Pope* (London, 1949), pp. 49–59.

8   Frank Brady, 'The History and Structure of Pope's *To a Lady*', *SEL* ix (1969), 439–62, has highlighted the dangers of making structural points about the poem: the ordering of the portraits differs between editions and the poem as we have it 'is no immutable "organic" whole' (p. 462).

9   'Running through the poem is an implicit analogy between the variability and ostentation of vain women and the broken light and color of dazzling but superficial painting' (*To the Palace of Wisdom* (1964), p. 160).

10 There is a close resemblance here to the art of Jane Austen's fanciful *Emma* (*Emma*, ch. 6) who in sketching Harriet Smith tries to catch 'a peculiarity in the shape of the eye and the lines about the mouth' but ends by making her subject 'too tall' (as the Johnsonian Mr Knightley points out). Her various attempts at sketching in different mediums (none of them finished) betray her as fanciful and impressionistic, though certainly not without a talent for detail.

11 Here I depart from Elizabeth Gurr: 'There is a sternness and physical repugnance in Pope's attack on the characters of women and none of the amused, forgiving tone of his attack on the characters of men' (*Pope* (Edinburgh, 1971), pp. 73–4).

12 The relationship between imagination and sympathy in moral and aesthetic theory is traced by Walter Jackson Bate, 'The Sympathetic Imagination in Eighteenth-Century English Criticism', *ELH* xii (1945), 144–64. The earliest formulation of this relationship, according to Bate, is that by James Arbuckle (*Dublin Journal* 1722). It is interesting to note how paradoxically Arbuckle treats man's capacity for '*Building Castles in the Air*': on the one hand, 'to give a loose to Fancy in its wild Rambles after chimerical Pleasure . . . may greatly perplex us in the Management of the common Affairs of Life, and divert us from pursuing them with due Intention and Application, by filling the Head with romantick Notions . . . and [be] productive of nothing but Disappointment and Repentance', and yet this 'Power of imagining fictitious Enjoyments' can express itself in identification (and therefore sympathy) with the circumstances of others – what he calls 'a kind of *Castle-Building* backwards' ('Hence we may see the Wisdom of our Creator in giving us this imagining *Faculty*, and such a Facility of placing our selves in Circumstances different from those we are really in . . .'). Although Pope does not take Arbuckle's 'benevolist' line he does make artistic use of the notion of the sympathetic imagination, and he does likewise balance it with an awareness of the follies of castle-building (the 'air-built Castle . . . The Maid's romantic wish', *Dunciad Variorum*, iii, 10–11). James Engell (*The Creative Imagination*, p. 145) misrepresents Arbuckle's view by including it in his section 'Faith in the Imagination' and by not

mentioning Arbuckle's insistence on the delusive nature of much imaginative activity.

13 *A Collection of Miscellany Letters, Selected out of Mist's Weekly Journal, The Fourth Volume* (London, 1727), p. 174.

14 Our first sight of the unfallen pair offers a significant contrast:

> 'Not equal, as thir sex not equal seemd;
> For contemplation hee and valour formd,
> For softness shee and sweet attractive Grace,
> Hee for God only, shee for God in him:
> His fair large Front and Eye sublime declar'd
> Absolute rule . . .' (*PL*, iv, 296–301)

15 *ARS* 180, introd. Felicity A. Nussbaum,

16 Pope's 'Argument' (added for the 1735 *Works*) categorizes the sketches: 'the *Affected*, Ver. 7, &c. The *Soft-natur'd*. 29. the *Cunning*, 45. the *Whimsical*, 53. the *Wits and Refiners*, 87. the *Stupid* and *Silly*, 101' (Twickenham ed., III, ii, 44).

17 Twickenham ed., vi, 286–7.

18 Perhaps the best known 'romantick' lady of Pope's day was Bridget Tipkin ('Parthenissa') in Sir Richard Steele's popular comedy *The Tender Husband* (1705), regularly performed in the 1730s. She is fancifulness personified, valuing everything for its appearance, and lives in a make-believe world of surfaces and gestures taken from her favourite romances: 'Since there is room for Fancy in a Picture, I wou'd be drawn like the Amazon *Thalestris*, with a Spear in my Hand, and an Helmet on a Table before me – At a distance behind let there be a Dwarf, holding by the Bridle a Milk-white Palfrey . . .' (IV, ii, 87–90). This fanciful attitude towards painting is recalled by lines 5–16 of Pope's *Epistle* ('How many pictures of one Nymph we view . . . If Folly grows romantic, I must paint it'). Bridget's aunt tells her that such romances are 'fit only to corrupt young Girls, and fill their Heads with a thousand foolish Dreams of I don't know what' (II, ii, 74–5). Much Augustan satire against romances and sensational novels was focused on the way such reading fed the imaginations of women, gave them false notions, played on their passions, and substituted a vibrant fantasy for a duller reality. The author of *Woman Unmask'd, and Dissected* (1740), for example, thought the matter simple: 'What most proportion's their exalted Fancies? / The Flash of *Novells*! Vapour of *Romancies*! (p. 67). See also Lady Mary Chudleigh on 'Romances and Trifles' (p. 87 above).

19 Johnsŏn, *Preface to Shakespeare* (1765). (*Johnson on Shakespeare*, ed. Arthur Sherbo (New Haven and London, 1968), i, 84).

20 See p. 88 above.

21 Seen from this angle the *Epistle* does not quite resemble a tour of a portrait gallery (see Pat Rogers, *An Introduction to Pope* (London, 1975),

p. 71; and Hagstrum, pp. 238–9). A closer analogy is perhaps a more informal one: Emma Woodhouse (*Emma*, ch. 6) displaying her sketches in turn – heads and full lengths, rapid drawings and almost-finished watercolours; she is pleased with her knack and her ability to capture elusive details, yet is aware that some of her sitters could not hold still. Among these sketches is one finished portrait sent off to be framed, but it betrays more zeal than skill and has sacrificed truth to flattery. (See n. 10 above).

22 An interesting perspective on this is given by Joseph Dorman's 'Ballad Comedy' *The Female Rake* (1736) published shortly after the appearance of Pope's poem. This displays Pope's line ('ev'ry Woman is at heart a Rake') on its title-page, and the contents show that the heroine, Sylvia, has benefited from reading *Epistle to a Lady*. Central to Dorman's piece is the contrast between Libertina, lover of masquerades, balls and operas, and Sylvia, who echoes the sentiments on which Pope's *Epistle* ends: 'When . . . a few Wrinkles shall succeed that Bloom, your Reason will be a faithful Guide to point you out that Calmness and Serenity of Mind which must for ever fix your Repose . . .' (p. 34), to which the restless Libertina retorts: 'ev'ry Moment, not bestow'd on Pleasure, is for ever Lost' (p. 34). It is left to Sylvia to point out (in song) the difference between their attitudes to life: 'While she pursues imaginary Joy, / My Time, in useful Studies, I'll employ . . .' (p. 34). Dorman's point is not subtly made, but his juxtaposition of restless activity and serenity of mind, of fleeting and lasting, of 'imaginary Joy' and the guidance of reason, show that he has understood the terms on which *Epistle to a Lady* is written.

23 In introducing the 'Ring' in Hyde Park (the parade-ground of fashionable society) in terms of fatiguing dazzle and glare, Pope may have been recalling *The Circus: or, British Olympicks: a Satyr on the Ring in Hide-Park* (1709) (See p. 95 above). That poem makes much of the glitter of clothes and equipages as they compete one against the other, and relates this to the 'fancy' which the scene of restless pleasure represents:

> 'A thousand diff'rent Whims possess the Mind,
> To Day they love, to Morrow are Inclin'd
> Fantastickly to vary like the Wind . . .
> The tinsel Harness glitters in his Eyes,
> And makes him fancy, as he's great he's wise.' (p. 6)

There is fierce competition between equipages in 'the Gilding, Carving, or the brightest Glass' and colours are used to lure the fancies of the opposite sex ('Ribbons singly prove / The Colour which conduces most to love', p. 12). The superficial dazzle of the scene makes the author cry out in exasperation: 'How strangely we're in Love with Colours grown?' (p. 13). Irrespective of Pope's knowledge of the poem, a scene such as this was probably in his mind as he turned from the busy, fatiguing parade-ring to the constant and well-tempered figure of Martha Blount.

CHAPTER FIVE

1 J. Philip Brockbank has said of *The Dunciad*: 'A laborious mode of analysis can never arrive at its art, for like the life and literature and language from which it emerges, it is not so much a structure . . . as a flux, refusing to stay for methodical inspection' ('The Book of Genesis and the Genesis of Books: the Creation of Pope's *Dunciad*', Erskine-Hill and Smith, pp. 192–211, p. 192.)

2 In his influential essay, 'Towards Defining an Age of Sensibility' (*ELH*, xxiii, (1956), pp. 144–52), Northrop Frye associates 'literature as process' with that age (*c.* 1750–1800). My analysis of *The Dunciad Variorum* suggests that Pope recognized this trend in his own age and was uneasy about its implications.

3 '*Nostoch* is that which we call a falling star, a kind of gelly or slime found oftentimes in the Summer in fields, and meadowes' (1650: *OED s.v.* 'nostoc'). See reference to Cowley below.

4 Dulness shares, for example, some of the qualities of the figure *Nemesis* as invoked by the chorus of Egyptians in Samuel Daniel's *Cleopatra* (1594):

> '. . . the worlds great Arbitresse
> And Queene of causes raigning here . . .
> Thou from darke-clos'd eternity,
> From thy blacke cloudy hidden seate,
> The worlds disorders dost descry . . .' (755–68)

5 Parallels between the Cave of Spleen and the Cave of Poverty and Poetry are discussed by Pat Rogers, 'Faery Lore and *The Rape of the Lock*, *RES* xxv (1974), 25–38, p. 32n.

6 A powerful use of *synteresis* occurs in Satire VIII of Marston's *Scourge of Villainy* (1598), in a passage close in theme and imagery to *The Dunciad Variorum*:

> 'Now doth the body, led with senseless will
> (The which, in reason's absence, ruleth still),
> Rave, talk idly, as 'twere some deity,
> Adoring female painted puppetry;
> Playing at put-pin, doting on some glass . . .
> Toying with babies, and with fond pastime,
> Some children's sport, deflowering of chaste time;
> Employing all his wits in vain expense,
> Abusing all his organons of sense.
> Return, return, sacred Synderesis!

Inspire our trunks! Let not such mud as this
Pollute us still. Awake our lethargy,
Raise us from out our brain-sick foolery!' (201–14)
Like Pope, Marston here draws together the ideas of anarchy, mud,
madness, infant games and misdirected activity. He pleads for the spark
of divine conscience to break through, and for men to turn away from
the false deity which deceives and enervates them.

7   'from the ardor of divine love, conceived in the intellect and in the will,
     there overflows into sense the heat which, with the consumption of all
     earthly humidity, kindles the heavenly thirst' (Pico, *De Imaginatione*, tr.
     Caplan, p. 97).

8   Spenser, *An Hymne of Heavenly Love*, 168; Milton, *Colasterion*
     (Complete Prose Works, ii (New Haven and London, 1959), 747).

9   Thomas Middleton, *The Ghost of Lucrece* (1600), 475.

10   Johnson's 'philosopher' uses the meteor image to contrast 'reason' and
     'fancy': 'He compared reason to the sun, of which the light is constant,
     uniform, and lasting; and fancy to a meteor, of bright but transitory
     lustre, irregular in its motion, and delusive in its direction' (*Rasselas*
     (1759), ch. xviii).

11   The commonest image for abiogenesis, or 'equivocal generation', was
     the 'serpent of old Nile' (Antony's name for Cleopatra, *Antony and*
     Cleopatra, I, v, 25; see above, Chapter One, n. 12). M. R. Ridley (Arden
     edition) quotes Sylvester's *Du Bartas* (1621 ed.): 'As on the edges of som
     standing Lake . . . / The foamy slime transformeth oft / To green
     half-Tadpoles, . . . / Half dead, half-living; half a frog, *half-mud*.' This
     is close to the imagery of the *Dunciad* passage. Pope used the image
     satirically in *An Essay on Criticism*:
     'Those half-learn'd Witlings, num'rous in our Isle,
     As half form'd Insects on the Banks of *Nile*;
     Unfinish'd Things, one knows not what to call,
     Their Generation's so *equivocal*' (40–3)

12   Crashaw describes the delusions of hope in similar terms, contrasting
     the North Star of Reason with the uncertain, misleading gleams of
     imagination; he addresses Hope:
     'Thine empty cloud the eye, it selfe deceives
     With shapes that our owne fancie gives:
     A cloud, which gilt, and painted now appeares,
     But must drop presently in teares.
     When thy false beames o're Reasons light prevaile,
     By *ignes fatui*, not North starres we sayle.'
     ('On Hope', 45–50)
     Milton expresses the delusiveness of Satan through this image, as the
     serpent leads Eve to the forbidden tree (*PL*., ix, 634–42).

13   *OED* (*s.v.* 'dull' 8) quotes: 'Dulle sighted or poreblinde' (Huloet 1552);

'A light Gray Gelding . . . dull Sighted, especially in the right Eye'
(*London Gazette* 1668); 'I'll not be made a soft and dull-ey'd fool'
(*Merchant of Venice*, III, iii, 14). John Russell Brown (Arden edition)
glosses the latter as 'easily deceived', quoting as a parallel Fletcher, *Elder
Brother* (1637), I, ii, 231: 'Though I be dull-eyed, I see through this
juggling.' Dull-sightedness therefore involves, literally or metaphori-
cally, an inability to see clearly.

14 Pope may, in part, be parodying this arrangement when he describes
Jove's privy in Book ii:

> 'There in his seat two spacious Vents appear,
> On this he sits, to that he leans his ear,
> And hears the various Vows of fond mankind,
> Some beg an eastern, some a western wind . . .' (ii, 81–4)

15 When Lady Mary Wortley Montagu tried to draft a riposte to the
original *Dunciad* she reworked this cave in a manner which turned the
poet's allusion back on himself. In her version Dulness's retreat is
identified with Pope's own grotto; it may glitter inside, but it is beneath
the mud and enwrapped in mist, so that the delightful Cave of Fancy
has become the dark, unhealthy den of the splenetic satirist:

> 'Her Palace placed beneath a muddy road . . .
> Here chose the Goddess her belov'd Retreat
> Which Phoebus trys in vain to penetrate,
> Adorn'd within by Shells of small expense
> (Emblems of tinsel Rhime, and triffleing Sense),
> Perpetual fogs enclose the sacred Cave,
> The neighbouring Sinks their fragrant Odours gave.'

(*Lady Mary Wortley Montagu: Essays and Poems, and Simplicity, a Comedy*,
ed. Robert Halsband and Isobel Grundy (Oxford, 1977), p. 247).

16 Clive T. Probyn, 'Pope's Bestiary: the Iconography of Deviance'
(Erskine-Hill and Smith, pp. 212–30) explores the theme of 'metamorphosis and mutation' in Pope's poetry, and he notes in this passage from
The Dunciad 'change, metamorphosis, mutation, the merging of
species into fantastic forms' (pp. 216–17). 'Pope's most subtle artistry
went into the cogent, imaginative re-creation of ambivalent, hybrid
imagery of man's weakness in the actual world . . . A conviction of the
reality of distinct boundaries between species provided Pope with the
confidence to create imaginative transgressors of those boundaries' (p.
221).

17 Ovid, *Metamorphoses*, i, 5–20. This chaos-passage was much imitated.
One little-known example which may be a further source for Pope's
passage is the Court of Chaos described by Sir Richard Blackmore (one
of the leading 'dunces'):

> '. . . ancient, barren Night did pregnant grow,
> And quicken'd with the World in Embrio.

The struggling Seeds of unshap'd Matter ly,
Contending in her Womb for Victory.
No Order, Form, or Parts distinct and clear,
Did in the Crude Conception, yet appear.
Thick Darkness did the unripe Light Embrace,
That faintly glanc'd on Chaos shady Face.
The unfledg'd Fire has no bright Wings to rise,
But scarce distinguish'd, with the Water lies . . .
Besides vast numbers of loose Atoms stray,
And in the restless Deep of Chaos play.
In dark Encounters they for Empire strive,
And gain what Chance, and wild Confusion give.'
(Sir Richard Blackmore, *Prince Arthur: an Heroick Poem: in Ten Books*
(London, 1695), ii, 25–52).

18 See Felicity Rosslyn, 'Pope and Cowley', *N&Q* ccxxii (1977), 237–8.

19 The indebtedness of Pope's 'chaos' passage to this description by
Oldham has been pointed out by Paul Hammond, *John Oldham and the
Renewal of Classical Culture* (Cambridge, 1983). See his discussion on
pp. 211–12.

20 The Dryden passage is discussed in relation to Pope's 'sense of non-
conscious life' in *The Dunciad*, by Emrys Jones, *PBA* liv (1968), 251.

21 Swift's bee accuses the spider of being a creature who 'by a lazy
Contemplation of four Inches round; by an over-weening Pride,
which, feeding and engendring on it self, turns all into Excrement and
Venom; producing nothing at all but Fly-bane and a Cobweb' (*The
Battle of the Books*, ed. H. J. Real (Berlin and New York, 1978), p. 10).
Leonard Welsted (for whom Imitation is 'the Bane of Writing') reverses
the image in praising originality in an author: 'that which truly and
lastingly pleases in Writing, is always the Result of a Man's own Force,
and of that first Cast of Soul, which gives him a Promptitude to excel; it
is his proper Wealth, and he draws it out of himself, as the Silk-Worm
spins out of her own Bowels that soft ductile Substance, which is
wrought into so great a Variety of Ornaments' (Preface to *Epistles,
Odes, &c.* (London, 1724), p. xxxviii). Such views consign Welsted to
the court of Dulness.

22 Dulness feels at home amongst children: 'The Taste of the *Bathos* is
implanted by Nature itself in the Soul of Man . . . Accordingly, we see
the unprejudiced Minds of Children delight only in such Productions,
and in such Images, as our true modern Writers set before them' (Pope,
Peri Bathous, p. 10).

23 Robin Grove, 'Uniting Airy Substance: *The Rape of the Lock* 1712–
1736', Erskine-Hill and Smith, pp. 52–88, p. 74.

24 *An Introduction to Pope* (London, 1975), p. 128. See also his *The Augustan
Vision* (London, 1974), p. 27.

25 See p. 44 above.

26 DePorte (p. 33) quotes two statements by Zachary Mayne: 'all Men do naturally Think and Reason alike', and 'yet there is no end of the Changes and Variations that may be made in Ideas, by Men's Imaginations operating differently in them . . .' (*Two Dissertations concerning Sense, and the Imagination* (London, 1728), p. 74).

27 E.g. i, 53–82; ii, 31–48; ii, 135–48; iii, 229–44. John E. Sitter, *The Poetry of Pope's Dunciad* (Minneapolis, 1971), touches on the issue of 'indiscriminateness' and 'verbal chaos' in Pope's descriptions (pp. 28, 30). Tony Tanner, 'Reason and the Grotesque: Pope's *Dunciad*', *Critical Quarterly* vii (1965), 145–60, links the mergings, monstrosities and dissolutions in the poem with the art of the grotesque.

28 Alvin B. Kernan, '*The Dunciad* and the Plot of Satire', *SEL* ii (1962), 255–66, pp. 259, 261.

29 Kernan writes penetratingly on the vortex image in the poem: 'Pope has so arranged his poem that this ultimate expansion is at once a contraction. At the very moment that dulness becomes everything, everything becomes nothing . . . The vortex is the figure Pope uses here, and it renders in geometrical terms the 'plot' of the poem. The turbulent outer lip swirls round and round growing ever larger and engulfing more and more. It sucks in water and rubbish and whirls them downward through narrowing circles, which end at last in the pinpoint of nothingness' (p. 262). Pope's interest in vortices is discussed by Marjorie Nicolson and G. S. Rousseau, '*This Long Disease, My Life': Alexander Pope and the Sciences* (Princeton, N.J., 1968), pp. 199–206; and J. Philip Brockbank, 'The Book of Genesis and the Genesis of Books: the Creation of Pope's *Dunciad*', Erskine-Hill and Smith, pp. 192–211, pp. 205–8.

30 'It is often said that self-referring fictions are peculiar products of the introspective "modern mind". But . . . Readers of Dante, of Chaucer, of Spenser, know that imagination's most appropriate personification has always been Narcissus' (Isabel G. MacCaffrey, *Spenser's Allegory: the Anatomy of Imagination* (Princeton, N.J., 1976), p. 10). Hobbes notes that 'when [fancy] seemeth to fly from one Indies to the other, and from Heaven to Earth . . . the voyage is not great, her self being all she seeks' (Springarn, ii, 59). The comforting and self-confirming implications of subjectivity are summed up in Sir Richard Steele's Mrs Clerimont, whose truest friend is her mirror: 'What pretty Company a Glass is, to have another self! (*Kisses the Dog*.) To converse in Soliloquy! To have Company that never contradicts or displeases us! The pretty visible Eccho of our Actions (*Kisses the Dog*.)' (*The Tender Husband*, 1705, III, i, 13–16).

31 See also iii, 247–8, where Settle replies to Theobald: 'Son! what thou seek'st is in thee. Look, and find / Each monster meets his likeness in thy mind.'

32 DePorte (pp. 30–48) explores the relationship between madness and subjectivity: 'the quest of thinking men in the late seventeenth and early eighteenth centuries for external standards by which to establish what was real or fanciful, good or evil, is closely connected with their identification of extreme subjectivity with madness' (p. 37), and he aptly quotes Shaftesbury (p. 44): 'spectres may impose on us, whilst we refuse to turn them every way, and view their shapes and complexions in every light. For that which can be shown only in a certain light is questionable. Truth, 'tis supposed, may bear all lights' (*Characteristics*, ed. John M. Robertson (Indianapolis, 1964), p. 44). Pope's Dulness exemplifies, in these terms, the subjectivity of certain types of imaginative activity.

33 Pope–Cromwell, 12 Nov. 1711 (see p. 17 above).

34 (i) Howard Erskine-Hill, 'The "New World" of Pope's *Dunciad*', *Renaissance and Modern Studies*, vi (1962), 47–67 (in *Essential Articles for the study of Alexander Pope*, ed. Maynard Mack (Hamden, Conn., 1968), 803–24, pp. 811–15); (ii) Emrys Jones, 'Pope and Dulness', *PBA* liv (1968), 231–63, pp. 252–6; (iii) Traugott Lawler, ' "Wafting Vapours from the Land of Dreams": Virgil's Fourth and Sixth Eclogues and the *Dunciad*', *SEL* xiv (1974), 373–86 (in *Pope: Recent Essays by Several Hands*, ed. Maynard Mack and James A. Winn (Brighton, 1980), 731–48, pp. 746–8.

35 Jones, pp. 256, 255, 252.

36 Mack and Winn, p. 747.

37 'Poetry is a *natural* or *morbid Secretion from the Brain* . . . there is hardly any human Creature past Childhood, but at one time or other has had some Poetical Evacuation, and no question was much the better for it in his Health . . .' (*Peri Bathous* (1728), pp. 12–13).

38 Erskine-Hill seems to me to strike the right balance: 'One can only conclude that here [the mud-nymphs passage], as in the other passages discussed, Pope wished to create and explore, for its own sake, an imagined world of folly, that he saw this "world" as something strange, fascinating and complex, surrealistically awe-inspiring or beautiful as well as ridiculous and offensive, and that he was concerned that it should not be presented as wholly repulsive' (Mack, p. 812). He adds: 'Pope may be said to observe the fantastic decorum of Dulness, and to make the world he is describing more immediate to the reader by permitting something of its irrationality to enter into the structure of his poem' (p. 814). Fredric V. Bogel, 'Dulness Unbound: Rhetoric and Pope's *Dunciad*', *PMLA* xcvii (1982), 844–55, tackles this problem of 'satiric contamination' by challenging 'the received image of rhetoric . . . [which] has kept us from assimilating the troubled responses of numerous readers of the *Dunciad*' (pp. 844–5).

39 Interestingly, Blackmore's poem *The Kit-Cats* (1708, reprinted in his

Collection of Poems on Various Subjects (1718), pp. 103–23) includes a
description of The Temple of Dullness, a place where thought is dulled
by the fumes of tobacco and Dullness's votaries are *lulled to sleep* around
his throne:

> 'The Vot'ries here eternal Silence keep,
> And unreproach'd their Worship pay asleep.
> The Idol is compos'd of Massy Lead,
> And Wreaths of Poppy-Flowers adorn his Head:
> Lolling and Yawning in his Chair of State,
> His Head reclin'd, the drouzy Figure sate.
> For Incense here, instead of *Indian* Gums,
> Kindled *Nicotian* spreads more grateful Fumes,
> Which lull the Senses vex'd with Care and Pain,
> Blunt the sharp Edge of Thought, and kindly cloud the Brain.'
>   (1718 *Poems*, pp. 114–15).

Blackmore's description of the Court of Chaos (from *Prince Arthur*,
1695) has already been quoted, n. 17 above. Such examples make his
place in *The Dunciad Variorum* an appropriate one.

40 Quoted by DePorte, p. 18.

41 See above, pp. 27–8. Thomas Tryon, in his discourse on madness
(attached to his *Treatise of Dreams & Visions*, 1689. *ARS* 160) defines
insanity as 'a *Watching* or *Waking Dream*' (p. 249), and he remarks that in
madness 'the Soul is unclothed, and all its Fantasies and Imaginations
become as it were substantial unto them, as material things are to those
that are in their perfect Senses . . .' (p. 253). He concludes that '*Madness
is nothing but an Erring Sleepifying Power*' (p. 288).

42 ''Tis by means therefore of a controller and correcter of fancy that I am
saved from being mad. Otherwise, 'tis the house turns when I am
giddy. 'Tis things change (for so I must suppose) when my passion
merely or temper changes' (*Characteristics*, ed. Robertson, 208; quoted
by DePorte, p. 45).

43 See *The Art of Sinking in Poetry*, ed. Edna Leake Steeves (New York,
1952), pp. xliv–liii.

44 Pat Rogers, 'Pope, Settle, and The Fall of Troy', *SEL* xv (1975), 447–
58, makes interesting points about Settle's role in *The Dunciad*, and is
especially illuminating on his links with the debasement of the Trojan
story through opera and fairground droll. He shows how the 'charged
exoticism' of Settle's theatrical works resembles the tone of parts of *The
Dunciad*, and he notes the appropriateness of Theobald's collaboration.

45 'As city poet, Settle was employed to devise pageants for all the lord
mayors' shows from 1691 to 1708' (F. C. Brown, *Elkanah Settle: His
Life and Works* (Chicago, 1910), p. 122). Brown gives some details of
these pageants, pp. 122–6. See also Frederick W. Fairholt, *Lord Mayors'
Pageants*, Percy Society Publications, x (London, 1843).

46 This was Settle's payment for the 1703 Vintners' Company pageant (Brown, p. 125). The description of the 1698 pageant is given in extract by Brown, with a contemporary print of the triumphal chariot (p. 124).

47 Brown, p. 63. A copperplate engraving of the entire procession is reproduced facing p. 62.

48 iii, 47–54. See p. 132 above.

49 'Admire' here is used in the sense of 'to wonder at' (*OED* s.v. 'admire' 2).

50 *The Terrors of the Night* (*The Works of Thomas Nashe*, ed. Ronald B. McKerrow (Oxford, 1966), i, 354).

51 *ARS* 178, introd. Antony Coleman.

52 Theobald's *Shakespeare Restored* (London, 1726), which pointed out the inadequacies of Pope's *Shakespeare* and secured Theobald his role as hero of *The Dunciad Variorum*, was dedicated to Rich. In his dedication Theobald recognises the irony of a 'restorer' of Shakespeare addressing someone 'who has gone a great Way towards shutting him out of Doors', and he admits that the Town's favourite pantomimes and Operas are '*Pleasures*, in which the *rational Soul* has no Share'.

53 This opera has been attributed, though not with certainty, to Settle. See Brown, pp. 95–7; and Franklin B. Zimmerman, *Henry Purcell, 1659–1695: an analytical catalogue of his music* (London, 1963), pp. 325–7.

54 *The Fairy Queen: an Opera: Represented at the Queen's-Theatre* (London, 1692), p. 40.

55 See Brown, pp. 100–3.

56 Brown, p. 101.

57 See R. F. Jones, *Lewis Theobald* (New York, 1919), p. 26.

58 *The Entertainments, Set to Musick, for The Comic-Dramatick Opera, Called, The Lady's Triumph: Written by Mr Theobald, and Set to Musick by Mr Galliard* (London, 1718), pp. 2, 4.

59 *Decius and Paulina, a Masque, To which are added, The other Musical Entertainments, As perform'd, at the Theatre in Lincoln's-Inn-Fields, in the Dramatic Opera of Circe: Written by Mr Theobald, and Set to Musick by Mr Galliard* (London, 1719), p. 15.

60 This mock-epic 'action', paralleling the removal of the empire of Troy to Latium in the *Aeneid*, is examined by Aubrey L. Williams, *Pope's 'Dunciad': a Study of its Meaning* (London, 1955), pp. 16–25.

61 *The Rape of Proserpine: As it is Acted at the Theatre-Royal in Lincoln's-Inn-Fields: Written by Mr Theobald: and Set to Musick by Mr Galliard* (3rd ed., London, 1727), p. 6.

62 Lady Mary Chudleigh, 'Of Pride', *Essays upon Several Subjects* (London, 1710), p. 24.

POSTSCRIPT

1 See Spence, *Anecdotes*, entries 634, 636 and 644.
2 'I look upon this as the declining age of English poetry; no regard for others, no selfish feeling, can prevent me from seeing this, and expressing the truth. There can be no worse sign for the taste of the times than the depreciation of Pope' (*Letter to* ★★★★ ★★★★★★ *[John Murray] on the Rev. W. L. Bowles' Strictures on the Life and Writings of Pope* (London, 1821), pp. 46–7).
3 *Byron's Letters and Journals* (12 vols, London, 1973–82), ed. Leslie A. Marchand, viii, 93–4.
4 *Letter to Murray* (1821 ed.), p. 49.

Index